Politics and Development in the Caribbean Basin

Politics and Development in the Caribbean Basin

Central America and the Caribbean in the New World Order

Jean Grugel

Indiana University Press
Bloomington and Indianapolis

Printed in Malaysia

Library of Congress Cataloging-in-Publication Data
Grugel, Jean.
Politics and development in the Caribbean Basin : Central America
and the Caribbean in the New World Order / Jean Grugel.
    p.   cm.
Includes bibliographical references and index.
ISBN 0–253–32683–4. — ISBN 0–253–20954–4 (pbk.)
1. Caribbean Area—Politics and government—1945–   . 2. Caribbean
Area—Economic conditions—1945– 3. Caribbean Area—Economic
policy. I. Title.
F2183.G78   1995
320. 9729—dc20   94–24352

1   2   3   4   5   00   99   98   97   96   95

Para Victor Silvio, con amor

Contents

List of Tables

Abbreviations

ACP	African, Caribbean and Pacific countries
ARENA	Alianza Republicana Nacionalista (El Salvador)
CACM	Central American Common Market
CARICOM	Caribbean Community and Common Market
CBI	Caribbean Basin Initiative
CDR	Committee for the Defence of the Revolution (Cuba)
CIS	Commonwealth of Independent States
CUC	Comité de Unidad Campesina (Guatemala)
ECLA/ECLAC	Economic Commission for Latin America/ Economic Commission for Latin America and the Caribbean
DLP	Democratic Labour Party (Trinidad and Tobago)
EGP	Ejército Guerillero de los Pobres (Guatemala)
EU	European Union
FDR	Frente Democrático Revolucionario (El Salvador)
FMLN	Frente Farabundo Martí para la Liberación Nacional (El Salvador)
FSLN	Frente Sandinista de Liberación Nacional (Nicaragua)
GATT	General Agreement on Tariffs and Trade
IMF	International Monetary Fund
JLP	Jamaican Labour Party
NAFTA	North American Free Trade Area
NJM	New Jewel Movement (Grenada)
OAS	Organization of American States
OECS	Organization of Eastern Caribbean States
PCN	Partido de Conciliación Nacional (El Salvador)
PDC	Partido Democrata Cristiano (El Salvador)
PDP	Popular Democratic Party (Puerto Rico)
PL	Partido Liberal (Honduras)

PLN	Partido de Liberación Nacional (Costa Rica)
PN	Partido Nacional (Honduras)
PNM	People's National Movement (Trinidad and Tobago)
PNP	New Progressive Party (Puerto Rico)
PR	Partido Reformista (Dominican Republic)
PRD	Partido Revolucionario Dominicano (Dominican Republic)
PRG	People's Revolutionary Government (Grenada)
PRUD	Partido Revolucionario de Unifiacacíon Democrática (El Salvador)
PSD	Partido Social Democrata (Costa Rica)
PUSC	Partido Unidad Social Cristiano (Costa Rica)
ULF	United Labour Front (Trinidad and Tobago)
UNO	Unión Nacional de la Oposición (Nicaragua)
USAID	US Agency for International Development

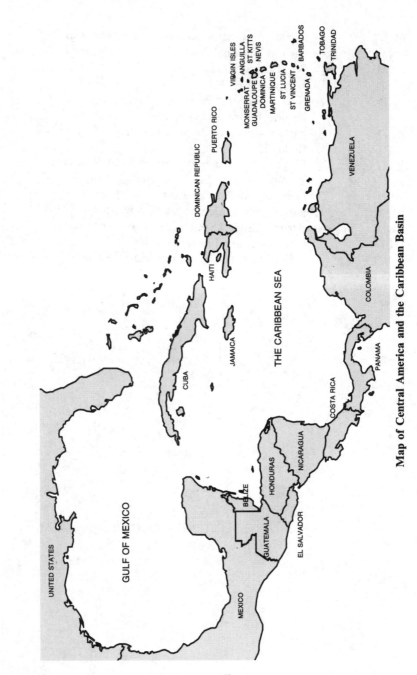

Map of Central America and the Caribbean Basin

Introduction: The Caribbean Model of Development

The aim of this book is modest. It does not attempt to cover political and economic development of the region in great depth. Instead, it is an introduction to the main issues and debates concerning the politics and political economy of the countries which make up the area. In particular, it offers, in an interdisciplinary fashion, the tools for analysis of the models of development in the region and their evolution through the twentieth century to students hitherto unfamiliar with the region.

The countries under discussion here are those of the Central American isthmus – Guatemala, El Salvador, Nicaragua, Honduras and Costa Rica – and most of the larger, independent island territories located in the Caribbean: Cuba, Haiti, the Dominican Republic and Jamaica; references are made, especially where comparisons with the rest of the region seem fruitful, to the smaller islands of the Commonwealth Caribbean, especially to Grenada and occasionally also to Trinidad and Tobago. We have included some discussion of Panama, but not a detailed study of its political economy because the relationship with the US makes it a case almost completely apart. Most of the countries – those located on the Central American isthmus, Cuba, Puerto Rico and the Dominican Republic – included here share a common hispanic cultural legacy. But Haiti and the Commonwealth Caribbean are the results of completely different historical experiences from the Spanish-speaking countries of the region. Our aim in including these case studies is to illustrate the complexity of political traditions and structures within a very small region of the developing world. We want to compare and contrast, to find similarities and differences within the national experiences of the region. The countries of Central America and the Caribbean offer an opportunity for fruitful comparison of the possibilities and the

1

limitations of political and economic policy-making on the periphery. It should be noted that our understanding of the Caribbean, a much disputed and highly ambiguous notion, is confined in reality to the geographical extension of the 'Caribbean Basin', a term which gained currency in the 1980s because of its use in US foreign policy circles.

The idea that we can profitably study the politics, and economics – and therefore the development process – of Central America and the Caribbean together is relatively recent. The similarities within the region have been overlooked by the cultural and linguistic gap which separates the Central American isthmus from most of the Caribbean states and the threads of common history have been obscured by the fact that Central America and the Caribbean belonged, as colonial territories, to different European empires. As a result, cultural difference has disguised the ways in which the countries of the region share similar obstacles to development as a result of history, politics and the pressures of the international system. In this book we therefore break with a tradition in Latin American and Caribbean social sciences by seeing Central America and the insular territories of the Caribbean as a sub-region within Latin America, itself fragmented by historical, geographic, economic, ethnic and cultural factors, characterized by smallness, extreme economic vulnerability, political and economic 'openness' to influences of bigger powers, especially the US, giving rise to political and economic systems which are penetrated and dependent.

A key concept in the book is that of 'model of development'. It is used in a broad sense and explained in more detail below. We use a discussion of the models of the development in the region to explain the cultural and social conflict which today characterizes most of the countries of the area. The term refers here not simply to how the economy works but to the linkages between political and economic decisions and decision-making. Although it is of course true everywhere that politics and economics exist in a dialectal relationship to each other, it is perhaps especially relevant to draw out the links between the two in the region under study. At the same time, we try and weave into the book the third strand of the analysis, as it were – a discussion of the impact of the international system on the development process. We trace the role of external actors on the political and economic processes in the region. There can be no doubt that this is a major input in the development process of the region because of the colonial past, the region's geographical location and the economic fragility of the countries which go to make up the region.

It is important to grasp at the outset that the present-day reality of Central America and the Caribbean is not a result of destiny or geography; it is a result of human history. In particular, the region today is the result of a combination of colonialism, the way capitalism expanded and took root in the area and the class structure it generated and the complex network of relations between external agents and internal elites. These three factors come together in the development models of the region. We now look at what this means.

The Caribbean Basin Model of Development

In the most general sense, the model of development throughout the region is one of peripheral capitalism and external dependence. All the territories of the insular Caribbean, whether part of the Spanish, English, Dutch or French empires, functioned as adjuncts of the international economy since their discovery and colonization. For countries on the Central American isthmus, full incorporation into the world trading system came later, with the liberal revolution after the 1880s. All Central American and Caribbean territories, however, became outposts of production of sugar, fruit, coffee, etc. for external markets. Throughout the region, the effect of this today is that the region produces what it does not consume and needs to import what it does consume. The most important characteristics of the Caribbean model of development are: (1) the smallness of the economies; (2) their acute economic vulnerability; (3) their location on the periphery of the international system; (4) an excessive influence of external agents; and (5) a tendency towards extreme concentration of power internally.

The countries we deal with in the book range from Grenada with a population of less than 100,000, covering only 344 square kilometres of land, to Cuba with a population of over 10 million, and Nicaragua with a population of almost 4 million but with a land extension of almost 120 thousand square kilometres (see Table I.1 at the end of the chapter). All the countries discussed in the book are small underdeveloped countries on the periphery of the international system. Of the 35 small peripheral states in Latin America, 32 are located in Central America and the Caribbean. What is meant by 'small' states? Does it refer simply to geography? We should beware of attributing the economic and diplomatic vulnerability these states share simply to their geographical size. With the exception of some tiny islands of the Caribbean perhaps, the countries of the region are undoubtedly viable politically and economically. Cuba, admittedly the largest of these countries, has a population greater than Portugal, for example, or, to take examples from Latin America, greater than Bolivia or Paraguay. Size *has* undoubtedly imposed certain structural limitations on the economic potential of the countries which make up the region, but smallness is not just a question of population or territorial extension.

'Smallness . . . is not derived exclusively from geography, but rather from their position with respect to the world system of economic and political forces. More specifically, smallness is a phenomenon determined by the historical development of the international division of labour' (Vuskovic and Escoto 1990: 9). Geographic smallness may make states tend towards economic vulnerability because of a dependence on primary commodity exports and a tendency to have only a small industrial base, but it is not necessarily a determining factor. External vulnerability and an absence of negotiating power or influence within the international system are more important. Smallness therefore refers principally to the size of the economic sector and to the position states occupy in the international system. For small peripheral states, as we shall see, it is particularly difficult to develop external policies which can break the cycle of dependent development. Some of the obstacles small peripheral states face include: limited natural, human, and technological resources; low productivity and low per capita income; low capital formation; dependence on foreign investment and aid; and a small internal market.

Economic weakness is linked to external vulnerability in the region. The impact of external actors on political and economic decision-making is a factor which pulls the region together and at the same time makes the individual countries interesting from the point of view of comparison for the researcher and student of development. In particular, Central America and the Caribbean suffer in the contemporary world from the effects of US influence, whether from government or large multinational investors. While parts of the Caribbean remained under European control, the US government felt its sphere of influence was confined to mainland Latin and Central America and the territories of the collapsing Spanish Empire – Cuba, Puerto Rico, the Dominican Republic and Haiti. However, European withdrawal from the region and an increased concern about security in the South have accentuated the tendency in Washington to design policy for 'the Caribbean Basin', treating it as a relatively homogenous whole, a sub-unit of Latin America. Since the time of President Reagan, US policy-makers refer to the Caribbean Basin as an identifiable, geographically bounded area. In reality, the term is less than accurate – El Salvador, for example, borders only the Pacific Ocean and is not washed by the Caribbean Sea – but it does serve to designate those countries which are a primary security concern to Washington within Latin America as a whole. Washington's security interests, today expressed more in terms of a fear of Caribbean immigration and the import of illegal narcotics than in the traditional discourse of external subversion, and the fact that the Caribbean has served traditionally as a significant area for economic expansion, together account for the imprint of the US on almost all aspects of political and economic life in the area.

It is the contention of this book that application of the Caribbean model of development has affected negatively the political and economic development of the region. It has meant production of raw or at best semi-processed goods for metropolitan markets, resulting in open and highly vulnerable economies; and technological dependence, technological backwardness or at best advanced technology limited to 'enclaves' such as free trade zones or mining, owned by foreign capital, without linkages to the rest of the economy. The economies of the region have been and remain rural or extractive and the dynamic sectors of the economy are not labour-intensive or only generate employment for a small part of the year. Within the restricted framework of this model growth is nevertheless possible and at certain periods has occurred: 1950–70 for example. But growth has not been self-sustaining and it depends upon cycles in the world economy. Internally, the model had been controlled either by the oligarchy, from outside by the metropolitan state, or by a local dominant class culturally and economically tied to the export model and the metropolis. As a result, benefits generated from exports have been concentrated in the hands of a restricted elite who have tended to opt for consumption over capital accumulation. Taxation is low, in some cases minimal, and savings and local investment in the national economy are also low.

This pattern has been sustained through different phases of development. In the first phase, the Caribbean Basin specialized in the production of sugar, coffee and bananas. In the 1960s – in the case of Puerto Rico slightly earlier – the region experienced the development of light industry. Throughout the region, foreign capital played a crucial role in industrialization. But export agriculture remained the foreign exchange earner for many countries, leading to a decline in subsistence agriculture and food production for internal consumption. Elsewhere agricultural production for internal consumption was systematically neglected by government. Despite industrialization, Caribbean Basin states have remained highly vulnerable to external fluctuations in demand and investment.

In the 1980s, the region entered a period of deep crisis, partly due to external factors – global recession and falling export prices, for example. But the crisis was not simply a result of a temporary slowdown in growth. Rather it was a result of the pattern of development itself which provoked a series of profound internal contradictions. Extreme polarization, marginalization and impoverishment had become in-built features of the model in most of the countries of the region. In some, the result was growing popular insurgencies, similar to that which had led to the revolution in Nicaragua in 1979. In Guatemala, and El Salvador where popular mobilization in 1980s was greatest, deepening poverty, violence and exclusionary politics, far from being short-term responses to the economic crisis, were the pillars on which the economic model rested. In Guatemala, for example, the benefits of the economic growth experienced in the 1970s were felt exclusively by the rich: the top 20 per cent of the population increased its share of national income in this period from 47 per cent to 57 per cent, while the poorest 20 per cent of the population was condemned to suffer a reduction of its share from a miserable 6.8 per cent to a pathetic 4.8 per cent (Flora and Torres-Rivas 1989a: 78).

Development policies in Central America and the Caribbean, then, have been characterized by extreme agrarian specialization and have always been subject to the demands for agrarian exports within the advanced regions of the globe. This has shaped the external sector and it has limited the possibilities for planning and reform. Economic expansion has also been conditioned by international demand and the cycles of the international economy. But the adaption, expansion and crisis of economic models have also been affected by, and at the same time have helped to condition, the political environment. The complex web of political and economic factors involved in creating the regional model of development is perhaps best illustrated in the crisis which overshadowed the region through the 1980s. Analysing and explaining this crisis is one of the goals of this book.

Many economists concluded towards the end of the 1980s that the economic structures of the region were no longer viable without radical political and economic reforms and without a new mode of insertion in the international economy (Gorostiaga and Marchetti 1988; Deere *et al.* 1990). However, the expected collapse of the model did not take place and the decade of the 1990s is witnessing a restructuring of the traditional model to fit with the demands of the re-shaped international system. In particular, the regional economies are becoming more open, according to the orthodox canons for capitalist economic growth. But unless the markets of the developed countries (the US, the European Union and Japan) also open up, there will be no sustained benefits at all from this policy. And even if opening up the economy leads to growth, there is no guarantee that growth will be translated into development. As the UN *Human Development Report* for 1992 warned: 'it is possible that the changes taking place in the external environment will be of help but they can never be a substitute for internal reform' (UN 1992: 1).

The Crisis of the 1980s

The crisis of the 1980s, which was most intense in El Salvador, Nicaragua and Guatemala, left nowhere in the region unscathed. It was a truly *regional* crisis. Even Costa Rica and Jamaica, long regarded as the only stable and solid democracies in the region, were beset by crisis, although the symptoms of crisis were different from the political polarization which took place in El Salvador or Guatemala. Cuba alone was able to postpone political and economic crisis because of its ties with the Soviet Union, but the problems faced by the Cuban regime today are a testimony to its inability to resolve the problems characteristic of the region permanently.

The 'Central American crisis' in particular, as it came to be known, has generated a substantial literature explaining the genesis of the crisis and prognosticating its final resolution. In this book, we see the crisis which tore the region apart after 1979, most graphically in the Central American isthmus, as a consequence of the patterns of development historically. That is not to say that factors relating to the international system of the time, to the 'hotting up' of the Cold War and in particular to (exaggerated) US fears of external subversion, did not play an important role in the crisis. They were especially influential by the end of the 1980s in determining its outcome. But international factors cannot explain the causes of the crisis. For that we must look in depth at the region's history.

In Central America, the origins of the crisis, which politically was characterized by popular resistance to the model of development implanted in much of the isthmus, lay in the economic and political changes of the 1960s and 1970s. Although there is a tendency to ascribe the causes of rebellion to the poverty of the area, this is only partially true. Poverty did indeed deepen, and living standards for many people fell in Central America in this period, but this occurred in the context of a period of economic growth. And it was the changes which were taking place, especially in the countryside, which give us the clues to understanding the kind of growth that the region experienced. To put it in its most simple terms, the Central American economies expanded in the 1960s and early 1970s through increasing agrarian production for export. Agricultural products for export remained central to economic expansion even when industrialization was getting under way since agriculture still constituted the key export sector. The need to bring more land under production for export, and the introduction of new products, including cattle-raising which requires large tracts of land, meant that many peasants engaged solely or partially in subsistence agriculture (it was common to survive through a combination of subsistence farming, supplemented by seasonal employment as labourers on export-agricultural farms) found themselves landless. In El Salvador, where population density had already placed strains on the peasant economy, the situation was explosive from the late

1960s, as the short war between El Salvador and Honduras in 1969 indicates, caused by the flood of Salvadorean migrants across the border. At the same time, the slowing-down of the short burst of industrialization which began in the early 1960s with the establishment of the Central American Common Market brought further strains on Central American societies. All in all, the description by Perez-Brignoli of the growth in Central America in the 1880s due to the coffee boom, 'impoverishing growth', could just as aptly be applied to the expansion of the 1960s and early 1970s (Perez-Brignoli 1989a: 98).

The economic growth of the 1960s, then, benefited only a small elite, especially those whose power lay in land for export, while the mass of the population, especially the peasants and the indigenous population, found itself excluded. But does this mean that the economic changes taking place rendered the political conflict of the late 1970s and 1980s inevitable and unavoidable? No, because the impact of economic change depends upon the political and social context in which it occurs. Costa Rica experienced economic growth through agrarian export diversification but this did not lead to the development of insurgencies and organized movements challenging the state. We must therefore look at more than the economic backdrop to explain the crisis. In fact, the roots of the conflict lie as much in the class relations – and in some cases, as in Guatemala, in the intertwining of class and ethnic conflict – which had developed in the countries under discussion. Growth activated the latent political conflicts which existed at the heart of Central American societies. Political systems are based on oligarchic rule or an alliance between the oligarchy and the military and rest on an authoritarian political culture requiring deference on the part of the poor and the peasants. These systems came to be questioned by subaltern groups. And popular demands for economic and political reform found in most cases that the state's only response was repression. We can therefore point to the ideology of the Central American elites, and in particular to their absence of flexibility, as one of the major causes of the Central American crisis. The important question of oligarchic ideologies is discussed in detail in Chapter 2.

The traditional model of development in Central America came under threat in the 1980s from a variety of directions: radical governments, guerilla movements, popular rejection of the model, and, last but not least, its own economic weaknesses. The crisis of the 1980s, which brought civil wars, foreign intervention and political violence to the region, was therefore about more than simply economic tensions. It was about questioning the viability of, and creating opposition to, the framework of politics which had sustained the models.

The link between economic changes and political crisis can be seen most clearly in El Salvador, Guatemala and Nicaragua. Here the transformation of the social structure in the period of industrialization and expansion of the agro-export economy led to the political activation of the working class and the poor peasantry. Yet the political exclusion of these groups in a kind of quarantine had come to be a *sine qua non* of these countries' respective political systems. In El Salvador and Guatemala, we could even say that political exclusion was the logical conclusion of the economic model in that its viability was sustained in the 1970s mainly by lowering wages and hence required authoritarian politics and the option of repression in order to enforce real wage cuts. Demands for political incorporation, participation and reform of the political system were a fundamental part of the crisis of the 1980s. It was more than merely an economic collapse.

In those countries affected by war and internal conflict, especially El Salvador, Guatemala, Nicaragua and Haiti, the costs of repression, militarization and war contributed to a deepening of the economic crisis in the 1980s. In fact Costa Rica alone of the Central American countries, with a style of development markedly different from that of its neighbours, did not experience disintegration, partial or total, of the state in the 1980s. In Honduras, where the economic crisis was less severe, democracy was weak and military influence significant until the end of the decade.

The Commonwealth Caribbean on the whole was able to escape the spiral of violence which engulfed many of the regional states. In Jamaica, for example, the political polarization which peaked in the early 1970s never spilled over into violent conflict as in much of Central America. The absence of violent solutions to political conflict in the Commonwealth Caribbean is in large part due to the emergence of political systems based on elite flexibility and the incorporation of organized subaltern groups, especially the trade union movement. The devastating economic crisis of the 1980s, however, did not leave the Commonwealth Caribbean unscathed. In particular, the difficulty of creating economies which generate secure employment prospects alongside viable export sectors constitutes the nub of the crisis today, not just in the Commonwealth Caribbean but in much of the insular Caribbean.

Throughout the region, the costs of confrontation contributed to a general trend towards a timid and partial revalorization of civilian and elected governments by the beginning of the 1990s. Washington was becoming by this time convinced that elected governments made for more stable regimes in the area and, supported by the Organization of American States, contributed to spreading a tentative wave of democratization. Democracies, however, are weak and far from being consolidated. Democratization is nevertheless an important regional issue. If the crisis of the 1980s was sparked by demands for political participation, its resolution depends on finding an effective way of organizing, channelling and representing the mass of citizens' public concerns. We return to democratization in the region at the conclusion of the book.

Profile of the Countries of the Region

What follows is a very short introduction to the most important countries of the region. We look briefly at the main economic characteristics and the political systems. Despite the similarities between the countries of the region in general, what should become clear is the considerable diversity within the region.

Costa Rica

Costa Rica is located on the Central American isthmus, with access to both the Pacific and the Atlantic Oceans, between Panama to the south and Nicaragua to the north. Because of its border with Nicaragua, the country acquired a geopolitical importance in the 1980s during the Central American civil wars. Officially, most Costa Ricans are of European or *mestizo* (a mix of European and Indian) extraction, though census data indicates 3 per cent African and 2 per cent mixed black and European/*mestizo*.

Costa Rican history followed the turbulent traditional pattern of the other Central American countries until the short civil war of 1948, which established the constitution in place today. The new constitution abolished the army and established the primacy of a civilist, democratic political system, with the *Partido de Liberación Nacional* (PLN) dominant. Perhaps the PLN's best-known leader, apart from José Figueres, the party's founder, is Oscar Arias, who pushed for a negotiated settlement of the Central American conflict in the late 1980s, known as the Arias Plan. But the economic difficulties and allegations of corruption against the PLN strengthened the right which, under the *Partido Unidad Social Cristiano* (PUSC) led by Rafael Calderón, won the 1990 elections. The presidential elections of February 1994 were won by José Figueres for the PLN, the son of the party's founder.

Long regarded as the most stable country in the isthmus, partly because income is less concentrated and the state assured the maintenance of an almost universal social security system after the civil war, the 1980s was a critical period for the country's economic development. The structural adjustment programmes of the 1980s have cut into the role of the state and lowered living standards.

Of all the Central American states, Costa Rica has been most successful at diversifying into non-traditional exports. Although it has pursued market diversification, the 1980s also witnessed an increased dependence on the US in economic and security terms.

Cuba

Cuba is the largest island in the Caribbean, located only 145 kilometres off the coast of Florida. The contemporary history of the island has been determined in great measure by its relationship with the US from the time of the Spanish American war of 1898, which freed Cubans from Spain. A sugar economy above all, the ethnic composition of the island has been shaped by the demands for cheap labour for the plantations, leading to slavery and later indentured labour: 51 per cent mulatto, 37 per cent caucasian, 11 per cent black, and 1 per cent Chinese.

In 1959, the 26th of July Movement led by Fidel Castro overthrew the dictator Fugencio Batista, creating a revolutionary state which still survives today, though facing immense difficulties due in part to US hostility and in part to the loss of trading and other economic preferences after the collapse of the Soviet Union. So far, the revolution has begun a timid process of economic reform, looking for joint ventures with European capital for example and expanding the tourist industry. Politically, the Communist Party remains in control, though the system also has elements of charismatic personalism.

After the revolution, economic diversification away from sugar was on the whole unsuccessful, but Cuba has managed to diversify its export base somewhat into citrus products, seafood, nickel and some medical products. The Confederation of Independent States (CIS) remains its most important trading partner, but China, Japan, Italy, Spain and Venezuela are also significant. Trade with China grew from from $180.1 million in 1986 to $420 million in 1990.

The Dominican Republic

The Dominican Republic occupies two-thirds of the second largest Caribbean island, Hispanola. Relations with neighbouring Haiti have often been strained as a result of economic tensions and immigration. Although independent from Spain since 1865, the Dominican Republic has been dominated by the US. The legacy of occupation is an economy shaped to producing for the US market and, politically, dependence on the US, which for example has meant a very minimal presence on the international scene.

Democracy in the Dominican Republic is weak. The long dictatorship of Rafael Trujillo (1930–62) gave way to a period of instability as the US intervened in 1965 to remove the victor, Juan Bosch, of the first democratic elections. The subsequent elections in 1966 brought Joaquin Balaguer to office, who later won elections again in 1982, 1986, 1990, and 1994, following a recount, amid accusations of fraud. The two most important parties in the country are the *Partido Reformista* (PR) of Balaguer and the *Partido Revolucionario Dominicano* (PRD) of Bosch.

An economy dependent on sugar, the country suffered badly from the 1980s recession and falls in the size of the country's US sugar quota. Structural adjustment policies were implemented. Diversification has been attempted through the promotion of Free Trade Zones and tourism.

El Salvador

El Salvador lies on the Pacific coast of Central America, the only Central American state without access to the Atlantic. It borders

Honduras to the east and north and Guatemala to the west. Despite its small size, El Salvador possesses extremely fertile land for agriculture especially in the valleys in the southern coastal region. In pre-colonial times, it supported a considerable population engaged in agriculture, with the result today that 89 per cent of the population are considered *mestizo*, 10 per cent Indian and only 1 per cent white.

El Salvador became a coffee exporting economy at the end of the nineteenth century, experiencing some diversification of agrarian exports after the Second World War, into cotton especially. Political and economic tensions throughout the twentieth century have centred on the struggle for land, as the landowning class sought to create ever-larger export farms at the expense of small-holdings. The result today is landlessness for a huge number of the peasantry. Since 1932, politics in the country have focused on the questioning of maintaining oligarchic dominance, if necessary through repression. By the 1980s, the oligarchy's intransigence, coupled with military repression, had brought the country to civil war in an effort to wipe out the opposition which had come together in the guerilla movement, the *Frente Farabundo Martí para la Liberación Nacional* (FMLN). The US, under President Reagan, committed unprecedented amounts of military and economic aid to El Salvador to prevent the FMLN taking power, despite consider-able international criticism (and at times from the US Congress) about the wisdom of supporting the Salvadorean Armed Forces, responsible for a huge number of documented human rights abuses. By the end of the 1980s, however, the US changed policies and began to support a negotiated end to the war.

Elections have in fact been held since 1982, but in an atmosphere of extreme intimidation, violence and repression and with the FMLN and their political associates, the *Frente Democrático Revolucionario* (FDR), excluded. The elections held so far, there-fore, cannot be regarded as democratic. The Christian Democratic Party, the party closest to the US, won the presidential elections until 1989, when the *Alianza Republicana Nacionalista* (ARENA), an extreme rightist party associated in the 1980s with the death squads, took office under Alfredo Cristiani. Since then, Cristiani has tried to change somewhat the image of the party and has enforced a political strategy as a way of maintaining elite dominance. An agreement was reached with the FMLN to end the war and begin a process of democratization in 1992. The elections of 1994, in which the left participated, were won by Armando Calderón for ARENA. The agreements also call for military reform and a series of other measures including reform of the judicial system.

Grenada

The small island of Grenada, the most southerly of the Windward islands, north of Trinidad, has been independent only since 1974. It shot to international prominence following the overthrow of Eric Gairy and the establishment of a revolutionary regime, the People's Revolutionary Government (PRG), under the New Jewel Movement (NJM), led by Maurice Bishop. In October 1983, amid internal struggles within the NJM, including the overthrowing of Bishop, the US invaded. In 1994, the New National Party, led by Herbert Blaize, won elections, but politics remained conflictive. Nicholas Braithwaite of the National Democratic Congress, was elected Prime Minister in 1990. The next elections are due in 1995.

Grenada is a member of the British Commonwealth, the Caribbean Community and Common Market (CARICOM) and the Organization of Eastern Caribbean States (OECS). The economy remains dependent on agriculture, especially nutmeg, bananas and cocoa. Unemployment is a structural problem on the island and the development of tourism has been a goal of all governments, including the PRG. The ethnic composition of the island has been shaped by slavery: 82 per cent of the population is African, 13 per cent mixed, 1 per cent caucasian and 4 per cent other.

Guatemala

Guatemala, the centre for the advanced Mayan civilization before the arrival of the Spanish, was also the administrative centre within Central American during the Colonial period. Many Indian communities survived the Conquest by retreating to the highlands, with the result today that the legacy of Mayan and Quiché civilizations are multiple, in language, culture and social practices. Almost 38 per cent of the population is Indian, retaining a traditional lifestyle. It is for this reason that literacy is low (55 per cent) because, for many Guatemalans, Spanish is a second language.

By the beginning of the twentieth century, the Guatemalan economy, the largest in Central America, was set in the mould of agrarian exports, primarily coffee and bananas. The 1930 depression brought a dictatorship to power, here as elsewhere throughout the region, which was overthrown in 1944 by the October Revolution, under President Arévalo (1945–50) and President Arbenz (1950–54). The process of economic modernization and social reform which the revolution signified was brought to an abrupt end with the US-backed invasion by counter-revolutionaries. The Armed Forces remained thereafter the arbiters of the nation's destiny.

In the late 1970s and early 1980s especially, under the military dictators Lucas García (1978–82), Ríos Montt (1982–3) and Mejia Victores (1983–5), repression, especially of the Indian communities, increased enormously. Outrage at the human rights abuses led to the suspension of almost all aid and cooperation agreements, assisting the movement towards a limited and partial transition. In 1986, the Christian Democrats won the elections bringing Vinicio Cerezo to office. In 1991 Jorge Serrano was elected president but ousted in an attempted military coup in 1993, bringing to power the civilian Ramiro de León Carpio. It is difficult to speak of democratization, however, in the country, because of the strength of the Armed Forces, the continued abuses of human rights and the corruption of the political elite. The country remains profoundly divided between a small elite and a politically dispossessed and alienated majority.

Coffee is the principal export commodity. Bananas and sugar production are also significant. There is in addition some assembling for export, especially in textiles, particularly in Free Trade Zones which guarantee income tax exemption. The US is the country's most important trading partner, receiving 41 per cent of the country's exports in 1991.

Haiti

Haiti occupies the western third of Hispanola, with Cuba less than 80 kilometres to the west. In the eighteenth century, it was the most important sugar producer in the Caribbean and was the first country to win independence from Europe. Haiti's ethnohistory has been shaped by slavery. On Independence, sugar collapsed as the ex-slaves fled the plantations to establish forms of peasant agriculture. Much of Haiti is today unsuitable for cultivation either because of its topology or because of severe land erosion. Agrarian plots are therefore small and uneconomic. The population is comprised of 95 per cent of African descent and 5 per cent mulatto.

Like its neighbour the Dominican Republic, early-twentieth-century Haitian history was marked by US dominance, with the US occupying Haiti between 1915 and 1934. This was followed by the long-lasting dictatorship of 'Papa Doc' Duvalier, who installed the principle of hereditary government and passed power onto his son, Baby Doc. The Duvaliers counted on the support, at times somewhat reluctant, of the US. In 1986, Baby Doc was overthrown by the army, which re-emerged as the arbiter of politics. The democratic elections of 1990, which led to the election of Jean-Bertrand Aristide, were cancelled by the military intervention of 1992, forcing Artistide into exile. The de facto government is under considerable international pressure to return power to the civilians.

Haiti's economy has wavered between economic stagnation and frank deterioration for most of the contemporary period. The size of the economy is small (US\$ 2 billion) for a country which supports over 6 million people. Subsistence agriculture on poor plots of land accounts for up to two-thirds of employment. Out-migration is common and increasing. The export sector is small, composed essentially of assembling. This has declined as foreign companies began to withdraw after 1992 with the end of the timid and weak start of a transition to civilian rule.

Honduras

Honduras, located on the isthmus, borders El Salvador, Nicaragua and Guatemala. Its strategic location was to turn the country into an important focus for the US military build-up in Central America in the 1980s. Its population is overwhelmingly *mestizo*, with some African mix on the Atlantic coast. The history of Honduras has been marked by foreign control and later the intervention of the Armed Forces. The state has historically been weak and the landowning class less powerful than in neighbouring El Salvador or Guatemala. Access to land for the peasantry was not a problem in the country until the 1960s.

The militarization of politics which characterized public life in the 1970s gave way after 1982 to civilian politics. In 1993, President Rafael Leonardo Callejas of the *Partido Nacional* (PN), elected in 1989, gave way to Carlos Roberto Reina of the *Partido Liberal* (PL).

Agriculture is the principal sector of the economy, accounting for 22.8 per cent of GDP. Agriculture is also the basis of the export sector, with coffee and bananas the main exports, with some diversification into non-traditional exports such as seafood and fruit. Manufacturing is weak though the government of Callejas especially tried to promote assembling for export through the creation of Free Trade Zones.

The US is the country's chief trading partner – with 45 per cent of exports destined for the US market – and international ally. The country was rewarded for its strict orthodox economic policies introduced after 1990, leading to a reduction in consumption and an increase in unemployment, by an inflow of international capital from the IMF, the World Bank and US AID.

Jamaica

Located 145 kilometres from Cuba and 160 kilometres from Haiti, Jamaica's culture and political system have none the less been marked above all by the effects of British imperialism. Jamaica was the principal British colony in the Caribbean and an important source of unrefined sugar in the eighteenth century. The decline of the sugar industry set in, however, with slave emancipation and the introduction of free trade in Britain. Although complete independence was not to be achieved until 1962, the years following the demise of sugar constituted a long period of economic decline. The 1930s were particularly critical years, marked by neglect from Westminster, an intensification of poverty on the island and an increase in violence. The collapse of sugar and the economic decline of the colony led to most of the white settlers leaving. Today the ethnic mix of the island is: African 76.3 per cent, Afro-European 15.1 per cent, East Indian and Afro-East Indian 3.4 per cent, caucasian 3.2 per cent and Chinese 1.2 per cent.

Jamaican government is based on the British parliamentary system. The system is bicameral, the Senate being appointed on the nomination of the Prime Minister and the Leader of the

Opposition. Two parties have dominated the island's political life: the Jamaican Labour Party (JLP) on the right and the People's National Party (PNP), somewhat more to the left. Michael Manley's PNP government in the early 1970s marked a radicalization of Jamaican politics, and the US, which has become increasingly important in Jamaican affairs since Independence, responded unfavourably. The 1980s were dominated by the JLP under Edward Seaga, with the PNP winning the elections in 1989 and 1993. The Prime Minister today is P. J. Patterson.

Since Independence, the Jamaican economy has continued to be troubled. Out-migration and unemployment are high. The structural adjustment programmes of the 1980s failed to generate growth although they were implemented with considerable support from international agencies and by the US. In spite of this, the government decided to press on in the 1990s with liberalization of foreign exchange, removal of price controls, elimination of subsidies and privatization. Economic growth, where it has taken place, has been in services and tourism. The export sector relies mostly on traditional goods – bauxite, alumina and sugar – with some diversification especially in textiles.

Nicaragua

Nicaragua lies between Honduras and Costa Rica, bordering the Pacific and the Caribbean. The Caribbean coast, for many years ignored by the politicians in Managua, has developed a culture of its own in which African elements remain important. The ethnic mix of the country is: *mestizo* 69 per cent, caucasian 17 per cent, African 9 per cent and Indian 5 per cent.

Nicaragua was the object of US attention from early in the twentieth century. The US occupied the country from 1912 until 1925, and again from 1927 until 1933. Before withdrawal, the US organized the National Guard under General Anastasio Somoza, who was to use the Guard to seize power in 1935. The Somoza family dominated political office and extended their influence into whole areas of the economy until the Sandinista Revolution of 1979. It was during the second period of occupation that the guerilla movement led by Augusto Sandino was formed to fight for national liberation, which later became the example guiding the

Frente Sandinista de Liberación Nacional (FSLN) in the campaign against the Somoza dictatorship in the 1970s.

In June 1979, the FSLN took power, the National Guard was dissolved and a new army was established from within the liberation movement. Relations with the US deteriorated quickly, especially after 1981. The increased hostility of the Reagan administration came together with internal opposition determined to overthrow the Sandinistas in the shape of US–financed *Contras* who operated from bases in Honduras, and later, to a lesser degree, from Costa Rica. The Nicaraguan conflict and US–Nicaraguan relations were to become a central issue in inter-American relations in the 1980s.

Despite broad reforms in some areas, the Nicaraguan economy started to deteriorate rapidly after 1985. This was due to a combination of factors, including the costs of fighting the war, *contra* activity which destroyed economic production in some areas, US hostility, internal opposition and errors in the implementation of political and economic strategy. In 1990 general elections were held which brought the newly formed heterogeneous anti-Sandinista coalition, *Unión Nacional de la Oposición* (UNO) to power under Violeta Chamorro. The Chamorro government has been plagued by internal political conflict and the economic problems left by the war. Unemployment remains high (40 per cent), the inflation which beset the last years of the Sandinista government is still not under control, and the export sector has not recovered. The next elections are due in 1996.

Panama

Panamanian history has been determined in large measure by its geographical location. It is the most direct land crossing between the Atlantic and Pacific Oceans. Panama borders Colombia to the east (of which it was a part until 1903), and Costa Rica to the west. Panamanians are 70 per cent *mestizo*, 14 per cent West Indian, 10 per cent caucasian and 6 per cent Indian.

The US assisted the Panamanian secession movement with the aim of using the new country to build a trans-isthmian canal. The Canal, which is owned by the US and was opened in 1914, is 82 kilometres long. The Canal thereafter became the mainstay of the economy and the means by which Panamanian dependence on the US was maintained. In 1977, the Panama Canal Treaty was signed between Presidents Torrijos and Carter which is to give the ownership and management of the Canal Zone to Panama by the end of the 1990s. Disputes about the implementation of the Treaty, along with allegations of narcotics dealings, were to be the backdrop to the US invasion of 1989 when the US troops arrested the then Panamanian president, Antonio Noriega.

The economy depends on services tied to transportation, international financial services and the Colon Free Trade Zone as well as the Canal. Cooperation and approval from the US has always been the key to economic growth – in Panama the dollar circulates freely as tender – which is why the economy collapsed at the end of the 1980s when the US decided to remove Noriega. The economic embargo implemented by the US caused severe disruptions and social instability. The government of Guillermo Endara, which replaced Noriega, presided over a period of economic recovery, based once again on services and transportation. The government also embarked on a process of privatization. Unemployment remains high at over 15 per cent and the reduction in government spending is affecting the living standards of many Panamanians.

Puerto Rico

Puerto Rico is an island in the Greater Antilles, 80 kilometres east of Hispanola. It was a Spanish colony until 1898, although in 1897 the island negotiated a form of autonomous government from the Peninsular. During the Spanish-American War, the island was occupied by the US and was subsequently governed from Washington. Its situation was partly formalized in 1917, when Puerto Ricans were given US citizenship. In 1947, the island was given the right to elect the Governor of the island, and in 1952 the present Commonwealth (Associated Statehood) status was granted under which Puerto Ricans retain control over internal affairs but do not vote in US national elections. Spanish remains the first language and Puerto Ricans are a mixture of European immigrants, with African and Indian influences.

Internally, the island has party-based representative government. The main parties are the Popular Democratic Party (PPD), the party that negotiated Associated status, the New Progressive Party (PNP) and the small Independence Party. Politics has recently been dominated by the issue of the island's political status, with voices in

Washington and on the island raised in favour of incorporation into the US. In 1992 Pedro Rossellou of the PNP became Governor of the island, replacing Rafael Hernandez Colón of the PPD. Although the PNP favours incorporation into the US, a non-binding plebiscite on the issue in 1993 rejected full incorporation.

The US supported industrialization on the island in the late 1940s and 1950s through 'Operation Bootstrap', which essentially encouraged US investment in tax-free assembling for consumption in the US market. In the 1970s, partly to fight increasing international competition, Puerto Rico began to encourage 'high-tech' foreign investment, in chemicals for example. Tourism is also an important contributor to the island's economy. Unemployment has been a structural feature of economic growth, remedied only partly by out-migration to the US and US federal assistance programmes.

Trinidad and Tobago

Trinidad and Tobago, to which we give only small attention in the book, are two islands forming one state located in the Lesser Antilles, with Trinidad separated from mainland Venezuela by only 12 kilometres; 30 kilometres separate Trinidad from Tobago. Fought over by European governments in the eighteenth century, Trinidad was ceded to the British in 1797 and Tobago in 1814. In 1889, they became a single colony. In 1958 they formed part of the Federation of the West Indies, seen by the British as the first step to independence, and in 1962, under Dr Eric Williams, the island became an independent state, a republic within the Commonwealth. Sugar plantations had led to the importation of African slaves and, after emancipation, of indentured labour, with the result that the population of the islands today is a mix of Africans (40 per cent), East Indians (40 per cent), mixed African and East Indian (16 per cent), Chinese (1 per cent) and European (1 per cent). Culturally, the islands are divided between Christians, Hindus and Muslims.

In the 1970s, the islands' prosperity increased considerably with the discovery of deposits of oil and natural gas. In the 1980s, the collapse of oil prices brought the county into recession and led to the implementation of austerity programmes. Recovery has been slow and unemployment remains high (18 per cent). In the 1990s, especially, the government began to promote growth through an increase in tourism as well as encouragement of non-energy investments.

We can see from the brief glance we have just taken at the countries which make up the region that the tendency to over-generalize in Central America and the Caribbean must be avoided. Diversity, in terms of production, social structure, ethnicity, political culture and language is the order of the day. Throughout the book, we concentrate instead on identifying the overall patterns of development in the region and then discussing differences between states.

As we said at the beginning, the goal of the book is to explain development patterns in the region. A main focus of the book is the crisis, political and economic, which erupted in the 1980s and which we contend has subsided but has not been resolved. It illustrates many of the features and consequences of the region's development model. We trace the origins of the crisis, insisting that the causes are multiple but related, through the contemporary history of the region, drawing attention to the idea of political and economic exclusion, which features as a constant characteristic of the countries which make up the area, though it is expressed in different ways and in different degrees.

Although the main body of the book deals with the region from the 1880s onwards, Chapter 1 sets the scene historically. It examines the most important features of colonialism which emerged in the area, analyses the different forms of international insertion which took place and points to the fragmentation of the region as a whole, and within the Central American isthmus and the insular Caribbean as a legacy of history. We look in some detail at the importance of the Liberal Reforms for Central America and the consequences for the insular Caribbean of the introduction of sugar and slavery and the later collapse of the plantation economies which took place in the nineteenth century.

Chapters 2 and 3 study the politics of the region. Chapter 2 introduces the reader to the framework of politics, understood broadly. We see politics as something more than just the formal political systems and look at the lines of conflict in regional societies. Social conflicts and exclusions, obviously, are reflected in the operation of the superstructures of politics – the political system – and the model of development generally. Important ideas introduced here are the state, class and ethnicity. The most important actors in Caribbean and Central American societies are identified. Chapter 3 continues the analysis of regional politics by examining the different political systems the contemporary region has produced. We try and explain the reason behind the authoritarian tradition, where it exists, and discuss the kinds of democracies the region has produced. Examples from El Salvador, Guatemala, Haiti and the Dominican Republic are used to illustrate different kinds of authoritarian politics extant in the region and introduce the question of democracy by analyses of the electoral politics of Costa Rica and Jamaica. We look at how the democracies of the area fared during the crisis years of the 1980s.

Chapter 4 is devoted to the international relations of the region. This constitutes a vital key to understanding development in the area given its historical dependence on advanced countries and its openness to penetration on the part of developed countries, whether economic or cultural penetration. Most attention is paid to the pivotal relationship with the US whose influence permeates the political and economic options, choices and decisions, large and small. We trace the history of US influence and assess the changing motivations of its policies over time. The role Europe plays today in the international relations of the region today is also discussed.

Chapter 5 concentrates on the genesis and development of the economic crisis which devastated the region in the 1980s. The origins of the crisis lie in the model of peripheral capitalism, which changed over time from one characterized by the dependence on agrarian exports, to one which incorporated some form of industrialization alongside agrarian specialization in the export sector. We look at the new models of political economy which have emerged as a result of the application of structural adjustment programmes, leading to a revived attempt at development through export promotion. We question whether this approach will solve the development problems which affect the region. Chapter 6 examines the attempts of some countries to break out of the region's established political and economic patterns of development and create new forms of organizing society. The revolutions in Cuba, Nicaragua and Grenada, where, in very different ways, new political elites tried to promote political incorporation and social wellbeing through a reorganization of society are the focus of the chapter. At the same time, the revolutionary states tried to tackle economic reform and design new strategies for integration into the international system. We assess, somewhat soberly, the results of revolution in the region.

Finally in the conclusion, we look briefly at the future of the region as international interest in the Caribbean Basin wanes. We question whether the development issues which gave rise to the crisis have been resolved and analyse to what extent optimistic forecasts for democracy in the region are justified.

Table I.1   Central America and the Caribbean: population and territorial extension

	Population	*Territory (sq km)*
Costa Rica	3,065,900	51,000
Cuba	10,732,037	110,860
Dominican Republic	7,321,000	48,422
El Salvador	5,376,000	21,393
Grenada	83,812	344
Guatemala	9,744,748	108,889
Haiti	6,647,000	27,750
Honduras	5,298,000	112,088
Jamaica	2,489,353	10,991
Nicaragua	3,999,000	118,358
Panama	2,476,281	77,082
Puerto Rico	3,294,997	8,959
Trinidad and Tobago	1,252,783	5,128

Table I.2   Social profile of the region

	Life expectancy (years)	Adult literacy (per cent)	Per capita income (US$)
Trinidad	71.6	96.0	6,604
Costa Rica	74.9	92.8	4,542
Grenada	71.5	96.0	4,081
Panama	72.4	88.1	3,317
Jamaica	73.1	98.4	2,979
Cuba	75.4	94.0	2,200
Dominican Rep.	66.7	83.3	2,404
El Salvador	64.4	73.0	1,950
Nicaragua	64.8	81.0	1,497
Guatemala	63.4	55.1	2,576
Honduras	64.9	73.1	1,470
Haiti	55.7	53.0	933

Source: *UN, Human Development Report*, 1993, UN Programme for Development.

Table I.3   Human development index: Central America and the Caribbean (scale 1–173)

High		*Medium*		*Low*	
		Grenada	59	Guatemala	113
Trinidad	31	Panama	68	Honduras	116
Costa Rica	42	Jamaica	69	Haiti	137
Cuba	75	Dominican Rep.	97		
		El Salvador	110		
		Nicaragua	111		

Source: *UN, Human Development Report*, 1993.

Table I.4   Unemployment in Central America and the Caribbean (1992)

Country	% of population unemployed
Costa Rica	5.6
Cuba	n/a
Dominican Republic	30.0
El Salvador	7.5
Grenada	25.0
Guatemala	40.5
Haiti	45.0
Honduras	7.6
Jamaica	15.4
Nicaragua	40.0
Panama	15.7
Puerto Rico	15.2
Trinidad and Tobago	18.8

Source: *The Caribbean Basin Basic Facts*, Washington, DC, 1993.

Table I.5   GDP (US$) and growth of GDP (1992)

Country	GDP	Rate of growth of GDP
Costa Rica	5.57 billion	1.0
Cuba	26.90 million	−1.5
Dominican Republic	4,816 million	−2.0
El Salvador	5.68 billion	3.5
Grenada	164.37 million	2.9
Guatemala	9.39 billion	3.3
Haiti	2.10 billion	−4.0
Honduras	3.90 billion	2.2
Jamaica	1,908 million	0.2
Nicaragua	1.90 billion	−0.7
Panama	2.00 billion	93.0
Puerto Rico	32.46 billion	0.0
Trinidad and Tobago	4.94 billion	1.8

Source: *The Caribbean Basin Basic Facts*, Washington, DC, 1993.

Table I.6   Urban population: Central America (1992)

Country	% of total population
Costa Rica	47.6
El Salvador	46.2
Guatemala	40.2
Honduras	45.3
Nicaragua	65.8
Panama	54.4

Source: *Instituto de Relaciones Europea - Latinoamericanas*, Madrid.

Table I.7   Density of population (1991)

Country	No. per sq km
Costa Rica	60.1
Cuba	96.8
Dominican Republic	151.0
El Salvador	256.8
Grenada	264.0
Guatemala	89.0
Haiti	239.5
Honduras	47.3
Jamaica	226.3
Nicaragua	33.8
Panama	32.7
Puerto Rico	368.0
Trinidad and Tobago	244.0

Source: *The Caribbean Basin Basic Facts*, Washington, DC, 1993.

1

The Historical Evolution of the Caribbean Basin

The countries of Central America and the insular Caribbean are extraordinarily diverse: in their political traditions, their external relations, in their cultures and in their social structures and ethnic compositions. The dichotomy in Central American history identified by James Dunkerley – that of unity and diversity – obtains all the more within the Caribbean Basin as a whole (Dunkerley 1988). The aim of this chapter is to identify the historical roots of the differences and similarities which we can perceive today, between Central America and the insular Caribbean on the one hand, that is between the different cultural universes which make up the countries of the Caribbean Basin which we are studying – Hispanic, Francophile and British – and, on the other, between the states themselves. History imposed a rigid separation for centuries within the region through the very different experiences of colonialism and the different forms of insertion into the international system. For this reason, in this chapter we deal for the most part with the colonial heritage and independence in the insular Caribbean and Central America separately. In time-scale, the chapter deals with the legacy of the past from the sixteenth century until the establishment of the framework of contemporary societies.

The 'Discovery'

The arrival of Christopher Columbus in the 'New World' is the starting point not only for the region's contemporary history but also for world history. The influx of gold from the colonies, the struggle for control of new lands and their products, and the mercantilist trade rivalries between European powers all contributed to the rise of capitalism within Europe. At the same time, Europe's discovery of America marks the start of modern imperialism. Capitalism and imperialism intertwine as the dominant threads within the history of the Caribbean Basin. The first colonies and the first jewels in the crown of the Spanish monarchs were in the Caribbean: the islands of Hispaniola (now divided between the Dominican Republic and Haiti) and Cuba, peopled originally by mainly Taino Arawaks or Amerindians.

The new lands were annexed by the Spanish crown for economic and commercial reasons. The Spanish tried to extract wealth from the islands through the imposition of taxes and tribute on the indigenous population. Plans were drawn up as well for the transportation of the Indians to Mediterranean Europe to be used as slave labour. However, neither of these options could be implemented in the long term and the Spanish were forced to look for a more viable basis for the sustained exploitation of the new colonies. As a result, the Crown, under internal pressure from the Catholic Church and the Spanish gentry who wanted a share in the wealth of the new territories, decided that colonizing the islands was the best way forward as a means of exploiting the gold that was thought, wrongly as it turned out, to be plentiful on the islands. A system known as the *encomienda*, that is dividing up the Indian population between the Spanish settlers for use as forced labour, was adopted officially in 1503. Bartolomé Las Casas, critical historian of the Conquest and defender of the rights of the Indians (though not the Africans who were later brought to the region as slaves) described the *encomienda* system as the Spanish 'eating from the sweat of the Indians' (Baez 1986: 45).

Hispaniola became the centre of Spanish colonies in the region due to the discovery of gold on the eastern part of the island. But the reserves were much scarcer than the Spanish had calculated and by 1528 were completely exhausted. Gold mining in Cuba enjoyed an even shorter history: the first discoveries took place in 1511 and by 1524 the mines were useless. Sugar was introduced to the island in the 1520s but was not intensively cultivated in this period because the colonies could trade only with Spain, and Spain did not control the European sugar trade. Another alternative crop was tobacco. Although it was a new crop with a growing European market, its expansion was once again limited by the trade monopoly established by the Spanish with the New World. In this way, the Caribbean island colonies lost economic significance and the attentions of the Spanish Crown shifted thereafter to the mainland. Hispaniola and Cuba entered a slow decline, a process which was not arrested until the eighteenth century in the case of western Hispaniola, later Haiti, and the nineteenth century in the case of the Dominican Republic and Cuba.

The 'Discovery' established the first linkages between the Caribbean islands and the European metropolis with major consequences for regional development. Firstly, the export orientation of the colonies was established from the outset and has remained the dominant feature of the regional economies. Secondly, and tragically, the early fever for precious metals and the use of the indigenous population as a source of unpaid and forced labour, a practice which would be repeated throughout mainland America, led to the extinction of the Taino Arawak people. The huge and sudden leap in the mortality rate of the indigenous population cannot be accounted for simply through the spread of European diseases nor through the rebellion and resistance of the Indians; rather the Indians died as a result of the imposition of the mining economy which demanded a permanent supply of labour in unsafe, uncertain and inhuman circumstances and necessitated a total transformation of social and cultural practices. It has been estimated that on Hispaniola, of a total population of around 300,000 in 1492, only 60,000 remained in 1508, 4,000 in 1519 and only 500 in 1548 (Baez 1986: 45). In Cuba, the indigenous population was similarly eradicated. Later, when sugar production took off in Haiti, the Dominican Republic and Cuba, the absence of indigenous labour led to the import of slaves from Africa, transforming permanently the ethnohistory of the islands. At the same time, the eradication of the indigenous peoples was an early demonstration of the racism and belief in white European superiority which underlay colonialism and on which ideologically the plantation sugar society which was to emerge later, rested. In Chapter 2, we will look at the importance of race and ethnicity in political conflict in the region. We should note here, however, that production in the colonial Caribbean was an enterprise founded on racial differentiation. Race therefore constituted the first line of conflict in colonial societies, determining access to goods, status and power.

The Mainland: Colonial Central America

Central America was colonized in the 1520s and the Spanish settled on lands where a variety of indigenous societies existed. Present-day El Salvador supported a relatively dense population dependent on intensive agriculture. By contrast, Nicaragua and Costa Rica were sparsely populated. By the time the Spanish arrived, the sophisticated highland Mayan civilization was in decline and Guatemala was dominated by people who had originally come from Mexico. In contrast to the fate of the Amerindians of the island colonies, the indigenous peoples were not wiped out completely by the Spanish, though their numbers were severely depleted.

Like the insular territories, the isthmus lacked significant deposits of gold and precious metals and was thus condemned to become a backwater of the Spanish empire. Interest centred mainly on Mexico and Peru. The degree to which the Spanish penetrated the existing social and economic structures, therefore, was partial. But changes there were, and highly significant ones, firstly in terms of political organization. Centralized rule was imposed through the establishment of the Captaincy General based at Guatemala City. Its importance was always eclipsed by Mexico City, the centre of the Viceroyalty of New Spain and the axis of the Empire in Middle America because of the riches of the Aztec Empire which, at the height of its glory, had fallen into the hands of the Spanish. Of the Central American states today, only Panama was outside the jurisdiction of Guatemala City and was part of a separate administrative centre stretching south towards Peru until the reorganization of the Empire in 1751.

The second major change that occurred with the arrival of the Spanish was the transformation of social relations and the ethnic composition of the region. *Ladinización*, the mixing of the Indians with the Spanish, occurred extensively, disrupting communal life. More than an ethnic category, *ladino* refers principally to Indians who have undergone a process of acculturation, those who have left the village and gone to form part of the economic and social system created by the Spanish. The Indian villages where the indigenous way of life remained intact, meanwhile, were marginalized from decision-making and resource control. And though the subsistence economy survived, the Spanish introduced a new code of social and economic behaviour based upon commercial not communal relations. As a result, the subsistence economy was put on the defensive and the Spanish reforms marked the beginning of the slow alienation of the Indian communities from the land.

The nature of economic production was transformed unevenly in the isthmus, however, because mercantilist links with Europe were weak. Agricultural production for internal consumption survived the introduction of crops for export, though the priority of the export sector was established. In El Salvador, the first commercial estates (*haciendas*) were introduced between 1590 and 1630 and constituted the beginning of a gradual encroachment on previously communal land. The expansion of indigo, the main export from El Salvador during the time of the Spanish Empire, depended principally upon the *repartimiento* system of tied labour until the beginning of the seventeenth century and thereafter on cheap, landless *ladino* labour. Indian villages coexisted alongside the *haciendas*, and in some cases even won legal recognition, but the competition for the limited land available in El Salvador for cultivation led to the gradual displacement of the village system, a process which started under the Empire and which lies at the heart of the conflicts in the country in the contemporary period.

In Guatemala by contrast, the Indian communities were able to retain greater autonomy by retreating to the highlands, causing a chronic shortage of labour for the *haciendas*. Nicaragua, with fewer Indian settlements, was a poor and neglected colony, producing mostly cattle, cocoa and food for the region. The largest Indian communities in Nicaragua, the Miskitos, remained undisturbed for the most part – by the Spanish at least, for in 1768, the British established an outpost for their Caribbean Empire on Miskito land which was to last until 1850 when the British ceded to the US the right to economic control in the area. Colonization in Costa Rica followed yet a different path. A combination of poor land for cultivation and physical distance from the main population centres, made worse by hazardous communications, increased its isolation and led to the retention of subsistence agriculture.

Independence in Central America

Central American independence occurred under unusual circumstances. Rather than engaging in direct combat with the Spanish forces during the Wars of Independence at the beginning of the nineteenth century, Central America found itself liberated as a result of Mexican independence. Initially the isthmus was annexed in 1821 by the short-lived Mexican Empire under Agustín de Iturbide following the defeat of the Spanish forces in the area. The collapse of Iturbide's empire just three years later led the five Central American provinces of Costa Rica, Guatemala, El Salvador, Honduras and Nicaragua to proclaim their independence in the guise of the United Provinces of Central America in a federation which was to last, unstable and challenged from within by centrifugal tendencies, until 1838.

The Federation was broken by the internal tensions generated by the intersecting struggles between centralism and liberalism on the one side and conservatism and regional parochialism on the other. These struggles constituted the meat and drink of regional politics until the beginning of the twentieth century. The Liberals triumphed at first in the Federation and sought to implement reforms which would modernize the region: education and legal reform, the end of the influence of the Catholic Church over the state, the intensification of methods of agrarian production etc. But the forces of regional conservatism eventually defeated them. The Federation was also bedevilled by its lack of financial resources, since the landed class, with only local loyalties, was unwilling to finance the new state.

At the time of Independence, the region was comprised of a series of local economies, and the creole class which came to power was not a single class united across the isthmus by common interests; instead, there were a number of competing creole elites, the roots of whose prestige and wealth lie in the different local economic structures which had emerged during the colonial period. As a result, Central American history between 1825 and 1870 is in effect a competition between these elites which ideologically was couched as a struggle between centralizing liberalism and conservative localism. We should not overemphasize the differences between the two ideologies, however, because they shared one very important characteristic which was to stamp its mark on the history of the isthmus. Both Liberalism and Conservatism were exclusionary ideologies in a profoundly racial and social sense. Both reflected the interests of the landowning and commercial classes, disdainful and ignorant of the Indian heritage and buoyed up by a conviction of their racial and cultural superiority. It hardly needs saying, therefore, that the symbols of pre-Conquest Central America could not be turned into factors for national unification within the new Republics and came to be revindicated only by cultures of resistance.

The Federation's collapse led to the emergence of weak national states. This weakness of central authority was intensified by an absence of national consciousness among the elites as opposed to local particularism. Independence had arrived almost fortuitously, with the effect that there was no prior development of nationalist sentiment to cushion the newly established nation state. At the same time, the absence of significant national markets for the exchange of goods, which would have promoted national integration and national sentiment, guaranteed the survival of localist tendencies. And, with weak central states, there was no possibility of a diffusion of nationalism from the state downwards. So the newly independent states came to represent the interests of different sectors of the local creole landed class.

In social and economic terms, Independence left unchanged the structures inherited from the colonial period. The power of the creole elite was untouched and it remained impermeable to other social sectors. There had been little mass mobilization compared with elsewhere in the Spanish colonies during Independence and popular participation in the process was minimal. As a result the social system was hardly altered. People of mixed race were freed from legal discrimination, and slavery (unimportant in economic terms) was abolished. These constituted two of the most important reforms inaugurated with Independence. The reality, therefore, of the period was that:

> popular sectors gained very little . . . The Indian communities and the poor *mestizos* of the ranches and other types of agrarian enterprises . . . felt scarce improvement in their lives and expectations. Creole opinion, with regard to the Indians, as Valle [leading liberal intellectual of the Federation] said, was that 'they existed only at the idiot stage of development'. (Lynch 1988: 189)

The dominant state, both in the Federation and in the isthmus following its break-up, was Guatemala. Its importance can be measured by the fact that in the first Congress of the Federation, eighteen deputies arrived from Guatemala while only nine came from El Salvador, six respectively from Honduras and Nicaragua and only two from Costa Rica whose population was a mere 63,000 in 1821. Guatemala was the only state in Central America where a dominant class expressed sufficient faith in its future to try and promote immigration from Europe, though the immigrants were to prove yet another divisive factor in a society already racially fragmented. And it is in Guatemala, the economic centre of the Federation, where the struggle between Liberalism and Conservatism could most clearly be seen.

The collapse of the Federation led to a conservative restoration in Guatemala under the *mestizo* Rafael Carrera who came to power in 1840. Carrera reversed the liberal legislation of the years immediately following Independence, brought back the religious orders and applied protectionist economic policies in an attempt to preserve the Central American market for Guatemala against an influx of European, primarily British, goods. His presidency rested on a peculiar alliance between the Church and the popular sectors who stood to gain little from the liberal reforms except perhaps greater insecurity with the deepening of the market. The ideological content of Carrera's rebellion against Liberalism, temporarily successful, is neatly summed up in the battle cry of his supporters: '*viva la religión y mueran los extranjeros*' ('long live religion and death to foreigners'). The impact of a Conservative Guatemala was felt throughout the isthmus: 'a Conservative Guatemala implied a Conservative Central America' (Dunkerley 1988: 15).

The Liberal Reforms

Liberalism, the ascendant ideology of the nineteenth century, could not be resisted for long, however, and we can date its triumph in Central America from around the somewhat arbitrary date of 1879. The imposition of Liberalism was to prove the most significant moment in Central American development. Why is this so? Liberalism formed a new ideological framework which determined the future pattern of Central American development. It shaped the socio-economic structures and the export model which survived, *grosso modo*, up until the Second World War. The liberal reforms paved the way for the advent of capitalist agriculture. Aimed principally at producing a capitalist land and labour market, the reforms constituted more than simply an economic project. And the reforms also affected the political framework of the region. The cumulative impact of the application of Liberalism was therefore tremendous. The imposition of the liberal model of growth is perhaps the most important single factor in causing the contemporary crisis in the isthmus.

As a philosophy, the origins of which lie in the period of European Enlightenment, Liberalism associated progress with the twin principles of private accumulation of wealth and private ownership of property. But in the context of Central America, Liberalism became a vehicle for the expression of a series of dogmas and prejudices about progress, development and capitalism. Liberalism in the region mixed devotion to free trade and economic development with a belief in the racial superiority of the creoles over the Indians and an admiration for North Atlantic societies. Taken in conjunction with the penetration of foreign capital at the beginning of the twentieth century, in fruit production in particular, the liberal reforms led directly to the subordination of subsistence agriculture in favour of the cultivation of products determined fundamentally by market demand, and provided the necessary environment for the implantation of the export-led model of development.

The reforms also constituted the starting point for the consolidation of the nation states of the region, which had not occurred, as we noted earlier, at Independence. Economic expansion and insertion into the international economy led to a strengthening of the state under the hegemony of an export-oriented agrarian dominant class. The model of insertion into the global economy can be best understood as an expression of dependent capitalism. 'External stimuli', that is the international system and the global market, played a vital role in the consolidation of oligarchic power. The oligarchic state, discussed in detail in Chapter 3, was based on the exclusion from power of all social groups except those which directly controlled the factors of production.

The modernization of the state, of economic infrastructure (the establishment of roads, railways, etc.), the imposition of wage labour were all part of the liberal oligarchical state. But the reforms were applied with different emphases and results in different countries, and the success of the reforms varied. Cardoso and Perez-Brignoli (1977) offer a typology of the impact of the various reforms according to the degree to which land was privatized, that is the amount of land brought under cultivation for export in comparison with the survival of both communal (land farmed by the indigenous village communities) and common land, used by the peasantry. The degree of social conflict associated with the expansion of export agriculture also varied, partly as a consequence. In Guatemala, for example, common forms of property-holding survived after the introduction of Liberalism, whereas in El Salvador, common land[1] was practically eradicated. Here, apart from the country's small size and high population density, the best coffee-growing areas were situated in the most populous parts of the country. In 1879, the dawn of the liberal era, 25 per cent of the total land area of El Salvador was common land. The liberal legislation of 1879, 1881 and 1882 prohibited the communal possession of land and opened the door to the monopolization of land by a small dominant class composed either of landowners who had previously cultivated indigo, or other groups, some urban, who used the new credit facilities to create coffee *fincas* (Cardoso and Perez-Brignoli 1977: 37). Access to land became impossible for thousands of peasants who were thus forced to live as best they could as labourers on the new coffee farms.

In El Salvador, Guatemala and Costa Rica, the liberal reforms benefited the coffee growers. Coffee was the 'liberal' crop *par excellence*. It transformed relations of production and became the first of a series of export crops to be produced using capitalist agriculture and created an agrarian bourgeoisie. In Guatemala, coffee production had taken root slowly from the period of the Federation, and created a small group of coffee growers with direct channels of access into government. By the 1860s, the decline of cochineal led to an increase in coffee production levels. As in El Salvador, this meant a transformation in how land and property were owned, the introduction of a system of banking credits, the creation of a network of infrastructure to transport the coffee and the creation of a workforce for the new expanding industry. One way more land was made available in the 1870s was through the privatization of Church property, the Church in Guatemala being a far more important landowner that in El Salvador because of its past as the centre of colonial power. In some cases, Church land was given free of charge to the landowners with the only stipulation that it be used to grow coffee. Previously uncultivated land was also privatized and brought into production. And a third way to increase the available land for coffee was through ending the right to pass the renting of plots of land from generation to generation although they had been farmed by particular families since time immemorial. This was known as the *censo enfiteutico*, or emphyteusis, and the problem with it, from the point of view of the Liberals, was that these plots were used for subsistence agriculture not export crops. Legislation passed in 1877 gave the tenants the right to buy within six months – impossible for most tenants who had neither sufficient money nor access to credit – or the land was to be publicly auctioned. It is estimated that 74,250 hectares of land were sold to coffee growers as a result (Cardoso 1991: 61).

The ending of the *censo enfiteutico* was also aimed at addressing the most serious obstacle in the path of the coffee growers in Guatemala – the shortage of labour. Proletarianization of rural labour had taken place slowly, mainly because of the retention of indigenous strongholds still farming communally and the existence of areas where food production for internal consumption remained important. The coffee *finqueros* opted for a system of guaranteeing a labour supply through a combination of returning to the colonial system of forced labour and deepening debt peonage. The new Labour Code of 1877 empowered the *finqueros* to use coercive tactics whenever necessary to obtain Indian labour from the highland communities for the coffee estates during the harvest. At the same time, many Indians had assumed debts for goods that they could not obtain within the communal village. They were therefore forced to work to pay off the debt. The result was a system of coffee production resting essentially on unfree labour. Consequently, in cases where paid labour was employed, the wages were low relative to the rest of the isthmus. Politically too, the impact of this arrangement was enormous. It established a system of social control which linked the landlord class to repression. It meant that from the 1870s onwards, the Indians came to be seen as a block on national progress by the Liberals and the landowners, a view that has made possible in the twentieth century the elaboration of strategies aimed at their elimination.

In Costa Rica, which was in fact the first of the Central American states to turn to the intensive cultivation of coffee because of the almost complete absence of other export crops inherited from the colonial period, coffee caused less upheaval than in either El Salvador or Guatemala. Coffee was produced in Costa Rica in a markedly different kind of environment. The most important differences were in access of land, the average size of the coffee *fincas*, the formation of the labour force and the relationship between the *finqueros* and the labour force. The absence of important export crops before the rise of coffee had made small-holdings too widespread for the concentration of land to be feasible; hence production was encouraged on farms far smaller than those which obtained in oligarchical El Salvador and even Guatemala through the use of credit and other measures adopted by the government. Carolyn Hall's study of Costa Rica demonstrates that the largest *fincas* (over 35 hectares) occupied only 25 per cent of all coffee producing land (Hall 1982). At the same time, the scarcity of labour – Costa Rica's population was small in relation to land mass – meant that wages were high relative to neighbouring countries.

These factors give us an indication of the roots of the exceptional nature of economics and politics in Costa Rica. Costa Rica has not experienced either prolonged armed struggle or violent confrontation for power, features which have characterized politics in Guatemala, El Salvador and Nicaragua. One explanation is that capitalist agriculture took root there differently. The onset of coffee production led to less concentration of land than elsewhere in the region and forced the state to adopt measures aimed at benefiting broader sectors of society than simply the largest landowners. In fact, the role of the state is at least as important in understanding Costa Rican development as the land question. The *cafetaleros* in Costa Rica were not able to establish exclusive control over the state after 1870. Colonel Tomás Guardia, who took power that year, established a tradition of relative state autonomy unknown elsewhere in the region.

Liberalism was weakest in Honduras. The liberal reforms were only partially successful, with the result that Honduras entered the twentieth century with an export base resting on foreign investment. Bananas, which became Honduras' main export, coexisted along-side subsistence agriculture. But bananas did not take land away from the peasants who engaged in subsistence agriculture. Nor did they strengthen the oligarchic elite which remained weak compared with its neighbours. Land for cultivation for internal use was available until the mid twentieth century. So struggles between the peasantry and the state were few, repression generally unnecessary – and the army therefore weak. National integration remained problematic in Honduras, as a result of the failure of Liberalism, compounded by the difficulties of geography which isolated the banana enclaves from the capital and from the areas based on peasant production. So Honduras, in marked difference to its neighbours, was characterized by fragmentation, a weak oligarchy, a subsistence peasantry unthreatened by export production, and the establishment of powerful outside influences over the state.

Green Gold: The Banana Companies

The banana industry established itself as an essential component in the development of the region at the turn of the century. It took off in those states with access to the Atlantic where ports were built to transport the fruit abroad. By the 1920s, bananas were an important part of the Guatemalan, Costa Rican and Honduran economies, and to a lesser extent in Nicaragua. The political economy of banana production was very different from coffee. For example, the banana industry was controlled by foreign companies not local bourgeoisies; and the companies tended to own all aspects of the industry from production to shipping, transport and marketing in a process known as vertical integration of production, magnifying the political influence of the companies. Rivalries between the banana companies were played out within the host countries and across the region, almost leading to war between Guatemala and Honduras in the 1920s. In this way, banana production also increased the fragmentation of the region.

It was in Honduras where the political impact of bananas was greatest. At the beginning of the twentieth century, along with Nicaragua, Honduras was the country where the agro-exports were most backward. Neither during the colonial period nor in the years following Independence, had Honduras developed a stable export product. Infrastructure, both financial and economic, was poor. Although the government of Marco Aurelio Soto (1873–83) introduced some liberal reforms, the dominant class was weak and relied principally upon external support from Guatemala. Soto himself was a mining entrepreneur and tried to promote the mining of precious metals in the country but was defeated by the difficulties of obtaining credit and falls in the price of silver internationally. By the 1890s, the dominant class remained without a solid economic activity to back its political power. It was in this context that the banana companies arrived and were greeted positively by Honduran elites who hoped that foreign capital would bring progress and development, while leaving them in charge of the state.

The first bananas in Honduras were in fact produced by national growers, principally small and medium-sized farmers. Only transport and commercialization were controlled by the foreign companies. Unlike in the past, however, these companies were no longer European but US-based and aimed at satisfying the US market. But in the 1900s, the Honduran government began to grant land directly to the banana companies, a policy which was eventually to make it almost impossible for the smaller producers to survive. The first grant in 1902 was to US citizen William Streich and was of some 5,000 hectares in size. It formed the basis of the Cuyamel Fruit Company of Samuel Zemurray. By the 1920s there were three large companies who controlled Honduran production: the Vacaro Brothers, later to become Standard Fruit, the Cuyamel Company, and United Fruit, a late entrant into Honduras. By 1924, however, United Fruit owned 161,800 hectares of land in the country, of which 70,882 hectares had been granted to them cost-free in return for the construction of railways (which were used for the transportation of the bananas) in the country (Castillo Rivas 1980: 42).

This was the beginning of a new and more exploitative relationship between the banana companies and the host countries, which was to earn Honduras in particular the name of 'banana republic', a derogatory term synonymous with an absence of national control over important political and economic decision-making. It is undoubtedly the case that the expansion of banana production had severe and damaging consequences for national development in Honduras. First of all, the banana companies used their economic weight to gain political leverage, in order to assure government decisions and contracts which would be beneficial to themselves. Economically, this led to the expansion of the companies into railways, transportation and ports. The entire process, from the plantation to marketing abroad, was in the hands of the companies. As a result there was no stimulation for the local bourgeoisie to expand its economic activities. An enclave economy was thereby created in which the circuit of capital formation was completely external. Hence the phenomenal growth of the banana industry had few multiplier effects on the economy as a whole and other areas of the country remained tied to pre-capitalist production. The political consequences of banana production were equally nefarious. The bourgeoisie was kept small and weak and the state remained rudimentary in its development.

The Consequences of Liberalism for Central America

Growth based on export agriculture imposed severe dislocations on the overall economic activity of the Central American states, which included dependence on external markets over which national control was minimal, either because the companies responsible for marketing were foreign (bananas) or because Central America did not produce the export good in sufficient quantities to influence price and demand (coffee). But external vulnerability was not the only weakness that export agriculture imposed on the region. It led to a concentration of investment in the export sector, with the result that production for the internal market declined steadily. This had negative consequences in particular for food production. At the same time, it created dislocations in the supply of labour, attracting labour into the export sector away from domestic agriculture. In the case of coffee, while prices remained high, it proved cheaper in the short run for planters to import food and bring more and more land into coffee production. When prices fell, however, rather than increasing the land available for the internal food supply, the landowners began a desperate search for new export crops. And politically, the state remained underdeveloped and badly financed as the political system was dominated by the struggles of the export groups for power and spoils.

It is little wonder, therefore, that overall the liberal reforms have been described as 'growth without development' (Hamnet 1988). Modernization in the liberal era signified an expansion of infrastructure and an increase in the volume of exports of primary goods. Liberalism contained no notion of the concept of internal development or of the development of the state. Only in Costa Rica did the state escape the tight control of the landowning class or foreign capital. Liberalism failed to promote national integration, as is demonstrated amply by its inability to integrate all social classes into the market economy. It led to a process which Bradford Burns describes as 'the modernization of underdevelopment' in that it created 'an aura of progress around the plantation homes and the privileged areas of the capital [but] it proved increasingly detrimental to the quality of life for the minority' (Bradford Burns 1988: 191). While the planters could afford to pay for imported food, the loss of land for subsistence farming or for local consumption meant increasing hunger and poverty in the countryside for the peasants and for the poor in the cities. This was the case even during the years of expansion and growth.

The fragility of export agriculture as a model of development for the region became apparent in the late 1920s. Dependence exclusively on external markets made the consequences of the international depression particularly acute. After 1929, the region registered a sharp decline in external trade, a fall in real incomes internally, unemployment in urban areas, lay-offs in the export zones, especially severe in banana plantations, and led to threatened, and in some cases actual, bankruptcies among the coffee *finqueros*. Rather than leading to a change in the development model, however, as occurred in the large Latin American countries, the Depression in Central America brought in its wake a restructuring of the state, better to defend the interests of the exporters from groups from below who urged change.

Liberalism also imposed a notion of development which became hegemonic in elite mentality in the region. Ideas about development in Central America essentially relate to how land and labour should be used, and liberalism insisted that land and labour should be deployed to increase production for export. National development therefore came to be synonymous with deepening an economic model which meant the improvement of the living standards only of the elites. Other ideas about how Central American societies should develop, which take into account factors like consumption among peasant families, job security, access to land, health and education, have been marginalized politically and have traditionally found little space within the political systems. These ideas have been described by the elites as subversive and have flourished only outside the established framework for taking political decisions. Until the 1979 revolution in Nicaragua, for example, only in Costa

Rica were living standards understood to be a measure of development.

Nicaragua and Panama: External Domination

Although development as it was understood by the Liberals became the goal for all Central American elites, the reforms were only partially carried out in Nicaragua and Panama. Nicaragua experienced an attempt at Liberalism during the government of José Santos Zelaya (1893–1909) during which coffee production expanded along with attempts to create infrastructure. But coffee was unable to replace cattle-raising, left over from colonial times, as the axis of the economy and remained far less important than in Guatemala and El Salvador. At the same time this weakened the Liberals politically since cattle provided the economic support for the strong Conservative faction within Nicaragua's elites. Santos Zelaya then tried to raise European capital to build a transisthmian canal, in an effort to shore up the Liberals against the conservative opposition by linking it to foreign capital. This move provoked the ire of the US as well as that of the Conservatives and led to the US intervention of 1912. The invasion opened a cycle of US intervention in Nicaragua which only ended with a shift in US policy after 1933 and the start of the 'Good Neighbour' period of US diplomacy. As a result Nicaragua came to depend to an extraordinary degree on Washington and at the same time full integration into the world market through exports was delayed until after the Great Crash of 1929.

Like Nicaragua, Panama attracted the interest of world powers because of its strategic position in the isthmus. Both were considered prime sites for an trans-isthmian canal. In fact, the transportation of goods had always been central to the Panamanian economy, from the time of the Spanish Empire, when silver from Potosí in the Bolivian *altiplano* was brought through Panama to be carried on to Europe via the Caribbean. An inter-oceanic railway was opened in 1855, built with US capital. A part of Colombia until 1903, both its isolation from the national centres of power and the nature of the local economy, dependent on trade and transport, created the basis for regionalism and separatist sentiment which led to an independence movement. Independence triumphed in large measure, however, thanks to the support of the US. When Colombia rejected US proposals to build a Canal across the isthmus, the stage was set for Panama's secession with US connivance. The Canal was opened in 1914, and its strategic importance to US and economic importance inside Panama turned the new state into an enclave of Washington. This process was possible partly because the development of export agriculture had been hindered in Panama, as in Nicaragua, though in this case by the strength of mercantilist groups inside the country. As a result, the local dominant class was weak, ineffectual and vulnerable to external pressure.

The Colonial Caribbean

The history of the insular Caribbean is marked, more than by anything else, by sugar and slavery. Sugar was introduced to the region to satisfy the tastes of the European market and its production required large amounts of hard labour in difficult and unhealthy conditions. This led to the forced importation of labour from Africa to carry out work it was thought that no 'civilized Christian' could be expected to do – that is, to slavery. The contemporary Caribbean, then, can only be understood as a product of the twin forces of sugar and slavery which give unity to the modern history of an otherwise fragmented area.

The islands were shaped by the economic and political imperatives of the metropoles to which they belonged. Inter-colonial rivalries carved up the region and led to its present-day fragmentation in language and politics. But sugar and slavery have also bequeathed a common legacy in terms of race and social structure. The importation of slavery on the scale witnessed in the region, coming on top of the genocide of the indigenous population, transformed the ethnic composition of the region and rendered particularly complex the issues of class and race.

The Caribbean is a mixture of Spanish, Dutch, French and English colonization and it is here where, perhaps more than anywhere else, the great European mercantile empires competed for control over global trade. The original Spanish settlements on Cuba and Hispaniola rapidly expanded to cover the other large islands in the Caribbean Sea: Jamaica was colonized in 1509 and

Puerto Rico was settled in 1512. For the Spanish, the decline of mining on the islands converted the colonies basically into ports of call for shipping from the mainland on their way to Europe. Sugar and bananas were cultivated on Hispanola by the early sixteenth century but only in modest quantities. Later, with the rising threats to Spanish New World possessions from other European powers, the Caribbean islands became military strongholds to protect the more valuable mainland colonies. From the point of view of the Spanish, their economic importance became secondary.

By the 1530s, Spanish ships in the area were regularly facing attack from pirates from England, France and Holland. In the 1560s, the English tried to break the Spanish commercial monopoly on trading with the Caribbean settlers. The 1588 defeat of the Spanish Armada signalled the decline of the Spanish sea-borne empire and heralded the start of other European settlements in the region. Over the next fifty years the English settled in St Kitts and Barbados (1624), St Nevis (1628) and Tobago, St Lucia and Montserrat shortly after. The French seized Guadaloupe and Martinique in 1635 and colonized part of Hispanola, later to turn it into a separate state under French rule, now Haiti. The Dutch, who also initially controlled much of the trade with the French and English settlements, were ceded Curacao, Aruba, Bonaire, St Eustatius, Saba and part of St Martin, all very small islands, in the 1630s. Jamaica, the most important of the British colonies in the area, was seized in a military operation from the Spanish in 1653.

The sheer volume of slaves transported into the Caribbean sugar plantations from this point onwards almost defies belief: it is estimated that between 1450 and 1900 around 11.7 million West Africans were taken by force to the Caribbean of whom 10 million were sold as slaves (Coote 1987: 21). And the legacy of slavery shapes contemporary politics in the region. It has led to the establishment of a colour hierarchy – white over brown over black. The plantation society in which sugar was produced was therefore only superficially 'European'. The planter class was composed of European settlers, many of whom spent large periods of time outside the Caribbean, whereas the workers, the social and legal framework of the plantation, family structure, religion and even language were non-European.

Sugar production also determined the social structure of the region. Controlled by metropolitan capital to serve the metropolitan economies, the sugar industry created weak dominant classes. The planters therefore could not accumulate capital on any scale and were unable to transform the economy away from sugar once its decline had set in. At the same time, their political weakness is revealed in their dependence on military support from the colonial power centres to maintain order on the plantation. The backwardness of the dominant class in the British Caribbean is clear in the widespread phenomenon of absentee landlordism, and in the British and Spanish Caribbean by the need for foreign capital within the economy into the twentieth century.

Slavery and the Plantation in the English Caribbean

By the 1670s, England was the major maritime force operating in the Caribbean and on the way to becoming a major supplier of sugar to Europe, a position it was to consolidate early in the eighteenth century. Sugar from the English Caribbean accounted for 9 per cent of the total volume of imports into Britain. Jamaica, where sugar was produced by a wealthy planter class, was by far the most important of the British Caribbean colonies. Between 1714 and 1773, 'Jamaica was as valuable as New England as an export market; Barbados and Antigua together were worth as much as New York to British exporters' (Williams 1944: 45–6). The planter class and sugar mill owners lived well, importing luxury goods from England, in marked contrast to the living conditions for the workers on the plantations and in the mills where sugar was produced, and indeed in contrast to the relative poverty to which the white elites declined after the ephemeral glory of sugar had passed. But the greatest profits were to be had by the refining industries based in England since sugar was exported semi-refined and processed on arrival. A tax was imposed on the importation of refined sugar from 1670 in order to guarantee that refining be carried out in the metropolis. In this way, accumulation of capital in the Caribbean was restricted and diversification hindered. By the same token, the planters were required to import nearly all their goods from England.

Plantation society rested on violence, threatened and actual, making the planters dependent on protection from England and the troops who were permanently stationed on the islands. In the last resort, slaves were to be kept in order by the army. Yet the demise of slavery in the British Caribbean at the beginning of the nineteenth century was neither a result of its inhumanity nor was it overthrown by the slaves themselves. Rather it was the result of economic change. The productivity of the islands was declining and sugar was becoming less important to the British economy. In Jamaica 'between 1799 and 1807, 65 plantations had been abandoned, 32 were sold under decrees of the Court of Chancery to meet claims against them, and in 1807 suits were pending against 115 others. In 1806, the price of sugar was less than the cost of production' (Williams 1970: 281). Sugar was suddenly unprofitable because of the rise in sugar beet production in Europe and because the plantation, in the new world of industry and efficiency, was economically irrational. It supported an excess of domestic slaves in particular who were unproductive and merely guaranteed the comforts of the planters. At the same time the Caribbean became less important to Britain as the Empire extended over the globe. Finally, the onset of industrial capitalism in Britain modified ideologies and beliefs, in the area of labour relations and ethics for example, leading to demands for the ending of the slave trade, which England had dominated, and of slavery itself. The end of slavery came with the Emancipation Act, passed in 1833 and imposed by England on territories under colonial rule. In Jamaica, the Act prompted a wave of protests from the House of Assembly which represented planters and slave owners. The opposition of the local dominant class was of course unable to stop emancipation but it put the issue of representative government for the colonies firmly on the agenda for the first time. It was to resurface throughout the nineteenth and twentieth centuries.

The end of slavery transformed relations of production as many of the ex-slaves fled from the plantation, turning to subsistence agriculture. This phenomenon occurred throughout the insular Caribbean where the end of slavery signified the basis for the reconstitution of a black peasantry. Problems with labour supply led to the decline in the large estates and contributed to further falls in production. However, this problem was not as acute as in other parts of the Caribbean, for example Haiti, and the English attempted to resolve it by introducing indentured or contract labour from Asia or China. None the less production never regained its previous importance, though colonial society was still preserved and the social dominance of the planter class was upheld by the colonial system. But technological backwardness, lack of investment and increasing competition from Cuba made it impossible for sugar to recover. Sugar only took off again in Jamaica in the early twentieth century when the United Fruit Company and the West Indies Sugar Company, a subsidiary of Tate & Lyle, moved in. The British Colonial Office meanwhile urged economic diversification on the planters to little avail, and the islands continued to depend on sugar and its by-products until the Second World War.

Haiti: From Sugar Island to the First Independent Territory

The richest sugar colony in the eighteenth century was Saint-Domingue, as it was known after its secession to the French in 1697, situated on the western half of Hispanola. Virtually abandoned by the Spanish, it had become a base for French pirates operating in the area. But after 1697, the French settlers immediately planted sugar cane. Higher yields were obtained there than anywhere else in the Caribbean and the fertility of the virgin soil then stands in sharp contradiction to the deforested and eroded land of today. By the 1790s, Saint-Domingue produced almost as much sugar singly as the total produced by all the British possessions together (Baez 1986: 67). Table 1.1 indicates the increase in production in Saint-Domingue.

Sugar was to transform the social structure of Saint-Domingue. It created a small class of white plantation owners, often absent, who had few links or loyalties to the colony and ties instead to France, and a small white artisan, professional or overseer class, none of whom exercised political power directly. The planters were known

Table 1.1   Sugar production, 1730–91 (metric tons)

	Jamaica	Barbados		Saint-Domingue
1730	16,263	12,731	(1726)	15,000
1760	39,841	7,589		56,646
1791	60,900	7,105		78,696

Source: Adapted from Baez 1986: 65 and 66.

as the *grands blancs*, a status they shared with the most important members of the colonial bureaucracy. The white artisan class was known, logically enough, as the *petits blancs*. The labour for the plantations was provided by African slaves. Starting from a mere 2,000 in 1681, the number of slaves in Saint-Domingue increased to 117,000 in 1730 and to 480,000 in 1791. The death rate was high in the plantations as evidenced by the fact that 864,000 slaves were imported into the colony over the same period (Prince 1985: 11). The slaves constituted 80 per cent of the colony's population on the eve of Independence. Wedged between the slaves and the white population was a small but growing mulatto sector, known in French as the *affranchis*, subject to political, social and economic discrimination legitimated in the *Code Noir*, the official French colonial code of practice. In contrast to other Caribbean islands, and as a result of the demand for sugar from Saint-Domingue, the mulattos were conceded the right to own plantations. This was to become an important factor in the internal struggles which erupted in the territory during and immediately after Independence.

On the eve of Independence, Saint-Domingue was a colony ruled by fear and violence. The eighteenth century had witnessed a series of slave rebellions which were crushed in blood by the military authorities. But the differences between white and black, the enslaved and the free, were not the only tensions in the colony. The *petits blancs* resented the incongruence between their high colour status and their low economic status; the *affranchis* opposed the limitations and restrictions on their political and economic rights; and there were divisions among the *grands blancs* as some of the planters resented the privileges and corruption of the colonial bureaucratic elite while they themselves were excluded from political power. Others objected to the *exclusif*, which meant that planters could only trade with France. These tensions were to erupt in the years following the French Revolution, the prelude to independence for the colony.

Following the Revolution in France, the *grands blancs* called a Colonial Assembly based on property rights (thereby excluding the *petits blancs*) in the town of Saint Marc, sided with the moderate factions in Paris and called for self-government. This was an attempt to keep plantation society intact, and therefore of course slavery, against the demands for liberty and equality from the revolutionaries. At the same time, the *grands blancs* sought to maximize their own power base by demanding an end to the *Exclusif*. The *petits blancs*, on the other side, tended to sympathize with the democratizing tendencies in the Revolution and therefore opposed the Assembly. The mulattos also sympathized with more radical factions in the Revolution because they would stand to gain full legal and political rights. The refusal of the planters to grant civil rights to the mulattos led to a mulatto rebellion in 1790. It was defeated and had gone unsupported in Paris but the issue remained, simmering under the surface. Hence when a slave revolt broke out in 1791, it plunged Saint-Domingue into a struggle where the intersections of race and class are difficult to disentwine and dealt a death-blow to colonial control.

The leader of the slaves, Toussaint L'Overture, assumed complete control of the colony by 1798 and defended it from attack by the English. Independence was not demanded, until Napoleon decided to reintroduce slavery into the colony and took Toussaint L'Overture, Haiti's first national leader, prisoner. A second revolt was then led by Jean-Jaques Dessalines and Henry Christophe, independence was achieved in January 1804 and Haiti became the first independent territory of the region. Haitian independence was only recognized by France, however, after the new government agreed to compensate the planters who had lost their land, leading to a debt which forced the country to raise loans which were not paid until 1922.

Independence left the economy in ruins. Toussaint L'Overture had wanted the retention of the sugar economy, though using free labour, and had encouraged the planters to return. Dessalines, in contrast, supported the trend which had emerged as a de facto reality during the Wars of Independence towards dividing the plantations up into plots of land for former slaves. A few large estates continued to produce sugar in the south under the domination of the mulattos, but the tendency towards subsistence agriculture was irreversible. Other export crops were attempted such as coffee and timber, but with little success. A return to subsistence agriculture responded to the cultural demands of the ex-slave population, and in any case the chances for export crops were limited by poor internal capital accumulation and a constitutional order forbidding foreigners to own property. By the 1820s, landless labourers constituted only a third of the rural labour force. For Haiti, then, Independence, the end of slavery and the collapse of the sugar industry did not signify a transition to capitalism; instead it meant the resurgence of an archaic mode of production. Production for export did not take off again until after the US occupation between 1915 and 1934.

The Rise of Sugar in the Spanish Caribbean

The exhaustion of gold reserves on Hispanola was the prelude to a long period of decline through the seventeenth and first part of the eighteenth century in Cuba, Santo Domingo and Puerto Rico. During this time, the costs of maintaining the colonies outweighed the benefits extracted from them and they served as military outposts to defend the wealth of Mexico and Peru from Spain's colonial rivals. Economic isolation had resulted in a measure of agricultural self-sufficiency in the colonies. The relationship between Cuba and Spain during the sugar boom differed significantly from that of Haiti and France or Jamaica and England in that the weakness of the Spanish Empire by the mid nineteenth century meant that it could have no pretensions to a trade monopoly.

Sugar was not cultivated intensely until the nineteenth century, when it was grafted onto an already established social structure. Before the 1820s, small-scale cattle farming, sugar and tobacco contributed to the formation of an economic system in Cuba based on access to land and the generation of a system of large estates, smaller farms and common land. This system led to the creation of a dominant landed class with few possibilities of capital accumulation given the small scale of production and the absence of external markets, supported by the other privileged classes on the island – the military, the colonial administration and the Catholic Church. The dominant class was closely tied to Spain and had not participated in the independence movements of the Spanish colonies on the mainland. The immense plantations which were created in Cuba later in the nineteenth century therefore took root in an already settled colonial society. As a result sugar did not lead to an absentee planter class along the lines of Saint Domingue and Jamaica.

Sugar boomed in Cuba after the independence of Haiti and its switch to subsistence agriculture, and by 1860 Cuba had become essentially a one-crop economy (see Table 1.2). More than 25 per cent of land was given over to sugar while cattle raising and crop farming were confined to the eastern part of the island and supplied the plantations on the west (Hamnet 1988). Labour for the plantations was assured, as on other Caribbean islands, through the importation of slaves on a massive scale. Slavery had existed on Cuba as early as 1515, and had been used as labour in both rural and urban areas, but it grew hugely with the expansion of the sugar industry, just at a time when the trend elsewhere in the region was towards emancipation. Estimates point to the arrival of perhaps 1,000 new slaves a month until the outbreak of Cuba's first attempt at independence against Spain in 1868. Partly to counter increasing international criticism of slavery, plantation owners began to turn instead to contract labour from China especially. Conditions of work were equally horrific for the contract workers which was in reality a disguised form of slavery. The following testimony from a Chinese worker is illustrative of the conditions under which they were employed:

> we are old and weak and it is only uncertain whether we shall die in a depot or in a fresh place of service or be cast out as useless by the roadside; but it is certain that for us there will be neither coffin nor grave, and that our bones will be tossed into a pit, to be burnt with those of horses and oxen and to be afterwards used to refine sugar, that neither our sons nor our sons' sons will ever know what we have endured. (Mintz 1987: 53)

The plantations continued to operate with slave labour until 1880. Unlike elsewhere in the Caribbean, the ending of slavery did not lead to a decline in production. Free labour replaced slavery without any disruption in production. In fact, the Cuban planter class had argued unsuccessfully with the Spanish Crown that the ending of slavery and the introduction of free labour relations would lead to an increase in output and efficiency. Cuba was therefore the first Caribbean island to introduce capitalist labour relations into the sugar industry. Cuban sugar production was also distinguished by its prompt adoption of technology (machinery and railways, especially) and by its close association with the US market, even before independence from Spain. In 1865, 65 per cent of Cuban sugar was exported to the US, rising to 82 per cent in 1877. In 1893, £64 million worth of sugar was exported to the US while exports to Spain were worth only £6 million. A new attempt at introducing protectionist policies on the part of Madrid led to a fall in demand in the US after 1894 and demands on the part of the planters for independence. It was the prelude to the Cuban struggle for independence which led to the Spanish-American war of 1898 for control of Cuba.

Table 1.2   Sugar production, 1815–94 (metric tons)

	1815	1882	1894
Puerto Rico	79,660	579,660*	1,079,660*
Grenada	11,594	1,478	3
Jamaica	79,660	32,638	19,934
Trinidad	7,682	55,327	46,869
Puerto Rico	——	65,000*	48,500*
Cuba	39,961	595,000	1,054,214

*For Puerto Rico, the figures correspond to 1886 and 1893–4 respectively.
Source: Adapted from Williams 1970: 366.

The 1898 war tightened relations between the sugar production on the island and the US. The US occupation ended in 1902, though the island remained under US indirect control. The US presence stimulated a further expansion and modernization of the industry, which led to a concentration and centralization in production on the plantation and a separation of the plantation from the mill or factory where sugar was refined. Capital investment in the industry increased, in particular investments from foreigners, mostly US citizens who took up residence on the island. The dominant class, which had not been able to win independence from Spain alone, was weakened in the process and reduced to a position of dependence on the US. As a result, the consolidation of an independent nation state under the control of a local dominant class was aborted.

The late nineteenth century also witnessed the spread of capitalist sugar production to Santo Domingo and Puerto Rico, though production levels were unable to rival those of Cuba. Puerto Rico, smaller and more insignificant in terms of its importance for the Spanish Crown, had depended economically on a combination of food production for internal consumption, cattle-raising and contraband. Coffee became its first important export crop in the nineteenth century. Coffee was grown profitably with free labour and the size of *haciendas* was small. Slavery existed on the island, but did not constitute a central element in production terms and, uniquely in the Caribbean, the white population outnumbered the non-whites. In both Puerto Rico and the Dominican Republic, agricultural capitalism spread out unevenly and the peasantry retained partial access to land, though output of traditional exports, coffee in the case of Puerto Rico and tobacco and cocoa in the Dominican Republic, began to decline. In the case of Puerto Rico, the US occupation after 1898 led to larger-scale production and to a loss of land for coffee, affecting *hacendados* and the peasantry. In the Dominican Republic, the expansion of sugar had a particularly negative effect on food production for local consumption, as the plantations, paying high wages relative to the peasant economy, attracted labour away from the food-producing areas, leading to food shortages, high prices and a national economy dependent on international rather than local demand.

Politics and Economics on Independence: The Spanish Caribbean

For almost all of the nineteenth century, Haiti remained the only independent territory within the Caribbean. But the economic decline of Spain created tensions between Madrid and the remaining Spanish colonies, which led to struggles for independence. Santo Domingo, which itself fell into economic decline and was dominated by its independent neighbour, Haiti, freed itself of Spanish control in 1865. Like the rest of the Spanish Caribbean, the newly independent territory of the Dominican Republic soon drifted into the sphere of influence of the US. For the decline of Spain coincided with the rise of the US as hegemonic power in the region and resulted in a steady transfer of the metropolitan pole around which the economies of the Dominican Republic, Puerto Rico and Cuba functioned from Madrid to the US. 'Independence' therefore was relative for these three territories, especially for Puerto Rico and Cuba which were occupied in the Spanish-American war of 1898, which occurred as the Cubans were engaged in their second War of Independence from Spain. The US ostensibly came in to support the Cubans but in fact provoked the war with Spain to assure themselves of control over the island. The US perceived Spain as unable to guarantee the stability of the region. Meanwhile, many of the planters inside Cuba felt their future was best assured by close ties to the US and supported US intervention and even the idea of annexation. As a result, the US came to control the destiny of the Spanish Caribbean to such a degree that the Cuban revolutionaries who took power in 1959 traced their lineage directly from José Martí, the leader of the Cuban Independence movement in the 1890s and proclaimed the second independence of the island.

The US victory was swift and inaugurated a military occupation which lasted until 1902. The withdrawal of troops took place after the passing of a new constitution which left Cuba under US tutelage; the 'Platt Amendment' granted stations to the US on the island, gave the US some influence over Cuba's management of its economy and granted the provision that the US could intervene in order to guarantee 'the preservation of Cuban independence'. The first independent government of Estrada Palma lasted only until 1905, when the US military returned. Meanwhile, the occupation of Puerto Rico in 1898 was to prove more permanent and led to annexation of this strategically important island which only a few years earlier had won the right to self-government from the Spanish. It was not until the 1930s that the status of Puerto Rico was to be discussed seriously again.

Politics and Economics on Independence: The British Caribbean

The decline of sugar and the end of slavery together constituted a watershed in the British Caribbean. Thereafter, the problems of governance within the territories and the relationship between Britain and the local dominant class became more complex. The forms of government which had evolved in the British Caribbean were based, on the one hand, on the dual principles of maintaining imperial domination and upholding white supremacy, which underlay the entire Empire, and on the other, on the tendency towards representative government which is a key factor in British constitutional development – that is, representation for the white local dominant class where it existed. Britain had decided early on in favour of granting representation to free citizens (i.e. whites) in the form of Houses of Assembly partly as a means of raising the funds for colonial administration. This contrasted with the tendency which emerged early in the nineteenth century for the Crown to retain decision-making powers in Westminster, with the result that eventually two different systems of government emerged: that of the Crown colony, ruled from Westminster, and the islands which retained a local legislature.

The tensions between the two systems intensified after emancipation. In Jamaica, the largest of the British possessions and with a well-established local Assembly, emancipation changed radically the existing socio-economic structure. A property qualification which restricted representation in the Assembly could no longer be relied on to keep blacks unrepresented since many planters pulled out of the island after 1833. This, coupled with the fall in sugar production, reduced land prices by a considerable amount. By the 1860s, blacks and mulattos formed a majority within the Assembly. It was in this climate of growing politicization of the non-white population that the beginning of open conflict with the metropolis began, in the form of the Jamaica Rebellion of 1865. The British troops responded with a wave of unprecedented repression, razing the houses of non-whites, hanging the leaders of the Rebellion and imposing the death penalty after courts-martial in 364 cases. As a result, Jamaica was turned into a Crown Colony, losing its assembly, in a reflection of the tendency of British imperialism at the time. Of the British territories, only Barbados retained a local legislature, whereas in Jamaica, ruled directly by the Crown after the Rebellion, a partially decentralized form of government was reinstituted after 1885 with the introduction of a Legislative Council.

But neither full Crown Colony government nor the modified version of Jamaica after 1885 were able to solve the problems of the islands, rooted as they were in the depression of the sugar industry, the absence of stable alternative products and the emergence of a low-wage high-unemployment economy. A Royal Commission was sent from Britain in 1938 to investigate the catastrophic state of the British Caribbean and the depression in the sugar industry. It concluded that the salaries and dividends which high-grade employees and share-holders received were paid by keeping local wages unacceptably low. Wages in the sugar industry in the British Caribbean were lower even than in Cuba or Puerto Rico: in 1938 an unskilled sugar worker in Jamaica earned between 48 and 60 cents a day, while the minimum wage in Cuba was 80 cents a day. And Jamaicans were better paid than labourers in Barbados, Grenada, Trinidad and St Kitts. The Commission also noted living standards in Jamaica for workers:

> people [were] living in huts the walls of which were bamboo knitted together . . . the ceilings were made from dry crisp coconut branches which shifted their position with every wind. The floor measured 8 feet by 4 feet. The hut was 5 feet high. Two openings served as windows and a third, stretching from the ground to the roof, was the door . . . In this hut lived nine people, a man, his wife and seven children. They had no water and no latrine. There were two beds. The parents slept in one, and as many of the children as could hold on in the other. The rest used the floor. (Williams 1970: 453)

Yet despite these conditions, decolonization in the British Caribbean, in marked contrast to Haiti and the Spanish Caribbean, was peaceful. Britain emerged from the Second World War economically exhausted, aware that the dismantling of the Empire was inevitable and only a matter of time. Only the form that independence would take and the post-independent political map of the region were in doubt. The biggest stumbling block to early independence lay in the small size of the territories. Independence, without some form of federation, was impossible from the point of view of the British Colonial Office, because it would leave the new, independent communities isolated diplomatically, weak economically and contribute to the instability of the region. Ten years of discussion were required to come up with a Federation of the British West Indies, dominated by the largest islands, Jamaica, Trinidad and Barbados, in association with the Windward and the Leeward islands. The Federation came into existence in 1958 with the idea that full independence would be granted four years later. But Jamaica seceded from the Federation in 1961 following a plebiscite on the issue. As a result, Independence, 'by default', replaced the Federation as official British policy (Payne 1988a: 15). Jamaican independence in 1962 was followed by Trinidad and Barbados. The smaller islands followed through the 1970s and 1980s.

Conclusion

We have reviewed briefly in this chapter the history of Central America and the Caribbean from its 'discovery' by the European powers to the onset of the contemporary period. There are obvious and major differences between the historical patterns of political and economic development of the societies which make up the region. Some countries achieved independence almost 150 years before others. The political influence of the colonial powers over the territories varied enormously as did the legacy they left behind. The economic potential of each country, its ethnic composition and political cultures also differ. But some threads of unity also emerge. All have developed small agro-exporting economies, vulnerable to outside pressure as a result of imperial or external control. All have had to adapt inherited and imposed political systems to fit new societies. And all found themselves pulled over time into the sphere of influence of their giant and powerful neighbour, the US. This has happened even in the British colonies, independent relatively late in the twentieth century.

Having seen the historical legacies of the region, in the chapters that follow we examine how political systems and models of economic development have been implemented. Development throughout the region in the twentieth century has been essentially about the usages of land and labour. The decisions of how to use land, what to grow, how to maintain a supply of labour in the export sector and the construction of national labour forces have corresponded in some cases to internal elites and in other cases, at least partially, to external actors. But above all, these decisions have been taken in the *political* arena, and have been the result of political motivations as well as the apparently neutral rationale of economic growth.

2

Making Politics: Class, Ethnicity and Nation

Politics everywhere is about power and the exercise of domination by some groups over others. Political conflicts reflect the tensions, alliances and negotiations which take place between groups in society. These conflicts are played out in the private and the public sphere – that is, within the framework of everyday social relations (for example, the workplace, the school and the family) and within the established arena for the resolution or mediation of conflict: the state. Most analyses of power and conflict from the perspective of political science concentrate on the state, with the result that some social scientists see politics as a struggle by contending social groups to control the state and thus assure the implementation of a particular model of development. There are many other arenas within the private sphere where domination is exercised or hegemony constructed because all social interaction has a political content. But in this chapter we concentrate on politics as it is played out in the public arena.

The construction of a public space and the organization of a political system mean the creation of a state and individuals and groups to operate it. The professionalization of political activity, the expansion of the functions of the state and the development of a complex bureaucracy have all meant that professional politicians (a 'political class') have come into existence everywhere and that the state has assumed some degree of autonomy from society. Today, even in the Caribbean Basin where political struggles are less 'mediated' than in advanced capitalist societies, those who operate the contemporary state are not necessarily members of the dominant socio-economic groups, though it is unlikely that they will be completely devoid of connections to them either. In Central America and the Caribbean, the political class remains ultimately dependent on and responsive to local socio-economic elites and in some cases the metropolitan state. But the political systems sometimes allow for a certain diffusion of power.

Traditionally, the state in the Caribbean Basin operated as an instrument of domination for powerful local socio-economic groups or the metropolis. However, elite groups have not always been able to exercise uncontested domination. Subaltern social groups have been able to challenge the ruling elite at a number of critical historical moments, though generally in an unorganized and spontaneous fashion. In fact, struggles to broaden participation and to construct polities representative of all its citizens are a feature of contemporary politics in the region. In the colonial Caribbean, for example, slave revolts were a constant threat to plantation societies. On the isthmus, the rise of export agriculture, the penetration of capitalism in the countryside and the beginning of wage–labour relations were accompanied by a violence which marked political systems and laid the foundations of the repression and marginalization which, with brief exceptions, have characterized state responses to popular organizations throughout the present century.

In this chapter we identify the main political actors in the region before examining the political systems in detail in Chapter 3. Regional politics changed rapidly in the post-war period and we therefore look at the way 'new' actors have emerged and the transformation of the traditional elite.

The Determinants of Politics: Class and Ethnicity

There are two major cleavages which explain the political behaviour of dominant and subaltern groups in the region: class and ethnicity. Ethnicity and class have been the major determinants of stratification and social identity in the region since colonization. Which is more important? There is no simple answer, though it is clear that in many countries the dynamic of politics depends upon the interaction of the two. Many sociologists, marxist and non-marxist alike, concur in ascribing class (stratification for Weberians) a primary role in social organizations, production and politics globally. For Marx, an irreconcilable conflict between producers and non-producers was at the heart of all political conflict and constituted the motor of history. But class formation is not an identical process in all capitalist societies. Class cannot be ascribed mechanically nor is it immutably fixed because societies are in a constant process of change and transformation. So we need to look at how classes are formed in Central America and the insular Caribbean.

According to Roxborough, 'the class structures of the Third World differ from those of the advanced nations in two principal ways: they are more complex and the classes themselves are usually weaker' (Roxborough 1979: 72). Historically, the local dominant class has been weak or has even been replaced by the metropolitan state or the bourgeoisie of the metropolitan power. In the insular Caribbean, dominant elites are even now highly dependent upon external support. Even in the isthmus, where in most cases the dominant class exercised power over the state independent of foreign powers and controlled production within the economic system (the exceptions are Honduras and Panama), the oligarchies have needed periodically to rely on external support. At the same time, the composition of subordinate classes is fluid. Finally, non-class cleavages, especially ethnicity but also gender, language and religion, cut across class lines.

In spite of these difficulties, many social scientists have continued to assert the primacy of class cleavages in the region. One of the most widely used analyses of class is that of Alejandro Portes (Portes 1985). He uses the following criteria to ascribe class: control over the labour power of others; economic remuneration; and position in the productive process. His conclusion is that there are five classes within Latin America and the Caribbean: the dominant class, which owns and controls production, controls the labour power of others and has the highest income through investment and capital, which at the same time ensure its retention of power; the bureaucratic-technical class, which does not own the bases of production but controls labour power and enjoys high economic rewards; the proletariat in the formal economy, which controls neither production nor the labour power of others but has a relatively regular income; the informal petty bourgeoisie, which controls production and labour power, but on a small scale and usually without earning a high income; and the informal proletariat, which has no control over production or labour power and enjoys no regular economic remuneration. While this analysis has the advantage of taking on board the complexity and fragmentation of peripheral capitalism, it concentrates essentially on class analysis within the urban economy. It assumes that the dominant class enjoys control over production and labour within agrarian capitalism as well as within the urban sector, but it fails to make distinctions within the peasantry and the rural poor. With this limitation in mind, however, it undoubtedly constitutes a useful focus for class analysis in the region.

The original determinants of social structure throughout the region were the plantation and the *hacienda*, which determined labour relations and access to and use of land. As a result a class structure suitable for export agriculture and the maintenance of colonial control developed. But class was associated with ethnicity from the earliest days of colonialization, for ethnicity was the key to the allocation of labour roles within the 'New World'. As a result, some social scientists have preferred to assert the central importance of ethnicity and talk of 'colour-class', especially in relation to the Caribbean. The class/ethnicity debate is particularly acute in ex-plantation societies which were organized around the guiding principles of racism and slavery and where social divisions based on race and culture are immediately perceptible. In the Central American isthmus, in contrast, the black legacy is less immediately visible and the cultural boundaries between the white settlers and the Indian population were somewhat more permeable. This led to the development of an overwhelmingly *mestizo* population and was accompanied by the retention of land rights by indigenous communities, allowing for the development of a separate economy (at least in part) until 1880s, when the intensification of capitalist agriculture brought this period to a close. But the Indian population has also been subject to a permanent process of structural racism and deculturalization. According to Stavenhagen, the Indians were subject to 'internal colonization' after the 1880s, when the loss of communal land meant their effective subordination to white or *ladino* new elites (Stavenhagen 1970).

The abolition of slavery in plantation societies did nothing to reduce the importance of ethnicity as a major determinant of stratification. Jacome noted:

the abolition had little influence over the social situation of the negroes given that legal emancipation did not produce substantial changes in their social reality. . . . In the British Caribbean, the difference between white and black, the first as elite and the second as a dominated group, was much more marked because of the absence of an important mulatto sector. (Jacome 1990: 54)

This, then, is the point of departure for sociologists who stress the importance of ethnicity for post-colonial societies from orthodox marxist analyses of society, which stress class. The most significant contribution to our understanding of the place of ethnicity in the contemporary Caribbean has been made by the 'pluralists'. The pluralist school insists that social conflict is a result primarily of racial, cultural or ethnic criteria rather than class; they contend that

societies are stratified into politico-racial (and cultural) sections, with class playing a secondary or tertiary role, either over-determining the race–culture hierarchy or stratifying, internally, contraposed segments (usually created when whites decolonise and leave the political battle ground to contending, co-ordinate racial categories). (Clarke 1991)

Hall's influential analysis of plantation societies of the insular Caribbean is important precisely because it tries to overcome the division between race and class. Instead he stresses the relationship *between* socio-economic and racial factors (Hall 1977). But he comes down on the side of a class analysis as the means to understand conflict in contemporary societies. He argues that the abolition of slavery operated as a transition to class societies in place of the caste system of colonialism. For Hall, the development of political parties, trade unions and parliamentary institutions in the case of the English-speaking Caribbean operated to strengthen class identification. Independence and the development of the nation state, in the Commonwealth Caribbean at least, brought to power a coalition of class forces which formed a dominant bloc tied to the emergence of a national bourgeoisie and coopted other politicized groups. His analysis stresses the importance of class in the context of societies where the ideological matrix of conflict has been created originally by ethnic and cultural conflict.

Class Actors in Caribbean Basin Politics

The Oligarchy or Plantocracy

The oligarchy, or the plantocracy as it is often referred to in the Commonwealth Caribbean, is the class of large landowners who produce for export. Traditionally it is the class which has exercised control over land and labour in the region. It remains the key to the dominant bloc in Central America, though not in Haiti nor in the English-speaking Caribbean where large export-oriented farms are mainly a thing of the past. In the Commonwealth Caribbean manufacturing, business interests and even commercial elites have largely replaced agro-exporters as the main internal economic organizations shaping the political agenda.

In the English-speaking Caribbean, the landowning class owed loyalty ultimately to the metropolis, even though it might have disagreed on particular policies implemented in the colonies or on the correct system of government to be pursued.[1] Its power was limited by colonialism, and so, although the basis of the political and economic elite until Independence, it was on the whole more permeable than the oligarchies of Central America. More than economic interests, the plantocracy by the end of the nineteenth century was united in defence of its whiteness. In Jamaica 'white society accepted a certain level of equality among whites, not because they believed that all whites were equal but because being white in the Caribbean meant above all *not* being black' (author's emphasis) (Bryan 1991: 67). As a result, though there were clear differences in income, education and culture between the plantocracy and the rest of white society, the elite was moderately open to entry from new sources of wealth such as merchant capital, investments in bananas or transportation and even to professionals such as doctors or lawyers – providing these individuals were white. This permeability was accentuated by the economic difficulties of maintaining sugar production in the British Caribbean. The divisions between rich and poor whites were sufficiently marked for the socio-economic elite to remain culturally homogeneous and retain a class identity. But undoubtedly the idea that the Caribbean was made up of racially divided societies and that the responsibility of the whites was to civilize and christianize the black population (as well as exercise economic domination over them) – central features of the ideological vision of the white elite and the imperial state – could sometimes divert inter-class rivalry and even blur class distinctions between the plantocracy and the new capitalist sources of wealth by the twentieth century.

Unlike the Caribbean economic elites which owed their existence to mercantile capitalism, the modern Central American oligarchies, emerging later, took shape alongside the full incorporation of the isthmus into the world economy in the 1880s. In some cases the new liberal dominant class absorbed the old conservative guard, while in others (Guatemala and Nicaragua) this was less marked; and in some cases too the new oligarchy proved permeable to foreign residents with capital (Cardoso 1991: 56). Coffee, and with it the decline in subsistence production and the creation of a rural labour force, was the main vehicle for oligarchic control over society. At the same time, coffee cemented the organic relation between the oligarchy and the state. Only in Costa Rica were the large coffee growers forced to share power with other socio-economic groups; elsewhere the oligarchies maintained their distance over other producers and middle class professionals until the 1930s.

Most sociologists have examined the Central American oligarchies as a closed socio-economic elite or class whose power rests upon economic control backed up by the diffusion throughout society, even among the dominated classes, of values and symbols which uphold elite power (for example land ownership, Western culture, dress, skin colour). This ideological control lies at the heart of the construction of oligarchic hegemony (Torres-Rivas 1990: 52–3). Family networks and kinship ties have also played an important role in maintaining homogeneity within the oligarchy and keeping it small and unified. For example, in El Salvador, the oligarchic elite is traditionally referred to as the 'fourteen families', and although today that elite is much larger, Dunkerley argues that twenty-five firms still account for 84 per cent of all coffee exports (Dunkerley 1991b: 160).[2] Extreme concentration of income, illustrated in Tables 2.1 and 2.2, remains an important feature of Central American economic and political life. Oligarchic ideology is also influenced by racist notions of white superiority, a rejection of the Indians as an ethnic group and of *ladinizacion*.

As well as forming the socio-economic elite, the oligarchies of Central America and Spanish-speaking Caribbean also constituted a political elite, the only group enjoying state power until after the

Table 2.1   Distribution of national income in selected Central American countries in 1989

| | Population sectors by quintiles (20%) | | | | |
	1st*	2nd	3rd	4th	5th
Costa Rica	4.0	9.1	14.3	21.9	50.8
Guatemala	2.1	5.8	10.5	18.6	63.0
Honduras	2.7	6.0	10.2	17.6	63.5
Panama	2.0	6.3	11.6	20.3	59.8

* The 1st quintile is made up of the poorest 20 per cent of the population; the 5th, of the richest 20 per cent.
Source: *Instituto de Relaciones European–Latinoamerican*, Madrid.

Table 2.2   Per cent of national income controlled by the top 10 per cent of the population (selected countries)

Country	%
Costa Rica	34.1
Guatemala	46.6
Honduras	47.9
Panama	42.1

Source: *Instituto de Relaciones European–Latinoamerican*, Madrid.

1930s. A very different situation existed in the colonial Caribbean, where the government was in the hands of the metropolitan state and its bureaucracy, and where as a result the planters did not assume direct responsibility for decision-making. Even in Honduras, where the liberal reforms were rendered somewhat vacuous by the absence of a strong internal class and the importance of foreign capital, the state was managed by members of the internal elite, albeit subject to pressures to make policy in favour of foreign capital. The absence of a political commitment to independent political management and statehood within the English-speaking Caribbean contributed to the decline of the white economic elite in most of the territories, accentuated by the steady falls in profitability of traditional export production in the region. Following independence in the Caribbean, given the weakness of the local leading class, the foreign bourgeoisie or even the metropolitan state remained central reference points for national decision-making.

After the 1930s, the power of the oligarchies was modified in Central America. Sometimes oligarchic domination was severely threatened and at times only restored with the assistance of the Armed Forces (El Salvador; Guatemala). We can also note the beginning of the process of reform of the political superstructures after 1945, which broadened the number of the enfranchized through the cooptation of some middle sectors, without providing any real reform to substantiate and legitimize the changes. The exception in this process, as in so many others, is Costa Rica.

Today, the oligarchy is less closed than in the past, when the source of its income was centred on agrarian production and where land fulfilled a second, non-economic function, conferring on its owners a series of political and cultural rights unquestioned within the confines of a deferential political culture. Now, the term 'oligarchy' refers to the political agreement between the export-oriented groups with the new urban businesses, both commercial and financial, tied to foreign capital, to exclude from effective participation other social groups and to maintain privileges reminiscent of pre-capitalist modes of production. The economic diversification of leading socio-economic groups, the professional-ization of politics, and the mobilization of subaltern groups together have challenged the oligarchies' exclusive hold on power. According to Bourricaud, the contemporary oligarchs are financial speculators, rather than simply agrarian producers (Bourricaud 1967). None the less, economic modernization has proved no barrier to the retention of traditional means of holding on to power, through corruption and clientelism as well as repression. Especially in El Salvador and Guatemala the oligarchies perfected capitalist methods of production and maximized profits from the export sector, without reforming either their political or social codes of behaviour. As a result there is no correlation between capitalism and democracy in Central America.

Nevertheless, the oligarchies and the dominant economic con-sortia in the region have been seriously threatened by the events of the 1970s and 1980s. The economic crisis of the 1980s weakened local capital, and increased the leverage of external actors over the state throughout the region. At the same time, the dominant economic groups were faced with fierce opposition internally from reformist and revolutionary groups, especially in El Salvador, Guatemala, Nicaragua and Grenada. However, the predicted collapse of the oligarchies did not on the whole come about. Even in Nicaragua, local capital has recovered much of its political control following the election of Violeta Chamorro in February 1990, and in El Salvador the oligarchy has survived the civil war as a major player in the political and economic arena, though the right-wing government of Alfredo Crisitiani, himself a coffee grower, was forced to make considerable concessions in order to bring the war to an end.

The Middle Class

There are considerable difficulties in conceptualizing the middle class everywhere, even in developed societies. For Marxists, the term is used to designate

> variegated groups such as the small producers, the petit-bour-geoisie, those engaged in the 'circulation of commodities' . . . the middle men . . . those who 'command in the name of capital' and their assistants, supervisors, secretaries, book-keepers and clerks, and finally an 'ideological' group embracing lawyers, artists, journalists, clergy and state officials such as the military and the police. (Swingewood 1979: 116)

It is difficult to define precisely who 'the middle class' are in the Caribbean Basin. We can usefully retain the notion of the middle class as sandwiched between the elite and the masses, rural and urban, and as weak and fragmented both in its ideological orientation and its politics. On the whole, the regional middle classes are less directly tied to capitalist production – manufacturing etc. – than in core countries and industrialists have tended to form part of the oligarchy or represent the interests of the metropolitan state. Some of the middle class of the region would fit Portes's 'technical-bureaucratic' class, though others – teachers, office workers, etc. – have undoubtedly been proletarianized.

It is important not simply to identify those groups who form part of a middle sector, but to assess their power within the political system. We can distinguish between those countries where civil society is relatively strong, the Commonwealth Caribbean and Costa Rica, where middle strata are clearly identifiable and occupy political and administrative roles within society and the state, and most countries of the Central American isthmus, where the power of the oligarchy combined with the Armed Forces has reduced the political presence of the middle class. In the Dominican Republic and even more so in Haiti, the absence of significant capitalist development beyond the free trade zones has hindered the development of a middle class. In spite of the proliferation of the state under Trujillo and the development of an intellectual and political consciousness on the part of a radicalized petite bourgeoisie leading to the growth of the *Partido Revolucionaro Dominicano* (PRD) in alliance with the urban poor under Juan Bosch, the middle class has proved unable to impose itself politically. It might be possible to identify Cuba's political elite as a middle class of the managerial or bureaucratic type, although a middle class occupying a space between private producers and owners of the means of production (who have themselves almost disappeared) and a salaried majority no longer exists.

The middle strata did not challenge oligarchic rule even with the rupture in export agriculture signified by the Great Depression, except in Costa Rica. There, however, after the civil war, a political and economic model was implemented in which the middle sectors emerged as a major component of the dominant bloc. The model privileged the growth of middle sectors, including the small producers for export in the countryside, by this time a strata unique to Costa Rica on the isthmus, and the urban and bureaucratic petite bourgeoisie, as well as industrial and agrarian bourgeoisies with links to foreign capital and the state. The state assumed a middle class ideology and development policy, prioritizing policies beneficial to the middle sectors in education, health, social security etc. (Rovira Mas 1988: 31–3). In Costa Rica, then, the ascendency of the middle class has depended on their absorption into the state and on relatively high state expenditure after 1948, although the recession of the 1980s threatened the state's capacity to protect and nurture Costa Rica's petite bourgeoisie.

Elsewhere in the isthmus middle class politics were defeated. A second opportunity appeared with the economic expansion of the post-war period and especially the 1960s. Significantly US policy in the region following the Cuban revolution claimed to have as its

goal that of producing middle class republics along the lines of
Costa Rica in order to stabilize the region and assure capitalist
development. But the economic growth of the period 1950–80 was
highly concentrated among the oligarchic groups and foreign
investors who entered the isthmus particularly after the start of
the Alliance for Progress. While industrialization and economic
modernization became part of the policies promoted by the state in
the 1960s, alongside proposals for regional integration, domestic
manufacturing growth was modest and by 1978 provided less than
one-fifth of total GDP (Dunkerley 1988: 203). Hence the growth of
the middle class, in terms of the power it wielded within the political
system, was limited.

Middle sectors in the newly independent Commonwealth Caribbean, made up primarily of the mixed race or black population,
constituted the new governing elite. In fact wealth had ceased to be
the monopoly of the white minority in the Caribbean in the
nineteenth century. The plantocracy in the English-speaking
islands had found its power diminished with the decline of sugar.
In Jamaica, some members of the mixed population acquired wealth
through the banana industry or through commerce. The ranks of
the middle class were further swelled by the arrival of Chinese and
Lebanese shopkeepers and merchants. Bryan notes that 'minority
layers of the coloured population extended their participation in
landowning, trading and dominated such professions as law' (Bryan
1991: 77). None the less, in spite of the material privileges enjoyed
by this middle class, the coloured and black population as a whole
continued to suffer up to Independence from the institutionalized
racism which was at the heart of the imperial system, which was
reinforced by differences between black and white in terms of
speech patterns, dress and education.

The founders of Jamaica's two principal political parties which
emerged in the 1940s, Alexander Bustamente of the Jamaican
Labour Party and Norman Manley of the People's National
Party, were representative of this middle class. Both parties
appealed to the black majority chiefly as voters to ratify the slow
process of decolonization decreed by the United Kingdom, rather
than as participants in politics, which remained a preserve of the
middle class. It is possible therefore to see the incorporation of the
middle class into politics in the Commonwealth Caribbean as a
brake on popular politics: 'a process of embourgeoisement and

elitism extended throughout both parties. In this way the changes imposed by constitutional change were more apparent than real, only the hegemony within the government changed from white to coloured, and the masses originally excluded from politics were invited to . . . applaud the authors of the national scene' (Munroe 1972: 84). By the same token, others have drawn attention to the generally conservative orientation of the new elites in the Commonwealth Caribbean, in questions of international relations for example. Most applauded the US invasion of the island of Grenada in 1983, a result of the fact that they identify 'their local class-national interests with what they perceive as the most friendly and powerful metropolitan power available. That power, of course, used to be Britain. But with the disappearance of the British Empire the colonial loyalty has shifted to the United States' (Lewis 1987: 137).

Elsewhere in the Caribbean, in Puerto Rico, Cuba and the Dominican Republic, the regional hegemony established by the US between 1898 and 1930 weakened the landowning class and strengthened the power to some extent of the middle sectors who were identified with the expansion of US capital. In Haiti a similar process occurred during the US occupation between 1915 and 1934, strengthening the black middle classes who came to be the proponents of a *noiriste* cultural nationalism. None the less, the identification between the growth of the middle sectors and the penetration of the middle classes by the black population did not occur everywhere: in Cuba and Puerto Rico, for example, the middle classes remained overwhelmingly white, with blackness remaining associated with subaltern groups.

The Urban Poor and Urban Working Class

The working class has been conceptualized by Marxists as a class of unpropertied wage earners compelled to sell their labour, ideologically disciplined by capitalism. It might be, however, that the term 'working class', developed for advanced capitalist societies, is inappropriate for Central America and the Caribbean and a more accurate term is the 'urban poor'. According to Portes' typology, the urban poor would form part of the formal and informal working class, with possibly a small number forming part of the informal petite bourgeoisie.

The slow and partial expansion of capitalism outside the agrarian export economies explains the weakness of the Central American working classes. The review of urban labour in the period 1870–1930 in the *Cambridge History of Latin America* makes no mention of Central American or Caribbean labour (Hall and Spalding 1989). The first signs of the development of an urban working class in the region occurred at the beginning of the twentieth century, and by the 1920s trade unions had been formed throughout the region and, in Central America and Cuba, Communist Parties had emerged. On the isthmus, the process was assisted particularly by the expansion of the proletariat in the banana enclaves where the first strikes were organized. But, with the exception of the banana workers, working class militancy was not a feature of politics until after the Second World War, and peasant mobilization, as in El Salvador in 1932, constituted the real threat to oligarchic domination.

Even today, it is difficult to recognize the urban poor as constituting a proletariat in classically marxist terms. Certainly in no part of the isthmus does a working class engaged in manufacturing predominate. Only in Nicaragua (65 per cent urban) is the urban population greater than the rural. Industrialization is weak and employs few permanent salaried workers, and the economic expansion of 1950–80 created few labour-intensive industries. On the eve of the Sandinista revolution in Nicaragua, for example, 'in the cities, the proletariat in productive enterprises and basic services . . . constituted 20 per cent of the urban economically active population; however the industrial proletariat made up less than half this figure' (Vilas 1989: 124). Urban employment did change in the period of growth between 1950 and 1980, even though the industrial proletariat grew only slowly. Dunkerley's research indicates an expansion of firms (often foreign-owned) employing more than 100 workers. Without suggesting that this workforce necessarily constituted a vanguard, he argues that the experience consolidates working class culture in the cities (Dunkerley 1988: 208). And elsewhere, on occasion, the employees of multinationals have played a leading role in struggles against oligarchic or military dictatorships – for example, the workers employed by Coca-Cola in Guatemala in the late 1970s and early 1980s. The urban workers in El Salvador, especially in 1979–81, also constituted one of the main forces behind the revolutionary insurrection of that period. We should therefore be wary of dismissing the urban poor as a non-revolutionary 'lumpenproletariat'.

Nevertheless, most urban workers, men and women, find employment in what some sociologists have called the 'informal sector', a term first coined by the International Labour Organization to refer to the 'employed poor' who did not fit either into the 'modern' sector of the economy or the 'traditional', i.e. agriculture. Informal sector employment is an intrinsic part of peripheral capitalism. It is composed of people who 'invent' their employment in order to survive: that is, the rationale of production in the informal sector depends on employment needs rather than market demands. Examples of informal sector employment include street selling, artisan production, motor car repairs, prostitution, paper recycling and rubbish-tip scavenging. Research points to it being a central and permanent feature of the life of the urban poor in the region and that it expanded enormously with the recession of the 1980s.

Although the poor in the cities in the Commonwealth Caribbean adopt similar strategies of survival to their counterparts in the isthmus, the forms of political organization and the relationship with the state are different. While the Central American urban poor have been excluded from the state by repression (except in Costa Rica), in the English-speaking Caribbean the tendency has been rather more to cooptation, especially of the political leadership and trade unionists. This reflects the application of state strategies based on British politics, which had assured a 'responsible' trade union movement concerned with bread-and-butter issues without questioning the validity of the political system or the mode of production. In Jamaica, Westminster decided to encourage a 'responsible and depoliticized' trade union movement after the riots of the mid-1930s, a recommendation of the Moyne Committee. In the period after 1945, the trade unions were associated with the demand for self-government in Jamaica and the first political parties were heavily associated with the trade union movement. While the trade unions therefore can be said to be responsible for opening up the Caribbean political systems beyond the closed elites of the imperial system, they were also responsible for moderating radical demands *vis-à-vis* the government in London (Serbin 1987: 199). As a result of the trajectory of working class organization, a critique of established labour practices and of political parties which had become electoralist machines formed a significant part of the ideology of the new left in the 1960s and 1970s.

The capacity of the trade unions to control labour and the poor in the Commonwealth Caribbean was weakened to some extent by the rise of radical groups who reject the Westminster model of politics, though within the insular Caribbean only in Grenada did they successfully challenge it. The economic recession of the 1980s and the implementation of economic models which generate less employment than ever in the framework of a neo-liberal reform of the state have also weakened trade unionism. In Jamaica, for example, unemployment in parts of the capital Kingston at the end of the 1980s was assessed at 70 per cent. Within the region as a whole approximately 40 per cent of the population are permanently occupied within the informal sector, or to put it another way, permanently excluded from participation within the economic model (Lewis 1991: 225–6). Women constitute an especially significant part of the Caribbean labour force employed in the informal sector; and since trade unions have traditionally ignored the role of women in production and politics, this operates as another barrier to effective organization by the urban poor.

The Peasantry and the Rural Poor

Marx devoted little time to analyzing production and class in the countryside; other sociologists have debated between seeing the peasantry as a class within the capitalist mode of production, suggesting that the peasantry is in fact part of a separate mode of production or arguing that peasants constitute a transitional class representing the vestiges of pre-capitalist production. None of this is especially helpful for understanding agrarian class structure in contemporary Caribbean societies, since it presumes few grada-tions in forms of production and access to land and it tends towards ignoring differentiation within the agrarian sector.

Caribbean Basin economies remain overwhelmingly rural. While the proportion of the economically active population engaged in agriculture has fallen steadily since 1945, dependence on agrarian products has declined much more slowly. This is not to suggest that the agrarian world has remained timeless and unchanged, however; the way goods are produced in the countryside and indeed the goods themselves have been in a continual process of transformation along with the deployment of rural labour. Changes in the rural economy have proceeded most rapidly in the Central American isthmus and the transformation of labour and land is at the heart of the Central American crisis. The success of export agriculture has reduced access to land and even food without creating possibilities of permanent and stable employment – most export crops, like coffee, sugar and cotton for example, require labour for only approximately three months in the year – and mechanization of banana production has lowered labour requirements in banana economies.

Social structure in the Central American countryside is complex because of the variety of different arrangements in access to land. The better-off peasants are those who have been able to keep some land, however small, to supplement wage earnings. Unfortunately, access to land for peasant production has continually declined since the mid-1960s. At the same time the size of independent plots has tended to shrink to the point of non-viability, increasing the dependence of the rural poor on seasonal wages, deepening the trend towards semi-proletarianization. During the 1980s, the situation for rural workers deteriorated dramatically, especially in El Salvador and Guatemala, as war, recession and political crisis led to unprecedented levels of open unemployment and poverty. In El Salvador, rural unemployment officially reached 50 per cent and underemployment was estimated at 80 per cent (Torres Rivas and Jimenez 1985: 40).

Furthermore, the wars in El Salvador, Nicaragua and Guatemala have led to the dispersion and displacement of large sectors of the rural population, some to the cities, others have fled to neighbouring countries and in some cases even as far afield as Mexico, the US and Canada. Peasants and the rural poor constitute the majority of the displaced and refugee population in the region. Perhaps of all the victims of the 'Central American crisis', their situation is the most tragic. They are the victims of a permanent 'competitive exclusion . . . the advance of agrarian capitalism caused the disappearance of the . . . peasant whose attachment to the land is permanent and substituted the temporary agricultural labourers whose position as such is not influenced by whether they own a small piece of land' (Torres-Rivas 1991: 100). UN statistics estimate that up to 10 per cent of the total population of the isthmus is displaced from its place of origin and that the majority are peasants escaping war or repression. Most are women, old people and children. In Guatemala alone, the number of internal displaced people has reached one and half million. In both El Salvador and Guatemala, the displacement of peasants is due fundamentally to 'the application of counter-insurgency strategies designed to destroy the logistical base, social support and probable sympathies of the civilian population [towards the guerillas]' (Torres-Rivas and Jimenez 1985: 43). Apart from physical danger and psychological damage, a result of violence, fear, insecurity, etc., the refugees and the displaced suffer an increase in poverty, having been forced to leave behind their possessions, and have no means to ensuring a livelihood in the future.

In the insular Caribbean pressure on land has been mitigated somewhat by out-migration. The transformation of the independent peasantry into a rural proletariat has not on the whole occurred, though plots remain small. The peasantry in the insular Caribbean is distinct from that of the isthmus in a number of other important ways too: for example, in terms of formation. The creation of a peasantry and a rural labour force occurred in a unique way in islands where slavery had been prevalent as a result of abolition. Rather than being made up of the remnants of pre-capitalist forms of production, a small peasantry was created in the wake of emancipation. In the case of Jamaica, the expansion of small peasant farms after 1840 led to a significant expansion of peasant production as a percentage of GDP and some degree of economic diversification by the end of the nineteenth century. Women were particularly important in peasant production, especially in their role as market vendors ('higgling'). By the 1880s, however, the expansion of the peasantry had ceased and access to land tightened considerably, partly to create wage labour for export agriculture. Export farmers had complained since before emancipation that it would reduce the availability of labour for sugar, although in fact the crisis of Jamaica's sugar industry had more to do with Britain's free trade policies rather than problems with labour supplies. Nevertheless, after the 1890s, the availability of labour for the plantations increased. Jamaica's inefficient plantations adopted a series of measures designed to cut costs and maintain profitability which centred on reducing the costs of labour. Hence a part of weekly wages were often in kind and wages were held level between 1870 and 1910.[3] In this way, the costs of inefficiency were passed onto the labourers.

Haiti and Cuba, for different reasons, constitute exceptions outside the established patterns of Caribbean rural economies. Haiti remains the most agrarian of the Caribbean countries, with three out of four Haitians still living in the countryside. The undeveloped nature of export agriculture has meant that most Haitians engage in subsistence agriculture and basic artisan production. However, land is poor and plots are small and overworked, leading to land erosion and soil exhaustion. The result is that production is woefully inadequate to provide even the basic needs of the peasantry itself, let alone provide for the urban areas. Hence Haiti needs to import food, in spite of its peasant economy. Furthermore, most peasants are without legal titles to the land they occupy and 'insecurity pervades social relations because the peasantry, huge in numbers but dependent at various levels, is dominated by a select minority of large landowners (by Haitian standards), big middlemen, notaries and politicians' (Girault 1991: 188). Haiti's peasantry also suffers from cultural and political isolation because transport is poor and access to news is infrequent. In the case of Cuba, rural structure has been transformed by the revolution which put into effect the most sweeping land reform in Latin America and the Caribbean. As a result, few independent peasant producers survive and most workers are employed directly by the state, or, in the case of farm cooperatives, sell to the state.

How important as a political force are the peasantry or the rural workers in the region? Undoubtedly the region 'is divided into citizens and the excluded' and the rural poor constitutes the most underprivileged of the excluded groups (Touraine 1989: 89). Peasants are the main victims of the agro-export model of development; of the repression and war which has become an institutionalized feature in Central American politics; they are the least privileged in terms of access to food, health care and basic services; and consistently register the lowest levels of literacy and the highest levels of infant mortality. Within the rural poor, peasant women constitute the most economically and culturally deprived. Has this contributed to turning the rural poor into a revolutionary force for change?

The answer depends on factors other than simply poverty since impoverishment by itself is not sufficient to politicize excluded groups. In the Commonwealth Caribbean, the agrarian poor have been marginal in anti-system political organizations. In contrast, in Cuba, the peasants of Oriente province, which registered the highest levels of rural poverty before the revolution, became one of the most important bases of support for the revolution.[4] And in parts of Central America, in Guatemala, Nicaragua and El Salvador, peasant organizations have proved to be an integral part of contemporary revolutionary struggles. Here, capitalist moderniza-tion of the agrarian economy combined with political exclusion of the poor to produce popular insurgency in which the peasantry has played a vital role. In Guatemala, where 2 per cent of the farms controlled 72 per cent of arable land in 1970, the *ladino* peasants went on to connect with indigenous communities which also found their access to land severely restricted (Handy 1988: 27). In Nicaragua, the FSLN grew in spite of relatively weak peasant organizations, building on the anti-US legacy of Sandino's insur-gency between 1926–33. In El Salvador, oligarchic fear of peasant mobilization after 1932 led to fifty years of military dictatorship while land concentration led to a situation of semi-proletarianiza-tion for most of the rural poor. But Honduras and Costa Rica have not experienced significant peasant revolutionary movements, though 'Honduras has the potential for serious domestic strife . . . unless reform policies are implemented' (Flora and Torres-Rivas 1989b: 48). In Costa Rica, not only have incomes for small and medium farmers been higher than elsewhere in Central America, but the state has also put into operation a number of policies which benefit the small and medium farmers in addition to offering incorporation into the system. At the same time, the impact of landlessness, which is traditionally higher than in neighbouring countries, has been mitigated by an agrarian system which offered higher wages and less unemployment.

Beyond Classes: the Armed Forces and External Influence

The Armed Forces

The armed forces are a major player in the politics of Central America, Haiti, the Dominican Republic and pre-revolutionary Cuba, in sharp contrast to the political tradition of the Common-wealth Caribbean, where the political system has largely gone uncontested since independence. What accounts for the militarism prevalent in most of the ex-Spanish colonies of the region and the very different tradition in the English-speaking Caribbean? Uni-causal explanations of military intervention – for example, cultural norms left over from the Spanish conquest or the weakness of civil societies, which is in fact as likely to be a consequence of militarization as much as a cause – tend to break down because of their very simplicity. There is no one, all-encompassing explana-tion of military intervention or militarism. The political predomi-nance of the military in Central America has been due to a combination of factors. Some of these factors include: the absence of national integration; uneven development; the immaturity of political parties; the separation of a political class and of political institutions from the rest of society; the internal divisions within the dominant bloc, leading to appeals to the army or to army intervention to impose control; and the effects of US intervention.

Military intervention occurred in the 1930s in support of oligarchic domination, and was very different from the military coups of the 1960s, when US backing for military take-overs became more important than ever before. And the counter-insurgency wars of the 1970s and 1980s can only be understood within the context of the threat posed by popular organizations coupled with oligarchic reaction, relative military independence and virtually unlimited external support. It is useful to distinguish between different forms of militarization; between a situation where the military overwhelm and occupy the state and state structures, and where civilian regimes rely on military backing in order to keep power. Guatemala in the 1970s and 1980s until the election of Vinicio Cerezo in 1986 would be a clear example of the first kind of militarization; and Haiti under Papa and Baby Doc and Guatemala after 1986, where army control of the highlands has continued unchallenged and abuses of human rights have gone unchecked, examples of the second.

The Liberal era brought the first professionalization of the Central American Armed Forces. But their real debut in politics came in the 1930s, when the military intervened to repress the popular protests which erupted in response to the disruptions the Great Depression left in its wake. On the isthmus, we have to distinguish between Honduras and Nicaragua, where the military and foreign-owned companies exercised a major influence over the state from the 1930s onwards, and Guatemala and El Salvador, where the economic recuperation of the oligarchy and its diversification into more lucrative commercial and financial enterprises with economic modernization after the Second World War went hand in hand with the entrenchment of the military within the offices of the state. In Nicaragua the personalist dictatorship of the army *caudillo* Anastasio Somoza García was able to assert control over the National Guard from the 1930s until 1956, while the Guard was even more clearly the political support of his son Anastasio Somoza Debayle's dictatorship (1967–79). Militarization of politics therefore became a constant in Central American political life as the army was used to repress popular movements. In Costa Rica the abolition of the army after the 1948 civil war effectively ended the threat of military intervention.

Although the Armed Forces have remained on the whole profoundly anti-communist and anti-popular, they have proved more than simply tools of the oligarchy. In some cases they have developed their own political project and vision of society, independent of and occasionally even in opposition to oligarchic domination, for example in Guatemala in 1944, when sectors of the army intervened to overthrow the dictator Jorge Ubico and install a democratic reformist regime. In Panama under Torrijos, the army became the channel for the articulation of nationalism, as well as the main vehicle for non-white upward social mobility, in a society where the white minority traditionally exercised economic power. In Honduras, the army was able to develop into an autonomous political force because of the weakness of the national economic elite which had been eclipsed by the US banana companies. After the military intervention of 1956, the army won the right to oversee the constitution and by the 1970s the Honduran Armed Forces was to demonstrate significant political autonomy from the major landowning, business and commercial groups.

The 'autonomy' of the Armed Forces from the oligarchy and indeed from civil society increased where the army became accustomed to government. In El Salvador, sectors of the Armed Forces were nurtured by the US, given privileged access to information, arms and training from the late 1970s onwards, and eventually went on to became a force beyond the control of their mentors (Castro and Barry 1990). In El Salvador and Guatemala, politicization weakened corporate control over the Armed Forces, encouraging decomposition and the emergence of groups who operate without direct reference to High Command. These groups, death squads, remain protected by corporate loyalty and a shared ideological conviction throughout the army that the Armed Forces are the frontier of the nation against subversion. The death squads killed around 300 people a month in Guatemala in the early 1980s and continue to harass the peasantry, the relatives of the disappeared, human rights workers and the Indian resistance communities.

There is yet another aspect to military autonomy: control of the state over long years led to the penetration of the military into the highest echelons of the economic elite. Nowhere is this more evident than in Guatemala. The process began in the 1960s and by the 1970s the army had established a substantial economic base with interests in at least 40 semi-autonomous state enterprises (Painter 1987: 47). At the same time, the Guatemalan military used their control of the state to ensure unjustifiably high defence budgets, reaching as much as a third of national expenditure in the mid-1980s, and generating a network of corruption and venality which benefited the army leadership. More recently, the army has been involved in the lucrative drug trafficking business. These interests have proved difficult to reduce and the military retain substantial privileges and power since the uneasy transition to civilian rule began in 1986.

External Agents

The influence of the metropolis over decision-making in the periphery has been incalculable in the past. Inevitably, its influence remains very significant today, whether exercised directly, through investment, or through international agencies or the banking system. Influence from outside economic forces has proved particularly influential in cases where the local dominant class is weak and production is in the hands of foreign companies (Cardoso and Faletto 1979). The importance of a 'world system' in which the winners are in the metropolis and losers in the periphery is such that some analysts have suggested that it would be more profitable to examine class formation at a global level than at the level of the national state (Amin 1974). The Caribbean Basin was one of the first parts of the globe to experience colonization and the region where British imperialism survived longest; it remains an area which the most powerful nation in the contemporary system, the US, defines as crucial for its national security; and as a region made up of small peripheral states, it is vulnerable to a variety of outside pressures in policy-making. These factors combine to give external agents an unusual degree of influence over politics in the region and to raise doubts about the sovereignty in the area.

British influence dates from 1625. Indeed, the sub-region of the insular Caribbean exists in its present form mainly as a result of the mercantile and capitalist policies of expansion of Britain and other European powers. The political economy of the region is a legacy of European greed and domination in which Britain played the key role. We can identify three phases through which British influence has passed: first the long period of colonization, when the economic and social structures of the contemporary period were created; second, the period of independence, after which the Commonwealth Caribbean was dominated by the ideologies constructed by Empire and which had penetrated the culture of the newly independent states, and by the retention of close links with Britain; and third, the current situation where the European Union (EU), with Britain as a member, still exercises a vital economic role in the region through trade, aid and investment. Now, however, Britain's role, and that of the EU, are small compared to the influence of the US. The US invasion of the island of Grenada in 1983, a member of the British Commonwealth and independent from Britain scarcely ten years, was strikingly illustrative of this fact.

None the less Britain has maintained an influence through the retention of some tiny dependencies: Anguilla, Montserrat, the British Virgin Isles, the Cayman Islands and the Turks and Caicos Islands. Investment, trade and aid and in particular the passage of illegal narcotics through the region en route to the US and Europe and the use of Caribbean banks to launder drug money, remain relatively important topics to British foreign policy. But it is the EU which operates today as the Caribbean's main partner in Europe. The struggle to deepen trade ties with Europe, determined by agreements known as the Lomé Convention, is particularly important for Caribbean countries in the agenda of Caribbean–European relations. The results of the four Lomé Conventions have been disappointing for Caribbean development. The framework of the relationship remains set in the colonial mould, with the Caribbean nations demanding significant trade concessions from the EU as part of a series of 'entitlements' which would go some way in ameliorating the costs of centuries of imperialism, and the EU talking instead of 'concessions' being made to 'underdeveloped' regions, as if Europe had played no role in the process of underdeveloping the Caribbean. Sutton sums up the Caribbean in its relationship with Europe as 'acutely dependent – a situation of which they are frequently reminded in their day to day dealings in Brussels' (Sutton 1991b: 122).

The influence of the major player in the region today, the US, is discussed in detail in Chapter 5. The US assumed the 'responsibility' for the Caribbean with the slow decline of Britain and its own rise to globalism. Although the US engaged in few examples of direct colonization, Puerto Rico being rather an exception to a general strategy of indirect control, a decisive influence over events in the region was established by the beginning of the twentieth century – via military intervention, economic pressure, and the buying of client politicians. The latter was particularly insidious, and much of the vigour and effectiveness of US control over regional politics has depended upon this strategy. By the post-war period, a more systematic kind of control has been established through the over arching framework of anti-communism. The 1960s witnessed the intensification of relations with the militaries of the area and control over the political elite.

The influence of metropolitan states over the politics of the isthmus is well illustrated in reference to Nicaragua. Confronting a long-standing threat to sovereignty throughout the nineteenth century because of British penetration of the Atlantic Coast region, which left behind a legacy of separatism and isolation, the new Nicaraguan nation was also weakened by US interest as the original site of the transisthmian canal. US tactics in search of control over Nicaraguan territory varied from outright invasion, to the buying of allies within the Conservative Party, to the creation of client governments and a close relationship with the Somola family. Despite occasional misgivings about the legitimacy of the dictatorship, the US upheld the family's rule, who in return served loyally through the Bay of Pigs crisis and the invasion of the Dominican Republic in 1965. Complete dependence on Washington was the result. In view of Nicaragua's history, it is not surprising that the *Sandinista* revolution was perceived as a threat to US domination throughout the isthmus. The US response in the 1980s must be seen within the pattern of historical relations rather than simply through the lens of the East–West conflict, as the US government insisted. By the same token, the defeat of the *Frente Sandinista de Liberación Nacional* (FSLN) in 1990 'for all practical purposes . . . signaled the reimposition of US hegemony' (Walker 1991: 169).

Interference by the metropolitan state in the internal affairs of the small states of the region under the guise of security concerns is not the only expression of external influence over regional events. We must include as well the role played by multilateral financial and economic institutions. The economic vulnerability of the region increases their leverage in the policy process. The World Bank and the International Monetary Fund (IMF) exercise a particularly significant influence over policy and the decisions taken by GATT (the General Agreement on Tariffs and Trade) are also important. The small Caribbean states have no voice at GATT although it determines access to markets for world goods and the degree of openness or protectionism of the big economies which are the main markets for Caribbean goods. The relationship between the international lending agencies and the countries of the region is skewed and unbalanced in favour of the lenders.

> Lending is in essence a game played out between a 'donor' who provides money and a 'recipient' who is expected, in return, to implement policy conditions . . . Recipients who are in a relatively weak bargaining position, whether because of the gravity of their economic position, their high financial dependence . . . or their inability to assert economic or geopolitical reverse leverage, [have] tended to have tight conditionality packages imposed on them. (Mosley 1991: 2)

An analysis of the impact of multilateral agencies on Jamaican politics illustrates particularly well the power of international institutions, because Jamaica received 'more IMF stabilisation packages since 1977 than any other country, three World Bank Structural Adjustment Loans and three Sectoral Adjustment Loans since 1982, and significant bilateral balance of payments support from USAID during the 1980s' (Harrigan 1991: 311). Harrigan charts the interaction between international lending and government fiscal and economic policies through the 1980s, after the loss of the elections by Michael Manley in 1980 following a much-publicized conflict with the US over bauxite policy and with the IMF over the conditions imposed on loans negotiated in 1978 and 1979. She demonstrates that the pressure from international agencies was particularly effective in the 1980s under the liberal-oriented government of Edward Seaga. In addition to the poor performance of the Jamaican economy and decline in living standards which resulted from the new policy orientation, Harrigan argues that Jamaica was caught between the conflicting demands of the IMF and the World Bank, the first demanding short-term stabilization and the Bank looking for signs of medium or long-term structural adjustment of Jamaica to the prevailing rules of the international system (Harrigan 1991). Throughout this period, the goal of the construction of a new international order, which would allow the Caribbean to trade on fairer terms with the powerful nations of the system, was abandoned.

Race, Class and Nation: Forces for Domination or Resistance?

Until after the Second World War and in some cases later, the metropolitan state and the local elites reserved the right to take all national decisions: they identified their own interests as those of the nation state or the colony. Recurrence to dictatorship, military intervention and repression in contemporary politics in the isthmus and the rather more latent threat of coercion within the English-speaking Caribbean illustrate that dominant class or metropolitan interests were imposed by violence whenever necessary. Today, power in the region remains for the most part an attribute of the dominant economic sectors. What ideological assumptions on the part of the dominant class underlie this determination to exclude popular classes from decision-making, even when recourse to violence and repression is necessary to sustain themselves in power?

The socio-economic and political elites of the Caribbean Basin have historically viewed subordinate social groups with hostility and mistrust. While the origins of this hostility, and indeed its *raison d'être*, lie in the system of exploitation through the plantation and the *hacienda*, that is in the maintenance of economic privileges, by the late nineteenth century it was also sustained by ideological and cultural assumptions in which images of ethnically and culturally inferior groups reinforced class differences. Many of these ideas were in fact derived from the ideologies of imperialism and racial theories of history which had emerged in Europe and in the US. Blacks and *mestizos* were viewed as barbarians, while it became the mission of the white elite to 'civilize' the area. Where the elite was itself racially mixed, it would often assume 'white' ideologies.

A belief in racial superiority was an important justification for the US intervention in the region. Late-nineteenth century imperialism rested on racist notions of white superiority and social Darwinism. 'The survival of the fittest' appeared as a convenient explanation of the status quo and white Anglo-Saxon domination. Until such time as the black and mixed race masses were 'civilized', elites and the metropolitan state accepted that coercion and force would be necessary tools of government. The white Jamaican elite expressed repeatedly the fear that the blacks were somehow 'combustible' (Bryan 1991: 22). In Central America elite images of the 'Indian' became associated with laziness, underproduction and untrustworthiness. Hence a dominant culture which rejected the black and Indian components of the nation, or rendered them as invisible as possible, was created, reinforcing the class and ethnic divisions.

Class and ethnicity are intertwined in the political struggles of the region with the idea of nation. Nation states and national myths are usually constructed to reflect and uphold the power of the dominant elites. The nation states of the region are still struggling to establish sovereignty, even as a reflection of the dominance of the leading socio-economic and cultural elites over the rest of society. This is partly because key roles in decision-making are still assigned to the metropolitan state, to international organizations or to elites allied to external markets, who view the masses of the region not as fellow citizens but as groups to be excluded from society and the polity. In these circumstances, nation-building is obviously incomplete. Touraine has gone as far as to suggest that these countries 'are only partly national societies . . . the privileges belong more to an economic system whose centre is outside Latin America . . . the excluded, the cities and especially the countryside barely participate in the national political system' (Touraine 1989: 52).

The struggle to create nation states from ex-colonies, in a geopolitical area constructed by imperialism has sometimes constituted a vital element in the political discourse of national leaders, enabling the ruling elite to articulate an ideology of national unity over ethnic and class divisions. Other versions of nationalism have emerged in the region which postulate a particular ethnic and/or class composition as integral to the nation state; the notion of what constitutes the nation itself becomes contested as groups in conflict seek to exclude others from membership. We can contrast the nationalism exhibited by the moderate independence leadership in the Commonwealth Caribbean who saw no contradiction in adopting the political system imposed by Britain with the nationalism of Black Power groups in the 1960s, emerging in Jamaica in particular, which rejected white elements as foreign to the Jamaican nation.

Class, ethnicity and nation constitute the building blocks of dominant ideologies. Ideologies of resistance which have been generated by subaltern groups also depend on the interplay between class, ethnicity and nation. We should note here, in fact, that the debate about the importance of race and class as primary cleavages in the societies of the Caribbean Basin takes place on two distinct levels: firstly, the academic debate outlined earlier; and secondly, a debate within the dominated groups and revolutionary movements of the countries of the region. Serbin argues that subordinate ideologies in the Caribbean

refer as much to the particular conditions imposed by interracial and interethnic relations, themselves a result of the plantation economy, slavery and colonial ties with the metropolis, as to the elaboration of the importance of racial and ethnic differences established by the racist ideology of the hegemonic sector and the responses of subordinate groups, producing a frequent identification between race and class in the formation of these ideologies. The result is that historically popular traditions in the Caribbean articulate in the first place ethnic and racial differences, in the framework of slavery, and later incorporate classist and national-popular elements in accordance with the political evolution of these societies after the abolition of slavery. (Serbin 1987: 89)

As an example of how these three factors interrelate over time within subaltern political movements, we can look at the discourse of revolutionary groups from Guatemala.

Export agriculture and oligarchic domination were imposed and upheld in Guatemala by military repression from 1880, with only a brief exceptional period between 1944 and 1954. In contrast to neighbouring El Salvador, where the generation of an agrarian economy based on an abundance of rural labour for coffee and the decline of viable small holdings produced an overwhelmingly *ladino* labour force in the countryside, dependent increasingly on wages, in Guatemala the Indian communities were able to survive and retain their own culture. Today more than half the population speak one of the twenty-two indigenous languages as their first language. The survival of Indian culture, coupled with the brutal repression the communities suffered in the 1970s and 1980s, has meant that an indigenist element has been incorporated into popular struggles. During the 1980s, the Indian 'communities in resistance' became a major force opposing the military. The massacre in Panzós in 1978 by the army of more than a hundred Kekchi Indians who had come together to protest against the expansion of cattle-raising on Kekchi lands, marked a turning point both in popular mobilization and Indian struggles in Guatemala. The combative peasant union, the *Comité de Unidad Campesina* (CUC), developed following out of the repression as an instrument of organization for the rural poor and the Indian communities. The CUC linked the Indian struggles with the *ladino* poor in a practical way for the first time: 'for the most politically active segments of Indian society, there seemed a practical convergence between cultural and class demands, all synthesized in a vision of the ancient Mayan civilisation' (Black 1984: 90).

However, the central importance of ethnicity today in Guatemala's popular struggles did not always find articulation within the discourse of revolutionary movements. During the Guatemalan revolution (1944–54), especially the first phase under Arévalo, socialism was articulated as developmentalist and utopian. It has little specifically indigenist content. Rather the main purpose of the revolution was to establish greater national control over natural resources, economic infrastructure and production and to redress the pressing issue of land tenure. The revolution was motivated by a particular vision of the nation – oppressed by outside economic agents in the shape of United Fruit, the owners of the banana plantations – and an idea of its own constituency as being made up of poor peasants without access to the minimum land required for sustenance. Gleijeses noted, 'agrarian reform . . . a sustained effort to modernise the country's physical infrastructure . . . were essential to the development of Guatelmala as a nation – to the transformation of its rural population from serfs into citizens' (Gleijeses 1989: 453). But the Indian communities were not yet recognized as principal losers in the expansion of agrarian capitalism.

Regis Debray's analysis of Guatemala in the wake of the overthrow of Arbenz recognized that popular struggles in Guatemala depended on the politicization of the Indian communities (Debray 1977: 307). But it was not until the 1970s that the guerilla movements first ascribed a protagonistic role to the Indian communities. The *Ejército Guerillero de los Pobres* (EGP), formed in 1972, recognized the profound ethnic divisions inside the country (Harnecker 1984: 294). The EGP was convinced that 'immersion in the Indian society of the western highlands in a prolonged campaign of political education and collaboration . . . represented the only viable strategy for a popular revolution in Guatemala' (Dunkerley 1991a: 142). As a result, particularly close contacts were forged with the CUC.

The central role of the ethnic question therefore in revolutionary discourse today in Guatemala has developed out of a new reading of revolution combined with the effects of military repression upon the Indian communities. As Handy has demonstrated: 'through much of 1982 and 1983, the military attempted to reform highland village society. By forcing the peasantry into military-controlled towns, enforcing a military monopoly over all services in the highland region, and establishing a rural militia closely monitored by the army, the military sought to ensure its dominance in the region' (Handy 1989: 112). The military's aim was threefold: to eliminate Indian culture (through forced teaching of Spanish, assassination, etc.); to subordinate the Indian communities economically to the *ladino*-controlled export model of agricultural production; and the separation of the Indians from any contacts with the guerilla forces. In the short term, through the control of many Indian villages and the dispersal of others through repression and violence, the military was successful enough to hand power back to the civilians in 1986 with the unspoken condition that they, the Armed Forces, remain in control in the peasant highlands. But peasant resistance to export agriculture and the Indian resistance to the *ladino* state continues. And within the resistance movement of the Indian communities, there is a vision of a new society, an alternative 'nation state', based on democracy, 'love of our land and our country' (Painter 1987: 119).

Conclusion

In this chapter, we have looked at the social structures of the countries which make up the Caribbean Basin and we have noted in particular the roles of class and ethnicity in determining social and political conflict. Until recently, the state defended exclusively the interests of the dominant socio-economic elites and/or external interests. Civil society is generally weak (with the partial exception of the English-speaking Caribbean) and in some cases the state is dominated by the Armed Forces or excessively dependent on external agents. Starting from the 1960s, however, the region witnessed a transformation of politics, with subaltern groups mobilizing, even in some cases at the cost of severe repression, to demand participation in decision-making and a fairer model of development. In some of the territories of the region which were still colonies, this movement coincided with the process of independence. At the same time, subaltern groups, excluded from meaningful participation, began to develop an alternative vision of 'the nation' in opposition to the dominant vision which condemned them to be little more than labour for production. This process contributed to the challenges to authoritarianism from popular movements and demands for social reform throughout the region.

We have tried to show in this chapter that class, or class and race together, constitute the primary lines of social division in Central American and Caribbean societies. How is this linked to the question of development? First of all, the plantation and export agriculture models of political economy have upheld the privileges of dominant elites and shaped contemporary social conflict. At the same time they have generated social groups who demand change in the way goods are produced and labour deployed. Secondly, there is a clear articulation between local politics and external influences on which implementation of the model of development rests. For some social scientists, the absence of national integration is at the heart of the external vulnerability which we have identified as an obstacle to the development of the region.

Notes

1. A good example of the disagreements which could occur between the plantocracy and Britain would be over Crown Colony Government implemented in Jamaica. The image the British government wished to present of the system was that of benign imperial paternalism over class loyalty to the white elite on the island. For the plantocracy the system of government was one which continually irritated because it placed bureaucrats from Britain in positions of power over the local elite.
2. In Jamaica, by the same token, it is traditional to refer to the elite as being made up of twenty-one families; in the Dominican Republic, twenty-five.
3. Importing East Indian labour was another device for maintaining costs low by creating an excess of labour; but on the whole the banana enclaves resorted to this more than the sugar planters.
4. Illiteracy in Oriente was officially 50 per cent before the revolution, while it was 24 per cent nationally.

3

The Political Systems of the Region

The oligarchy, the plantocracy or the metropolitan state have controlled the political systems of the region and assured the continuance of policies – economic, cultural, social and political – which benefit them, in spite of periodic challenges to their power. Nevertheless, the dynamics of regional politics, in the course of the last thirty years especially, has meant a reorganization of the state to take into account the internal changes which have occurred in the region and also as a result of external pressures. In Chapter 2, we looked at class structure in the region. In this chapter we examine in detail some of the different ways dominant groups have established control over the state apparatus. In particular, we look at examples of the oligarchic militarized state (El Salvador and Guatemala) and the personalist dictatorship (Haiti and the Dominican Republic). But dictatorship, in different guises, is not the only form of organizing the state in the region. In fact, an almost bewildering variety of political systems has developed in the Caribbean Basin. In particular, the region comprises the only area of the so-called Third World where representative democracy has developed alongside brutal, militarized regimes.

How can we explain such a broad spectrum of systems within a small region? Are the explanations for the different political systems economic or cultural? Are they rooted in different class formation and class structure? Does the answer lie in the historical processes which divided the Spanish-speaking world from the English? We will go some way to answering these questions by looking in detail at the authoritarian systems of the region and then at how the democracies of the region work.

94

Two Regional Traditions: Authoritarianism and Democracy

Authoritarianism and democracy represent opposing ways of managing social conflict. Conflict does not disappear within democratic societies but is institutionalized and mediated by the state. The outcome of conflict in democracy is not completely certain because democratic politics always contains elements of uncertainty. That is, democracy means that the dominant class is able to recognize and accept the possibility of ceding power to others, or at least sharing it out. Authoritarianism, by contrast, tries to eliminate conflict by repressing any manifestation of dissent. An authoritarian state cannot, by definition, ever acknowledge even the possibility of error. And crucially, it tries at all costs to retain a monopoly on political power.

The most outstanding feature of regional politics is the contrast between the political systems in the Commonwealth Caribbean, and the Central American mainland and the Spanish and French-speaking insular Caribbean. Westminster systems prevail in the Commonwealth Caribbean whereas on the isthmus the only consolidated democracy to be found is in Costa Rica, where there is a tradition of unbroken elections since 1953. In the English-speaking Caribbean politics is based around representative democracy, meaning regular free elections, a competitive party system and the peaceful handing over of power from one party to another. Democracy here is understood in more than merely a formal sense. Violations of human rights are relatively few and civil liberties in general respected, in sharp contrast to the conflictive and violent politics of much of the rest of the region. Paradoxically, late independence from Great Britain may help to explain the persistence of formal political democracy within ex-British colonies.

It has been suggested that what constitutes the regional contrast between democratic and authoritarian styles of government are the legacies from the past; that Britain inculcated a respect for democracy into its colonial subjects whereas Spain bequeathed a legacy of *caudillismo*, militarism and authoritarianism. But can we really hold the Spanish responsible for the political traditions of countries that have been independent for over 150 years? Beyond the cultural explanations, there are two lines of argument which political science has tended to use to explain the emergence of stable democratic systems: democracy has been associated with the development of stable capitalist development and/or with an absence of significant or independent military power. The first idea, relating democracy to economic development, does not take us very far towards understanding the political systems of the region. It is impossible to demonstrate any relationship between economic growth and democratization in the region. Indeed, the relationship would seem at times to be the reverse: in Central America, in the 1960s substantial economic growth took place but did not lead to democratic polities. Instead it deepened social and economic conflict which the state tried to resolve through violence and repression everywhere except Costa Rica. On the other hand, economic growth within the English-speaking Caribbean, where democracy is stable, is sluggish, and the Caribbean Community (CARICOM) states suffer from extreme external vulnerability.

Is the idea of weak military forces of any more use in explaining the democracies of the region? This argument implies that democracies can survive even when there is a less than full commitment in society, providing that there is an absence of alternatives. It is not a completely convincing argument for the Commonwealth Caribbean where there have been occasional threats of military intervention – in Trinidad in 1970, Barbados in 1979, in St Vincent in 1979, in Grenada in 1983, and in Trinidad in 1990. These have always been defeated and the military subordinated to the civil elite. It may be a more helpful focus in Costa Rica, where the absence of an Armed Forces has been an important factor in explaining the legitimization of the democratic system.

A more recent explanation of democracy versus authoritarianism relates the establishment of democracy to elite behaviour. Particularly important is the concept of unity or convergence within dominant socio-economic and political elites (Burton, Higley and Gunther 1992). Legitimization of democracy rests in large measure with the elite groups who historically have managed the state, and in particular their response to social change. If the elite is prepared to share power and to institutionalize conflict, confident it can maintain its influence within the political system, then the outcome is more likely to be a democratic one. If, on the other hand, elites are unprepared to cede any power, then the outcome is almost inevitably a recourse to repression. In Costa Rica, after the civil war of 1948, the elite moved toward convergence on the principles of the new political system: a narrow-based democratic system, which excluded Communist participation, but absorbed the non-Communist left and legitimated itself through reform (Peeler 1992).

Within the English-speaking Caribbean elite agreement on the essential framework of the political system comes from two sources: first, the relatively recent process of independence, which gave cohesion to the nationalist elite; and, second, the establishment of the Westminster system of government and of a political tradition inherited from Britain. The imperial legacy in the English-speaking Caribbean stresses the supremacy of civil society, links democracy with a tradition of popular participation through trade unions and delegates to the state some limited but key functions in the provision of welfare services and in the redistribution of income. Democracy could be said to deliver moderate material gain in the Commonwealth Caribbean and this fact has served to legitimize the system.

Authoritarian Politics

Authoritarianism has been the dominant state form in the region in the twentieth century but the forms of domination and popular exclusion have varied from country to country. On the isthmus, the most common form was oligarchic domination. By the end of the nineteenth century, the power of the oligarchies was established over production (land and labour) and over the state, in the Spanish-speaking areas of the region, thereby guaranteeing the reproduction of their own privileges. According to Torres-Rivas, oligarchic political domination rested on

the perception, shared by the dominated classes, of the social superiority of a few individuals, with a status assured simply through a surname. This preeminence was reproduced . . . through wealth, made easier by skin-colour and established through a monopoly of skills (such as reading and writing) . . . It rested on rents from land, labour from the peasantry, a monopoly of water, credit and marketing, all of which came together in an oligarchic culture. (Torres-Rivas 1990)

Elsewhere in the region, in those societies where the local dominant class was weak and/or the export sector underdeveloped or exclusively in the hands of foreign capital, authoritarian politics took shape in the personalist or *caudillista* mould – the Dominican Republic and Haiti, for example. In both cases, the Armed Forces and sometimes external forces have played a significant role in upholding the authoritarian state when it has come under threat from popular opposition – El Salvador, where the oligarchy sought the protection of ultra-right military groups, and Dominican Republic, where Joaquin Balaguer, ex-dictator and reluctant democrat, has relied on the support of the US.

The Oligarchic–Military Alliance: El Salvador and Guatemala

Oligarchic power is most deeply entrenched in El Salvador and Guatemala. In both countries the original oligarchic nucleus of large landowners expanded to incorporate new sources of wealth throughout the twentieth century, strengthening its hold over production and the state. And in both countries, oligarchic domination rested on the state's preparedness to use violence, repression and torture. In fact, the establishment of the oligarchic state after the liberal reforms has been graphically described as constituting simply 'an interminable monologue by the dominant classes with themselves' (Perez-Brignoli 1989a: 85). However, in El Salvador the civilian socio-economic elite has maintained greater autonomy from the Armed Forces than in Guatemala, partly because of the advantages resulting from the economic success it enjoyed in coffee production.

Following the peasant uprising of 1932, the Salvadorean oligarchy called on the military to participate in government. General Maximiliano Hernandez Martinez was to remain in power from 1932 to 1944, and although pressure for reform finally forced him from office, no civilian candidates stood in the 1945 elections. During the 1940s, the personalist style represented by Martinez slowly gave way to government by the Armed Forces as the military created an official party of government, *Partido Revolucionario de Unificación Democrática* (PRUD) in 1949, which changed its name to *Partido de Conciliación Nacional* (PCN) in 1969, and which controlled government until ousted by a reformist military coup, allied to the Christian Democrat Party (PDC), in 1979. While the successive military governments were in general repressive and anti-communist, the chief targets were the peasants and peasant union leaders, as the countryside was the site of social conflict and coffee production which constituted the basis of oligarchic accumulation. The controlled and corrupt elections limited power to military and their civilian allies in a 'facade democracy', characterized by the preservation of legal formalities.

The oligarchy–Armed Forces tandem had come under severe strain in the 1970s, with the rise of the Christian Democratic Party (PDC), leading to open government interference to ensure the victory of the official candidates in the elections of 1972 and 1977. But it was the 1979 military coup which was the start of a radical transformation of politics. The 1979 Junta contained both reformist and conservative army elements, a contradiction which was eventually resolved in favour of the diehard conservatives. But the intra-government conflicts now took place against a society polarized between an elite unprepared to yield an inch and a rapidly expanding and well-organized popular movement. The guerilla and the political fronts of the popular movements coalesced in 1980, and the *Frente Farabundo Martí para la Liberación Nacional* (FMLN) and the *Frente Democrático Revolucionario* (FDR) called for popular resistance to the government. By 1981, when the FMLN staged a 'final offensive', El Salvador had begun the descent into an unequal war which pitted the oligarchy and the Armed Forces, who could count on the resources of the state and the support of the Reagan administration in Washington, against a guerilla army supported by the peasantry and popular organizations including trade unions and sectors of the Catholic Church.

After 1982, government remained formally in the hands of the Christian Democrats, though the Army was free of government control. Dunkerley describes the politics of the 1980s in the following way:

the form of the dominant bloc shifted from the post-1950 'dual system' of military government and oligarchic economic control to a fitful tripartite arrangement whereby the military retired from office but was assured full operational independence and US backing, the PDC was permitted to assume office and parade its reformist policies, and the landlords were deprived of the advantages of electoral fraud but also protected from any major

realization of the reforms upheld by its newly privileged political
competitor. (Dunkerley 1988: 382)

The intensity of the struggle and seriousness of the popular
challenge led to a transformation in the political strategy of the
oligarchy. Unable to trust either the Duarte government, which had
committed itself to land reform,[1] or the US, which backed Duarte
and funded the war against the FMLN, sectors of the bourgeoisie
formed the *Alianza Republicana Nacionalista* (ARENA), led by ex-
officer Roberto D'Aubisson, in September 1981. ARENA's political strategy throughout the 1980s was a double one. On the one
hand, ARENA was associated with the death squads which
operated with almost total immunity after 1980 to the degree that
it was possible to murder even Oscar Romero, Archbishop of San
Salvador. On the other hand, ARENA also developed an adroit
electoral strategy which allowed it to capitalize on dissatisfaction
with the Christian Democrats, who could neither win the war nor
negotiate peace nor control the deteriorating economy.

ARENA won 26 per cent of the vote in 1982 and in 1985 secured
control of the Constituent Assembly. In 1989, Alfredo Cristiani
replaced D'Aubisson as party leader, signalling ARENA's growing
emphasis on a 'political' solution to the war over a military one and
was able to win the presidency, convincing Washington and ex-
PDC voters as well as the conservative right that ARENA in
government would end the war. Cristiani won the 1989 elections
with 53.82 per cent of the vote compared to 36.03 per cent for the
Christian Democrats. While Cristiani was forced to confront the
conservative wing of the party over the negotiations with the
FMLN which led to a peace treaty negotiated at the end of 1991
and signed in Chapultepec, Mexico in January 1992, he was also
able to guarantee the survival of the socio-economic elite and their
privileged access to power and wealth.

How can we describe the political system which took shape in El
Salvador during the 1980s? It is, of course, impossible to see El
Salvador as in a process of democratization during these years
despite elections in 1982, 1984 and 1985, although it suited the US
strategy for the isthmus to insist that electoral politics equalled
democracy. For the opposition front, the guerilla movement, the
FMLN and most international observers, the elections held were
fraudulent because of army intimidation and the exclusion of the

FMLN from participation. Low voter turnout, which in 1989 was down to around 40 per cent, is an indication of the absence of legitimization of the electoral process. And how can democracy, which rests on the negotiation of conflict, be built during a civil war? But it is also clear that outright repression and the authoritarian system constructed by the oligarchy and the military were exhausted as a political option. And by 1989, if the army could not defeat the guerillas, it was also clear that the FMLN could not take power either. The FMLN occupied the capital San Salvador for 11 days in November and December of 1989 which demonstrated that the army could not militarily defeat the guerillas; but the occupation did not inspire a popular insurrection nor was it a prelude to a guerilla victory. Meanwhile, Cristiani, elected in 1989, adopted a new strategy which did not diminish state violence but subordinated it to the long-term idea of constructing an electoral system which is capable of *demobilizing* popular opposition. So politics, while far from democratic, did signify a break with the past. And the new strategy under Cristiani, which fortified the civilian elite over the army, lent sufficient internal and international credibility to the system to force the FMLN to negotiate an end to the war in return for a guarantee of participation in the political system.

It is difficult to predict whether the peace agreement signed at Chapultepec heralds a genuine democratization of the political system. The FMLN obtained a series of guarantees from the Cristiani government in areas where reform was a prerequisite for political transformation: restructuring of the Armed Forces; guarantee of human rights for all Salvadorean citizens; constitutional reform which acknowledges the FMLN as a political party; and some socio-economic reforms. The most important reform of all perhaps is the creation of mechanisms of civil control over the army, a *sine qua non* of democratization. Part of the reform of the Armed Forces includes the dissolution of some of the branches most connected to the repression and the 'dirty war' and their replacement with a National Police Force which, in theory, ex-guerillas may join. For the FMLN, the peace agreements signify concessions in particular in the area of economic reform, regarded until 1992 by the FMLN as the only effective way of democratizing Salvadorean society. Instead, the FMLN has agreed to participate in a political system which essentially leaves unreformed the economic structures of production, prioritizing the building of a liberal democratic system.[2] As a result, after signing the Agreement, the FMLN redefined its ideology as 'revolutionary, democratic and profoundly Christian' (*El Nuevo Día* Mexico, 29 January 1992). But for the Agreement to signify a new chapter in El Salvador's political history, it must be accepted and respected by all Salvadorean society, not simply the FMLN. Cristiani has demonstrated that ARENA has better control over the extremist elements of the Armed Forces than the Christian Democrats had throughout the 1980s, but the minimum economic reforms contained in the Agreement – ceilings of land holdings and land for ex-guerillas as well as the incorporation of the guerilla army to the task of national reconstruction – are running into more vigorous opposition. And the resurgence of labour demands may intensify elite distrust of democratization. For while ARENA may try to build a demobilizing democracy, any process of opening up an authoritarian system carries the risk of the elite losing power. Elite response to that uncertainty, therefore, will determine the political outcome in postwar El Salvador.

In Guatemala, the relationship between the socio-economic elite and the military is somewhat different. Firstly the elite is considerably weaker as a result of its historical development. The Guatemalan oligarchy never established the exclusive right to control the state and Guatemalan-controlled coffee production has competed with foreign-owned banana enclaves for influence. The oligarchy was much slower to move into capitalist production of coffee and established instead dominance through a combination of the establishment of racist ideology from within the state and the insistence on non-capitalist seigneurial rights – the use of forced labour and the militarization of workers on coffee plantations. At the same time, the Guatemalan Armed Forces, required to play a role in upholding the state from the time of the liberal reforms which created the modern army, were also legitimized as a political actor in the nineteenth century through Guatemala's insistence on its role as regional power and pole of Central American unification. The Army has kept hold of its image as that of the guardian of the nation.

The oligarchy came under severe threat during the reformist period of Arévalo and Arbenz (1944–54), which attacked the basis of domination through a redistribution of land. Twenty-eight plots to overthrow Arévalo alone were discovered and Arbenz was finally overthrown by a combination of US intervention, landowner opposition and military uprising. After 1954, dominant groups needed open repression to stay in power with the result that the army has remained at the centre of state power. By the 1970s the Armed Forces had overwhelmed the state to such a degree that some analysts have talked of its 'colonization' or 'militarization' (Lowy and Sader 1985). As in El Salvador, the army installed a facade democracy after 1954, with monitored elections, unrepresentative parties controlling Congress and Congress itself watched carefully to ensure that the military's allies were in a majority. The right to executive office was retained by the military itself. At the same time, the Armed Forces were modernized and professionalized throughout the 1960s, partly in response to guerilla activity which began between 1964 and 1968.

Guatemala's militarized state entered crisis beginning in the late 1970s. The crisis was provoked by the strength of the combined guerilla factions, amounting to approximately 8,000 in 1980, who were able to count on the support of around a quarter of a million peasants and Indians in the highlands. The reaction of the military was neither to offer partial reforms nor to open the system up but rather to design policies aimed at the elimination of opposition and in particular the destruction of the indigenous culture based on the village. Around 100,000 Guatemalans were estimated to have been killed in anti-guerilla campaigns by 1983, during which over 400 indigenous villages were destroyed and half a million people displaced. By the mid-1980s, unable to win decisively the military conflict with the guerillas or eradicate their bases of support among the peasantry, with the country in deep economic crisis and internationally isolated because of the extraordinary level of state violence, the military changed tack and allowed the Christian Democrats to take power. The civilian governments of Vinicio Cerezo (1986–90) and Jorge Serrano (1990–93) represented only a marginal redistribution of power within the state. The military remain in control of the countryside and the economic power of the landed and business groups remains intact and unreformed. Serrano was forced from power in May 1993 after attempting to stage a coup with the collaboration of the Army. Its failure makes only slightly more possible a further attempt at democratizing Guatemala society.

The transition from military rule in Guatemala has led to the country's reinsertion in the international community, and to a certain degree of stability, though both Cerezo and Serrano headed shaky governments. But the institutions of the political system remain extremely weak, the executive office concentrates political power, and since 1986 little or nothing has been done to legitimize the new democratic system through socio-economic reform. The civilian political elite remains dependent on the army to retain office. Nor has the introduction of electoral politics in Guatemala been able to eliminate the violations of human rights, disappearances and murders, and without this being achieved it is impossible to talk of a transition to democracy. Approximately 650 people were murdered by death squads and over 140 disappeared between January 1988 and April 1989 alone. Victims of human rights violations overall totalled 1,145 in this period (Casaus and Castillo 1991: 92). And the Armed Forces not only retain considerable autonomy from civilian control, but still have evinced no clear commitment to the democratic system. Coups were attempted in 1988, 1989 and 1993. The party system remains permeable to the Armed Forces with the result that several generals were pre-candidates for the 1990 presidential elections, including General Ríos Montt, who organized the coup of March 1982, supported by the parties of the extreme right. In these conditions, it is impossible to talk of the construction of anything other than a facade democracy.

The Personalist Dictatorship: Haiti and the Dominican Republic

Personal or even family dictatorships are another kind of authoritarianism. Power is concentrated into the hands of one person in association with a close-knit circle of personal advisers or relatives, the state becomes a personal fiefdom, often used for private gain, and the country is generally run along the lines of a large landed estate. Rarely do these dictatorships embark on modernization, and when they do, as in the case of Jean Claude Duvalier in Haiti, it usually ends in the collapse of the regime. They can be very effective vehicles for demobilizing opposition over a long period because of their absolute control over access to the state. Because of their resolute anti-communism, the personal dictatorships could count on support from the US especially after the onset of the Cold War, a commitment renewed after the Cuban revolution. The US was an important prop of the personal and familial dictatorships of the Somozas in Nicaragua, of Trujillo in the Dominican Republic and of the Duvaliers in Haiti. However, the survival of these regimes for so many years was due to more than external support. We now examine in more detail two of those dictatorships.

Contemporary history in the Dominican Republic begins with the US occupation from 1916 to 1924, which consolidated American control over the Dominican economy. This process had begun earlier in the twentieth century when national ownership of production and infrastructure gave way to US ownership. In 1907, the US intervened in the internal running of the country in order to ensure payment of the external debt with the US. Coffee and tobacco cultivation, along with the small manufacturing sector, declined in favour of sugar production, controlled by US companies. It is in this context, of extreme external dependence and a weakening of the national socio-economic elite, that we have to understand the emergence of *caudillista* politics. External dependence strengthened the authoritarian tradition in the country, which has meant that between 1882 and the present day, three presidents between them have shared out 79 years in power: Ulises Heureux (1882–99), Rafeal Leonides Trujillo (1930–61) and Joaquin Balaguer (1966–78; 1986–). Of these, two, Heureux and Trujillo, were removed from power by assassination.

Rafael Trujillo, an officer in the Dominican army which had been professionalized and trained during the US occupation, seized power in 1930 while the Dominican economy was reeling from the effects of the US recession. Trujillo imposed a model of development which by-passed the old socio-economic elite, centralized the state and used it as a motor of capitalist accumulation, the benefits of which remained in his own hands. Peace with the US was guaranteed since the structure of the sugar industry was untouched and remained controlled by US companies. Opposition was almost impossible because of the weakness of Dominican social forces: the oligarchy had lost economic power, the working class was small and the peasantry isolated and engaged in mainly subsistence production. In effect, the Trujillo dictatorship replaced the role of the bourgeoisie which as a class had proved unable to promote the capitalist development of the country. As a result, the Dominican social elite remained tied to agrarian production, mainly outside sugar, and commerce, and was unable to move into the more dynamic sectors of the economy. At the same time, this separation between social status and real economic power emasculated any elite opposition that arose and thus served to maintain Trujillo in power.

Trujillo was able to survive the demands for democratization that swept the region in 1944, partly thanks to the support from the US, notable especially after 1947 and the onset of the Cold War, and partly because Trujillo extended his political base within the Armed Forces. From 1950 onwards, in addition to external diplomatic support and a loyal Armed Forces, Trujillo was able to legitimate authoritarian rule through the implementation of a nationalist economic policy. Imports were restricted in order to stimulate internal economic expansion, which led to the development of cement, glass and processed foods industries; the external debt with the US was settled; and Trujillo brought the sugar industry, previously almost the exclusive preserve of US companies, into national hands, extending the area of cultivation and significantly increasing the volume of agro-exports. Unfortunately, however, much of what was presented as national (or state) ownership actually came to be owned and controlled directly by Trujillo himself, his family or his private associates.

Throughout the 1950s, Trujillo remained comfortably in control of the country through a skilful use of anti-communism (thus keeping the US happy), nationalism and corruption. The dictatorship came to an end in 1961. In part this was a consequence of the slow-down of growth after 1958, but the more immediate cause was a sudden wave of confidence within the popular opposition to the dictatorship in view of the revolution in nearby Cuba. In the midst of an internal crisis and facing growing international criticism, Trujillo was assassinated by ex-associates. The political system created by Trujillo, however, has proved more resistant. Trujillo's successor, Joaquin Balaguer, was prepared to limit the extent of the economic acquisitions of the Trujillo family and open the system partially to include the main opposition party, the populist *Partido Revolucionario Dominicano* (PRD), but essentially he sought to maintain the economic and political policies inherited from Trujillo in coordination with a pro-US policy in international relations.

There was no miraculous transformation within the political system which remained closed and exclusionary after the death of Trujillo. The social and economic structures which had given rise to the dictatorship in the first place were unchanged. Civil society was weak and disorganized; the economy remained externally dependent and vulnerable, with foreign investment playing a major role; and the US, an actor of enormous importance historically and sensitive to any possible challenge to its domination in the region following the Cuban revolution, preferred repression to the dangers of opening the system up, as the invasion of 1965 by US marines indicated. Balaguer remained in the presidency after the invasion, concentrating power in his own hands and relying on corruption and electoral malpractice until 1978. Congress was not closed but was carefully controlled by regime supporters, aided in practice by a timid legal opposition. The system respected the trappings of a democracy, then, but underneath remained strictly limited.

Until 1978, Balaguer engaged in policies of economic modernization, and the small private business sector on the whole cooperated with the government which excluded the popular sectors. But after 1978, international pressure and internal opposition, including elite opposition, pushed for change and Balaguer stepped down in favour of the PRD. The failure of the PRD government under Jorge Blanco to promote serious reform damaged the possibilities of democratic construction, however, and contributed to the political disarray in the country today where official political movements remain clientelistic and mass movements organize outside the parameters of the official political system. So in spite of the introduction of alternation in power between the two main parties, politics remains locked in the model of exclusionary-repressive politics: popular demonstrations are severely repressed – as with the 1984 protests over food price rises; the state demonstrates an excessive preference for dialogue with business groups, domestic and foreign, and popular groups, including trade unions, have little or no access to the state; and, perhaps most symbolic of all, there has been little generational renewal within the political elite, and Balaguer, himself Trujillo's heir, and Juan Bosch, the historic leader of the PRD from the 1960s, remain the central figures within the country in a kind of political gerontocracy. It is a democracy 'that is always at stake, always in crisis, awaiting a resolution that fails to emerge' (Espinal 1991: 163).

Even more than the Dominican Republic, the dictatorship of the Duvaliers, father and son, which spanned the years between 1957 and 1986, is an example of a personal dictatorship which created a predatory state for private gain, impoverishing in the process the vast majority of Haitian citizens. Perhaps more than almost anywhere else in the region, elite political culture and the deep social divisions within the country made possible an authoritarian culture which permitted the Duvaliers' long hold on power. According to Christian Girault, the tradition of an authoritarian state has resulted in a 'chasm . . . between a ruling elite, heavily militarized and the rest of the nation made up of landless rural workers and peasants' (Girault 1991: 191). This is the central reason for the survival of Duvalierism and the main reason why, even after the exile of Jean-Claude, democracy remains a remote possibility. General Namphy spoke unconsciously from within this authoritarian culture when he declared after overthrowing the elected government of Leslie Manigat in 1987, that 'constitutions are not for Haiti' (Rotberg 1988).

Francois Duvalier, or Papa Doc as he was universally known, came to power in 1957, with the acquiescence of the US, an external power of enormous significance after the occupation between 1915 and 1934. But far more importantly, Duvalier's power was based on Haitian underdevelopment – its overwhelmingly rural population of subsistence farmers living on tiny individual plots of land, and its historic cultural divisions: between the city and countryside, French and Creole culture, and mulatto economic power versus black poverty. Finally, the dictatorship was cemented by corruption, in particular in smuggling and drug traffic, and institutionalized violence, less by the Army itself, which finally overthrew Papa Doc, but by a personalized police force, loyal to the family, the Tontons Macoutes.

Papa Doc's early political career and his rise to power can be explained partly by his staunch opposition to the creole elite and his defence of black peasant culture. However, although he was never to renounce completely *noiriste* and patriotic rhetoric, Duvalier came to power thanks to the support of sectors of the army, always influential in Haiti and at crucial moments the arbiter of politics. It was to be some years before Papa Doc could build up an independent armed group, the Tontons Macoutes, and lessen his dependence on the Army, but by 1960 the Tontons Macoutes outnumbered the regular Armed Forces and the Army was weakened. The subsequent subordination of the Army to the Duvalierist state accounts in part for its survival.

The longevity of the dictatorship, however, is also a consequence of the closed and personal system of government which Duvalier constructed. It culminated in his declaring himself president for life in 1964 and in 1971 assuring the transference of power to his son through the establishment of the principle of hereditary rule. This was achieved through the destruction of the independent organisms of the state, the absolute suppression of civil liberties, mass terror aimed at eradicating real or imagined opposition, including that of the Catholic Church, the projection of the figure of Duvalier himself as a predestined leader of Haiti's people, endowed with mythical powers, and the establishment of privileges for Duvalier supporters. Duvalier remained in power by neutralizing the autonomy of the state and handing it over to groups personally loyal to himself and the Tontons Macoutes. Inevitably, his policies, which closed the country off from the rest of the region, devoted government expenditure to the buying of allies through clientelism and corruption, and refused to consider economic planning and development as tasks of government, were to impoverish Haiti. In contrast to the regional tendencies in the 1960s, the Haitian economy slowed and exports shrunk. Haiti had earned 40 million US dollars from exporting its products abroad in 1955; by 1969 it earned only 33 million US dollars. At the same time, the country's diplomatic isolation increased after the US withdrew support in 1963 and began to encourage the formation of a centrist, democratic opposition.[3] Mass immigration was an inevitable consequence of the system which generated economic deterioration coupled with brutal terror.

Jean-Claude Duvalier, who came to power after his father's death in 1971, was to alter the major components of the dictatorship in some key areas. He improved relations with the US by playing with the notion of liberalization of the political model, though never seriously. In fact, repression under Jean-Claude, though more selective, was equally effective, at least until 1983. The new opening to the US led to a flow of foreign investment, mostly in off-shore assembling plants which took advantage of Haiti's cheap labour. In the 1970s, this new model guaranteed a certain degree of economic growth, though this was accompanied by a general increase in poverty as income concentration increased to the point at which 1 per cent of the population received 44 per cent of national income, paying only 3.5 per cent of its earnings in income tax in the mid-

1970s (Ferguson 1987: 70). The agricultural economy was in ruins and mass emigration to the US and the Dominican Republic continued. Jean-Claude also changed the composition of Duvalierism inside Haiti. In particular, after his marriage to the daughter of a mulatto millionaire, Michelle Bennet, the dictatorship was reconciled with the mulatto elite, whose wealth had been accumulated in the new financial and service sectors rather than in land ownership. This distanced Jean-Claude from the black middle class, an important source of support for Papa Doc, and divided Duvalierism itself. The splits within the governing camp were evident in ministerial changes of the early 1980s. The dictatorship was finally overthrown through popular unrest and struggle between October 1985 and February 1986, encouraged by the Catholic Church. But the departure of Jean-Claude for exile in France did not end the Duvalierist system. The army, which came to power in the wake of the dictatorship's collapse, has returned to its traditional role as arbiter of the country's destiny, closing off the possibility of a genuine democratization of politics, as demonstrated in the overthrowing of the popularly elected President Jean-Bertrand Aristide in 1990. At the same time, government through violence, terror, repression and patronage, the system bequeathed to Francois Duvalier and refined by him into an effective system of government, remains in force.

Although the overthrow of the Duvaliers led to the emergence of new political parties, trade unions, etc., the army and to a lesser extent the Supreme Court, which played an important role in 1989 in particular following the overthrow of the military government of Prosper Avril, have been able to determine the terms of the post-Duvalier system. They have operated from a very restrictive and cynical notion of what constitutes democracy. Rather than accepting that any transition to democracy in Haiti, if it is to have any possibility of success, must limit authoritarianism, clientelism, control the death squads run by the Tonton Macoutes and subordinate the Armed Forces to civilian authorities, democracy is equated with simply holding elections, with little guarantee that those elections will be free, fair and respected by the groups loyal to the overthrown Duvalier family or the Army.

Another obstacle to the transition in Haiti is the legacy of the past. The parties are weak, with scant support in Haitian society, little more than organizations which have mushroomed around individual politicians. The real organs of representation of Haiti society after 1986 have been the popular organizations in the countryside, the trade unions, neighbourhood committees and church groups. These were ignored until the election of Jean-Bertrand Aristide and repressed after his removal from power. Their importance can be measured in the fact that Aristide, whose power base lay in the popular organizations which emerged after 1986 and not in the party system, was elected into office with 67 per cent of the vote. It is obvious that the possibility of creating a legitimate and stable political system, therefore, without taking into account popular organizations in Haiti or channelling them into the party arena, is remote indeed. The military coup of September 1991 which led to the downfall of Aristide left a political vacuum, in which the military have been unable to stabilize their political power in spite of their neutralization of opposition through repression, because of international opposition, from the US, the Organization of American States, Latin America and Europe. But the creation of even a formal democracy remains a distant goal.

Democratic politics: Costa Rica and the English-speaking Caribbean

The political tradition of the English-speaking Caribbean following independence in the 1960s and 1970s and that of Costa Rica following the civil war of 1948 stand in glaring contrast to the authoritarian systems installed in the states we have dealt with so far. In these countries, electoral politics is the norm and the state has demonstrated a consistent commitment, in theory at least, to the democratic rights of its citizens. Obviously, all the democratic states of the region fall short, considerably in some cases, of being 'ideal-type' democratic states. Yet a commitment to creating and maintaining a democratic system, to seeking outcomes to conflict through negotiation and bargaining rather than through the use of force, is consistently displayed by almost all influential political and social groups. None the less democracy is expressed differently from country to country in accordance with factors such as inherited political traditions, the influence of interest groups in the political system, the social structure and the nature and depth of social and political conflicts.

Costa Rica: Democracy through Elite Agreement

Explanations of Costa Rican democracy, unique in comparison with the other Spanish-speaking countries of the region, are various. Some explanations have taken the country's nineteenth-century development as the starting point. While some historicist explanations have remained at the superficial level of attributing the contemporary political system to the introduction of free obligatory primary education in the 1880s, or to the relative absence of ethnic conflict compared to Costa Rica's neighbours, other historians have analyzed in depth the pattern of economic and political development during the liberal reforms as a key to twentieth-century Costa Rican political culture. Hector Perez-Brignoli argues that Costa Rica displayed more egalitarian land-tenure patterns necessitating less repression than the rest of the isthmus, and that by the end of the nineteenth century the state rested upon implicit collaboration, agreements and conciliation between different social classes (Perez Brignoli 1989b).[4]

But contemporary politics and the dynamics of the system are perhaps more the result of the settlement of the 1948 civil war than of past traditions. The civil war led to the establishment of a new constitution in 1949 which remains in force today. The length of time the constitution has lasted is itself something of a record in the region. The new regime imposed by Jose Figueres was based on an anti-communist but reformist vision of democracy which came to be seen as the political platform of the *Partido de Liberación Nacional* (PLN) formed in 1951. But the stability of the system is due to more than the reformist strategy of the PLN. It is the result of the elite agreement which took place after the civil war (Peeler 1992). This agreement neutralized the contending social forces through a pact between the victors of the civil war, essentially conservatives and social democrats, who were themselves divided ideologically and socially. After 1948 the democratic system was used in an effective way to limit in practice popular access to the state and to prevent any redistributive policies being adopted, ideas associated with the overthrown reformist coalition around Rafael Calderón Guardia. It was, in its beginnings, therefore, a democracy which offered certain reforms instead of sharing out power beyond the elite, heavily dependent on obviating rather than negotiating social conflict and on the active intervention of the state.

Initially, then, the legitimacy of the post-1948 democratic system rested less on popular sovereignty and more substantially on offering material benefits – pensions, health care, public services – to a majority of the population while preserving the economic interests of the elite. Organized labour in particular remained weak and fragmented, and even today levels of unionization remain low, as business groups and even the state tend to see unions as potentially disrupting the consensus between social groups imposed and maintained after 1948. By contrast business organizations are strong and have direct channels into the state and the press.

Nevertheless, to see Costa Rican democracy as no more than an arrangement between different sectors of the elite to exclude the possibility of mass participation would be erroneous. Although there are limitations on the system – there is little political debate, and little space for dissent since the newspapers, radios, and political parties all express similar views – democracy has evolved over time into a less rigid framework with real possibilities of reform. Important reforms took place after 1960 especially, which have meant that 'in the last three decades the country advanced considerably along the road of political democracy' through social reform, and a broadening of the suffrage (Rojas 1988: 190). And the democratic system has also served as a device for social integration and has legitimized itself through social policies. For example, income is less concentrated in Costa Rica than elsewhere in the isthmus, and state policies, at least until after 1983, have redistributed national income downwards towards the poor. Social policies and income subsidies from the state meant that by 1983 'the total proportion of families in poverty declined from 26 per cent to only 10 per cent. The [impact of the subsidies] is felt most among the poorest, who fall to only 3 per cent of the population as a result' (Trejos *et al.* 1988).

Elections enjoy a high turnout (around 80 per cent) and the system, once dominated almost exclusively by the PLN, now revolves around opposition between the party of the revolution and its conservative opponents. The PLN won the presidential elections in 1953, 1962, 1970, 1974, 1982, 1986 and 1994; it lost in 1958, 1966 1978 and 1990. Moreover, until 1986 the PLN controlled Congress, the judiciary and the directorates of most para-statal companies. In spite of the articulation of opposition, both from the right and far more fragmented opposition from the left, the PLN became the dominant party in a multi-party system. In particular, its dominance within the state economic institutions determined relations between the public sector and the private and made the PLN the focal point for private business lobbying and pressure. This in turn has led to allegations of government corruption and clientelism.

It was not until the turbulent decade of the 1980s, however, that the system came under serious strain. Despite the regional crisis and deepening international interest in the conflict, Costa Rica at first sought to maintain its traditional neutrality. But the country came under pressure from its most important ally, the US, to adopt a less ambiguous anti-Sandinista stance; at the same time, the economic crisis of the region led to a fiscal crisis of the state and forced the government to adopt a series of measures to stabilize the economy and reduce public expenditure.

Costa Rican democracy has consistently been backed by outside powers, especially the US, and to a much lesser degree, in the 1980s, the European Union (see Table 3.1). In spite of its neutrality, the country has operated as a traditional ally of Washington for whom maintenance of the democratic system in the country is a strategic necessity as the only stable political system in the isthmus. While this has given Costa Rica some autonomy on occasion in its dealing with the US, in the 1980s the US was able to use the country's economic problems, in particular its acute shortage of foreign exchange, to pressurize the governments of Monge (1982–6) and

Table 3.1   US military and economic assistance to Costa Rica, 1988 and 1989 (millions of dollars)

	1988	1989
Development assistance	8.50	11.00
Food aid	15.08	15.00
Economic Support Fund*	90.00	57.00
Other economic assistance	3.41	—
Military aid	0.23	1.75
Total	117.22	84.75

*Most flexible aid, to support allies through balance of payments difficulties.
Source: Casaus and Castillo, 1991.

Arias (1986–90) to support Washington's attitude to the Sandinistas in Nicaragua. In effect, therefore, Costa Rican democracy became more dependent and more closely associated with the US in this period.

But the strains on the political system in the 1980s were more than simply the result of the economic difficulties facing the country and the pressure exercised by the US. We look in more detail at the economic aspects of the crisis in Chapter 5. We should note here that the political system itself entered a period of exhaustion and the statist model of development was called into question. The crisis also opened a debate about public morality and in particular the attitudes of the political elite towards using the state for private gain. Congressional hearings were set up in 1989 into the links between public figures and drug laundering and implicated members of the PLN in particular, though high-ranking members of the opposition *Partido Unidad Social Cristiano* (PUSC) were also implicated. Ex-President Daniel Oduber (1974-78), then Director of Planning for the PLN and Latin American Vice-President of the Socialist International, was forced to resign all public offices as a result. The revelations about the involvement of the PLN in drug laundering may have helped the conservative candidate, Rafael Angel Calderón of the PUSC, to win the presidential elections in 1990. But the operation of the Commission also illustrates how the system accommodates the political elite, who are seen as the guarantor of democracy. It would seem that members of the Committee negotiated with both the PLN and PSUC to limit the damage done to the party leadership, and in particular to keep the PSUC presidential candidate Calderon and the PLN government of Luis Alberto Monge outside the brief of the investigation. It was felt that with presidential elections in February 1990, the damage done to the political class should be limited in the interests of political stability. So, the legitimacy of the system was never seriously questioned and the end of the crisis of the 1980s, coupled with the reform of the state, has endowed the system with a new legitimacy in the eyes of the elites. And although the material benefits of the system diminished substantially for lower and middle income groups, social protection has remained much higher than in neighbouring countries, ensuring that dissatisfaction with the system was limited.

The English-Speaking Caribbean: The Westminster System

Political systems in the Commonwealth Caribbean operate in a significantly different way from that in Costa Rica, though both types are democratic. This is partly a result of separate ethno-histories and different social structures. We can also trace the influence of the colonial and cultural norms imposed by the British Empire on the political systems in the English-speaking area. This process of acculturation began as an imposition from the Empire and went on to become part of the ideological legacy passed on to the local elite which became the political elite on Independence. The English colonial administration was structured around central ideas of British political culture, which became embedded inside the new political systems of the recently independent territories. As a result, the political systems of the Commonwealth Caribbean are based on the Westminster model – a two-party system, with tendencies to alternation in power between the parties; a system which awards a high priority to the concept of individual freedom; and which, at least in principle, upholds the independence of civil society from the state.

However, for a number of reasons the Westminster system in the Commonwealth Caribbean does not function exactly as had been anticipated. Instead there are flaws in the system which limit democracy and popular control over the political elite in practice. The political systems tend towards clientelism, and a concentration of power. Democratic theorist Arend Lijphart noted that the Westminster model permits 'the governing majority or popular leaders to carry out excesses easily' and suggests that this is a particular danger in numerically small societies and in pluralist societies, that is, societies which are profoundly divided culturally (Lijphart 1990: 364). In this case, he suggests, minorities will find either little chance to express their democratic demands or few possibilities that those demands will be attended to by the state. In a 'winner takes all' system, the votes of the minorities can be ignored because they are not needed to form a stable government. This suggests that the Westminster system depends upon the principle of exclusion of minorities. It is an inherent feature in the system, which can sometimes undermine its legitimacy and which accounts for the vulnerability of Caribbean democracy.

Colonialism did not create a sense of region-wide nationalism in the British Caribbean. Hence demands for independence were expressed by each island individually, initially by the largest islands in the West Indian Federation, created in 1958 and conceived by the British as the first step to staged sovereignty. Let us look briefly at the operation of Westminster democracy in the largest of the islands of the Federation, Jamaica and Trinidad, which together possessed 83 per cent of the land mass incorporated into the Federation and 77 per cent of the population. Jamaica and Trinidad received independence with the break-up of the Federation in 1962, Trinidad forming a two-island state with nearby Tobago. We can then contrast the political problems of these larger states with those of the smaller, and more recently independent territories of the Eastern Caribbean.

In Jamaica electoral politics began in earnest in 1944 with the introduction of universal suffrage, the beginning of the process of independence. The new political system was based on the two political parties which had emerged in the 1930s, the Jamaican Labour Party (JLP), an anti-communist party occupying the right of the political spectrum despite its trade union links and the People's National Party (PNP) a party of the centre-left, also enjoying trade union links.[5] The JLP was in power from 1962 to 1972, when it handed power over to the PNP which remained in office until 1980. Edward Seaga's victory in 1980 brought the JLP back into government; in 1989 the PNP was returned to office, first under Michael Manley, later replaced by P. J. Patterson. The PNP, under Patterson, won re-election in April 1993. Apparently, therefore, the system created was essentially stable: alternance in power, free and fair elections (though often with a tendency toward street violence), and the rapid development of strong party identification across the electorate, had become central motifs of Jamaican political culture. The commitment of the new political elite to the two-party system meant care was taken on Independence to try and ensure its continuity. Special functions were granted to the Leader of the Opposition. For example one-third of the members of the second chamber, the Senate, was to be appointed by the Governor-General on the nomination of the Leader of the Opposition, and it was expressly written into the Constitution that it was the duty of the Prime Minister to consult with the Leader of the Opposition. At the same time, a Bill of Rights was incorporated into the Constitution.

But democracy has displayed systemic weaknesses in Jamaica from its inception. In particular, the functioning of the system came to depend on an implicit trade-off between stability and democracy, understood in this context as representation of the citizenry. Anthony Payne suggests that the parties did not concern themselves in any serious way with mass politicization. Rather they developed into 'electoral machines led and dominated by educated professionals who acted as brokers and bargainers in an attempt to assemble multiple-class coalitions' (Payne 1991b: 35). There is a deep gulf which separates the political elite, composed of important members of both parties and their allies in the trade unions, business and the administration, and the mass of Jamaican citizens. Politics 'at the top' has very little relevance to the needs and concerns of the ordinary Jamaican citizen, with the parties functioning to ensure votes and to promote party identification but without creating channels for the incorporation into the political agenda of demands from the party bases. The parties operate from the top downwards. As a result, Jamaican politics acquired a markedly elitist character and the problems inherent in the system came to a head in the years after 1968. With the exception of the period 1972–88, years of ideological conflict in Jamaica and throughout the region, the parties have differed on very few issues of importance.

Until the 1970s, no Jamaican government was forced to address seriously the most pressing issues of concern to the electorate: the urgent need for social reform and measures to reduce urban poverty, and the eradication of racist social structures. The two issues are of course related: it is worthy of note that Jamaica's business class is ethnically mixed but includes few representatives of the black majority, while the urban poor are almost exclusively black. Race was to be the key to opening up political debate in Jamaica at the end of the 1960s by presenting the political system with a series of challenges, riots and protests against racial discrimination. Riots in 1966 led to a Declaration of Emergency. The 'Rodney Riots' broke out in 1968, led by Black Power activists, and culminated in police repression and the loss of the lives of three people. The riots revealed the fragility of a system based on elitism.

A genuine ideological debate opened after 1972, as the PNP inaugurated a more populist approach to politics combined with promises of 'democratic socialism'. But the costs of putting issues like political renewal and representation on the political agenda were enormous: the 1976 and 1980 general elections took place within an atmosphere of confrontation and violence and amid allegations of externally provoked destabilization. The defeat of socialist ideas inside the PNP, coupled with domestic and international preoccupations about the increasing levels of violence in Jamaican society in the 1980s, has tended to unify the Jamaican political class once again. The 1989 elections were preceded by a pact signed by the leaders of the JLP and the PNP, Seaga and Manley, which had as its aim the avoidance of political violence but which also symbolized the end of real ideological debate between the parties. A return to stability, therefore – but at a price. Jamaican society remains troubled by the elitism of the political class. This has contributed to one of the pressing problems of Jamaica – the formation of a subculture of violence as a response to conflict. Only a small proportion of violence is related directly to politics and the 1989 pact has largely eliminated partisan violence between the PNP and the JLP. But violence is becoming endemic in Jamaican life, especially in Kingston, a reflection of systemic failure. On the one hand, recourse to violence as a solution to individual problems reflects an enormous lack of faith in state institutions, and on the other the state's evident inability to protect people from indiscriminate attack, indicates a gap between the state and the mass of the citizenry, marginalized from full participation and representation.

More recently, the political elite of Jamaica has developed beyond the confines of the two-party system to incorporate a new technocracy. This has not broadened the political class, however; quite the reverse. According to Francine Jácome, this tendency became region-wide in the 1980s because of the need to implement new programmes of political economy based on neoliberalism and has intensified the distance between government and the mass of the population. Not only have the policies of readjustment hit the masses particularly severely but the policies have encouraged a tendency towards 'decision-making at the level of the political system being concentrated within an elite reduced to a technocracy which is outside public debate and unknown to the public. "Specialists" discuss and resolve . . . problems . . . as the only sure way to overcome the current economic crisis' (Jácome 1991: 177). The result is a political crisis, with a huge number of citizens apathetic about formal politics, signifying a crisis in particular for the party system. A poll in 1992 revealed that 47 per cent of the

Jamaican electorate are disillusioned with the two main parties and 41 per cent would prefer to support an alternative (Wedderburn 1993).

The problems facing the political system in Trinidad and Tobago are of a different type. As in Jamaica, independence signalled a transference of power to new political elites who had for the most part been educated in Britain and who accepted without question the suitability of the Westminster system. Again as in Jamaica, the political system which developed does not articulate the concerns of a majority of the citizenship, with politicians forming another segment of the elite. But in Trinidad and Tobago, the party system is also a faithful reflection of the racial divisions within the islands, in particular the dichotomy between 'Creole' (mostly black but with some mixed or brown population) and the Indian population which arrived originally as indentured labourers after the abolition of slavery in 1834. Conflict, therefore, has centred more on racial and cultural divisions than on economic issues. Social demands from trade unions, and public protests from the poor, have generally met with a state response aimed at a partial 'solution' through a temporary increase in state spending possible because of the substantial wealth which Trinidad's oil reserves generated through the 1970s and 1980s.

Race, then, rather than class has proved the organizational framework of Trinidadian politics, with racial division itself institutionally cemented by the Westminster two-party system (Clarke 1991: 69). The People's National Movement (PNM) created by Dr Eric Williams dominated government, contesting the elections essentially on questions of racial affiliation, receiving support from the black lower class majority but representing in government the mixed-race middle class. Indian support was channelled, by contrast, to the Democratic Labour Party (DLP), of conservative orientation in spite of its name. After 1976, opposition to the PNM was directed through the United Labour Front (ULF), a conservative party which replaced the DLP as the main channel of Indian opposition. It might even be more accurate to characterize Trinidad and Tobago as a monoparty system since the PNM was in power continuously until 1986 and Eric Williams Prime Minister until his death in 1981 (Serbin 1984). In addition, between 1970 and 1976, the PNM governed without opposition because of the collapse of the DLP. The experience of this two-island state would seem to confirm Lijphart's contention, whereby Westminster-style democracy, with its 'winner takes all' approach, enshrines the domination of the majority over the minority in culturally pluralist societies because the construction of alliances are for the most part unnecessary. The domination of the PNM finally came to an end in 1986, when A.N.R. Robinson became Prime Minister with the National Alliance for Reconstruction, a alliance between the rest of the political parties in the system against the PNM.

The problem facing the democracies of the Eastern Caribbean are of yet another kind: how to develop responsive and representative government in micro-societies. Antigua occupies only 108 square miles, with a population of only 80,093; Grenada occupies 133 square miles and has a population of 120,000; St Kitts/Nevis, a two-island state altogether occupying 103 square miles, has only a population of 44,000 people. Indeed the size of the islands and doubts about the economic viability of such small states meant that these islands received independence later than the larger islands of the Commonwealth Caribbean. Grenada became independent in 1974; Dominica in 1978; St Lucia in 1979; and Antigua in 1981. Tony Thorndike has demonstrated that the Eastern Caribbean microstates have hardly any conflictive political issues:

> political culture is essentially inward-looking and insular, where the surrounding sea is a barrier rather than a highway. It is also conservative in tone and expression, and where there was once strong fidelity to the British Crown there has developed a growing identification with the United States, its values and interests ... Notable by their absence are ethnic factors ... neither are class differences so pronounced as in, for instance, Jamaica. (Thorndike 1991: 110–11)

The absence of serious conflict is a brake on the emergence of a competitive party system and on politics generally. Government therefore has come to depend as much on clientelism and connection, and displays a marked tendency towards excessive presidential authority. Many people are employed by the government, from white-collar employees to manual labourers, which mutes criticism in these societies where alternative employment is hard to find.

Criticism of government is also difficult because of the absence of serious independent newspapers, radios and television channels. Public debate about political issues occurs at the margins of the political system. This tends to mean that governments, once the elections are over, pay little attention to popular opinion and can afford to practise paternalistic top-down politics. Political leaders such as Eugenia Charles, Prime Minister of Dominica, or V. C. Bird of Antigua exercise iron control over their parties, blocking internal discussion. How therefore can we describe these political systems? Elections are fair and governments have changed hands; the possibilities for successful destabilization or military intervention, though they exist, are poor. Democracies, undoubtedly, but with strong authoritarian components.

Conclusion

The many political traditions within the Caribbean Basin are a reflection of the fragmentation and diversity of the region. In the 1970s and 1980s, the region's political systems, whether democratic or authoritarian, came under severe strain. Popular demands were made for a sharing out of power and the economic resources of society. In much of Central America, after years of bitter struggle, this has led to a tentative move towards the creation of democratic systems, but elsewhere – the Commonwealth Caribbean and in Costa Rica – the crisis of the 1970s and 1980s and demands for participation have revealed the weaknesses and limitations of the existing democracies, though without necessarily calling into question the bases of the political system itself. In general, the idea of democracy is becoming stronger in the region, both as an alternative to repression and exclusion and as a means to negotiate consensus over difficult political choices in society. But in much of the Spanish-speaking countries of the region, only very recently indeed have political elites given any indication of their conversion to the idea. In the Spanish-speaking world in particular, civil society is weak and there remains a huge gap between the formal political system and the unofficial marginalized world to which most people belong.

Regional democracy has been shown to be stable primarily where it is related to the establishment of concrete material gains for most of the population. It is for this reason that we should be careful not to exaggerate the stability of the democratic systems where they exist and not to fall into over-optimistic expectations of the fragile trend towards democratization, for the region's ability to provide basic services has come under severe strain since the 1980s due to the combined effects of the debt, economic recession, fiscal crisis and austerity programmes which make any form of redistribution impossible in the short to medium term. We come back to the question of democratization in the conclusion of the book.

Notes

1. In fact only phase I of Duarte's land reform, which expropriated holdings over 500 hectares, was carried out. Phases II and III, which would have expropriated holdings over 100 hectares, the size of most coffee and cotton haciendas, were suspended, shortly after the Director of the Institute of Land Reform was murdered.
2. The Chapultepec agreement does have some socio-economic clauses: individual property is limited to 245 hectares of land; land is to be made available to some of the guerilla fighters, in areas which were under FMLN control and where the legal owners had fled; the government undertook to study the question of agrarian reform and to consult with labour organizations as well as business interests in the design of economic policy. However, in practice less attention was paid to the economic issue by both sides in the negotiations and the implementation of these clauses are less important for international observers of the peace process than the political reforms.
3. The US attitude to Duvalier was always to be ambiguous, however. Until 1963, the US administrations had seen little to object to in Duvalier's government and, indeed, Duvalier received substantial aid in this period. Motivated by geopolitical concerns and a fear of another Cuba in the Caribbean, the US abandoned Duvalier in search of other more presentable allies in Haiti. But the role of the US ambassador in Port-au-Prince, independent of policy in Washington, was generally one of support for the dictatorship; for example in assuring a smooth transition of power after the death of Francois Duvalier to Jean-Claude Duvalier.
4. In fact, prevalent ideas about land tenure in Costa Rica are often misconceived. Mitchell Seligson noted the concentration of land ownership as a feature of the country's agrarian development. He

writes: 'the Gini index of the overall distribution of land for 1973 is .86, which ranks it sixth most unequal of the fifty-four nations studied by Taylor and Hudson' (Seligson 1980).

5. A third party emerged after Independence, the Workers' Party of Jamaica, but it has never achieved many votes, and its expansion is hindered by the Westminster system which guarantees the dominance of the two large parties.

4

The International Relations of the Caribbean Basin

The international relations of the states located in the Caribbean Basin are dominated above all by the presence and power of the US. This is as true today for the countries which once formed part of the British Empire, as it is for the countries of the isthmus, from Guatemala through to Panama, and the islands of the Spanish-speaking Caribbean, which experienced direct US domination and in some cases intervention at the end of the nineteenth century. Internal politics, economic policies, development strategies etc. are designed with reference as to how they will be received in Washington. In all the states of the Caribbean Basin, therefore, decision-making internally, political and economic, is permeated with US influence.

However, the US is not the only outside power which has shaped the international relations of the area. In the first instance, the Caribbean, like all of the New World, is a 'creation' of Europe. Europe remained the determining influence until the twentieth century and still today directly rules in some micro-territories. In addition, the newly independent states of the Commonwealth Caribbean constructed a network of institutional relations with Britain and the European Union (EU) which keeps Europe as an important point of reference for Caribbean politics and economics. The Cold War has also left its mark on the international relations of the region, though in a more marginal way, with the Soviet Union playing a pivotal role in Cuban politics in particular between 1961 and 1990.

In this chapter we examine the contemporary influence exercised by outside players, especially the US, in the development of the region. The European presence has been outlined historically in Chapter 1; however, towards the end of the chapter we also look at the contemporary relationship between the EU and the region. And finally we explore the possibilities for regional cooperation as a way of reducing dependence.

The 'Hovering Giant': The US in the Caribbean Basin, 1880–1945[1]

The Caribbean Basin has been an object of US interest from the first formulations of US foreign policy. In effect, the Caribbean was taken to constitute the United States' third border, and as such it had to be made secure in accordance with national interests. This is the origin of the Monroe Doctrine of 1823, which asserted hemispheric sovereignty and declared that the intromission of external forces in the hemisphere would be regarded as dangerous to US 'peace and safety'. With the Monroe Doctrine, the cornerstone of US policy in the region was laid. By the end of the century, US interest in the region increased, as a result of a growing perception that Europe was withdrawing from the area and a fear that the region, without strong external control, would fall prey to anarchy and instability. The policy's ideological justification sprang from a deep mistrust of 'Latin' culture, which was perceived as irrational, backward and barbaric and also from an unshakeable conviction in the United States' own 'manifest destiny'. Interest was centred on the independent territories of the Central American isthmus and the islands of the weak and collapsing Spanish Empire.

An unusual degree of concern was evident in events in Nicaragua from early on. Attention was first directed there because of interest in locating part of a highway linking Eastern US to California after 1848 and the US annexation of Mexican territories; around the same time, the US mercenary, William Walker, was 'elected' President of Nicaragua, almost certainly with the direct connivance of Washington. This was the beginning of a tradition of intervention in Nicaraguan affairs, periodic invasions and military occupation that formed an essential element in Nicaragua's construction as a nation-state and constitutes a backdrop both to the Sandinista revolution of 1979 and US-Nicaraguan relations in the 1980s. Later, Nicaragua was under consideration by the US for the location of the planned trans-isthmian canal. When the decision was taken to construct the canal in Panama in 1914, the US bribed the Nicaraguan government with 3 million dollars to ensure that no rival canal was built through Nicaragua. The US desire to expand its influence in the region was viewed with alarm throughout the isthmus. In 1855, the Costa Rican Ambassador in Washington wrote: 'This Nation [the US] finds itself overwhelmed by an insatiable passion for expansion and riches . . . which seem to have weakened her notion of what is just and what is unjust' (Solis 1990: 28).

It is only with the growth in investments in the region and the building of the Panama Canal that we can talk about an active policy in the region. US policy stressed the need to 'civilize' the independent Central American states, but underlying this was a wish to make the area safe for international exploitation. In its origins, therefore, the policy rested on racist and imperialist assumptions, with the result that the US 'executed foreign policy without reference to the demands and responses of the [Central] American nations' (Tulchin 1971). The most celebrated aspects of US policy in this period were, on the one hand, the gunboat politics of the 'big stick' era of President Theodore Roosevelt in the early years of the twentieth century, and, on the other, the political clout of US business over policy in the 'dollar diplomacy' of the 1920s. With the perspective of history, however, we can see that US economic interests remained sectoral and limited and US investments only outstripped in number those from Europe in the 1920s. In practice, US interest remained reactive and erratic until the end of the nineteenth century. The end of the First World War saw the establishment of a clear tendency on the part of the US government to support business interests in Central America.

US capital did not spread out evenly throughout the isthmus. Where coffee production remained dominant (e.g. El Salvador), capital and banking remained under local control, though not always the transport infrastructure. The banana industry, which took off at the turn of the century, soon came to be dominated by US companies, especially in Guatemala and Honduras. The banana companies were able to obtain considerable economic privileges such as tax concessions or cheap land for cultivation, and political leverage over governments in view of their importance in the export economy of the region and the weakness of the Central American states. The political influence of the banana industry was notorious in Honduras during the almost constant civil wars between 1883 and 1933, which included rival companies as well as factions of the ruling class.

Even more aggressively expansionist policies were pursued by Washington in the remaining territories of the declining Spanish Empire. The US manufactured a diplomatic incident in order to 'assist' Cuba, Puerto Rico and the Philippines in winning independence from Spain in 1898. The short Spanish–American war marks the beginning of a period of unchallenged US hegemony in the region. The US was motivated to assure its own control over these islands by a combination of factors. First, it needed to reduce European influence in the region to a minimum. In order to avoid any outbreak of instability which might contribute to an increase in European activity, Washington saw tight US control over the future of these territories as highly desirable. Second, the US was in a phase of expansionism accompanied by a limitless faith in its future and a belief in the rightness of its actions. And third, the policy was underwritten by racist stereotyping of the Caribbean population as poor and ignorant and of the 'Latin' (i.e. the Spanish or the Creole) as barbaric and cruel. Important sectors of US society came to believe that the US must carry the 'white man's burden' in the Caribbean, a view with lasting consequences for US–regional relations. As a result of the war, Puerto Ricans found US citizenship thrust upon them in 1917, the first stage in the road to associated statehood, and Cuba was brought under the direct control of the US until 1934. Henceforth the Cuban economy was to be oriented almost exclusively towards sugar production for the US market. Even Haiti and the Dominican Republic, independent since 1825 and 1865 respectively, came under the US eye in this period. The US marines invaded Haiti in 1915 and stayed until 1934. The Dominican Republic was occupied in 1903–4, invaded in 1905 and again occupied between 1916 and 1924. By the time the troops withdrew, Haiti and the Dominican Republic were also inextricably tied to the US economy.

Regional Policy through the Cold War Lens: Containment

Greater attention was paid to security south of the US border during and following the Second World War. The US perceived threats from the Axis powers first, and then later identified what was believed to be a more enduring threat from 'international communism'. Attention was focused on the mainland states and the Spanish-speaking Caribbean. Other Caribbean islands, still part of European empires, were thought to be the concern of the Western allies. It was only with the start of de-colonization in the 1960s that the US spread its net towards the rest of the Caribbean.

Rather than simply reacting to events, Washington now began to pay some considerable attention to the design and content of a hemispheric policy. For Central America and the Caribbean, this policy meant US support for personalist dictatorships and *caudillista* politics and a deepening of the ties between the US and the agrarian elite and the military. A premium was placed on 'hemispheric solidarity' which was in fact a shorthand for loyalty to Washington. Within the policy, Latin America and the independent Caribbean was viewed as a homogeneous region, presuming a shared and almost total social, economic, cultural and political unity which was and continues to be false. It meant that the US policy-makers missed the specific characteristics of societies in the region which are the key to understanding political processes and social changes. Instead of understanding regional politics as a result of regional or national developments, the US came to see Latin America in static terms in which any kind of change was promoted by outside elements and 'external subversion'.

The new relationship was institutionalized through military cooperation agreements, cemented with the signing of the Treaty of Reciprocal Assistance (TIAR) in 1947, military and economic aid, closer contacts between US government and Latin American heads of state, and a new diplomatic framework, the Organization of American States (OEA), created in Bogatá in 1948. The OEA has become a fundamental instrument of the Inter-American system and has served mainly as a rubber stamp justifying US policy in the region. After the US-backed coup overthrowing President Arbenz in Guatemala in 1954, the OEA justified the action, ratifying the struggle against communism in the Americas; in 1962 Cuba was excluded from the organization because of US hostility; and the 1989 invasion of Panama met with swift OEA approval.

The overarching framework for US policy in the region was containment. It presumed that the Soviet threat was global. Policy came to rest exclusively on a bipolar vision of the world, in which any process of change became a manifestation of attempts by the Soviet Union to undermine the US. A key document from the period states 'the assault on free institutions is world-wide now, and in the context of the present polarization of power, a defeat of free institutions anywhere is a defeat everywhere' (Gaddis 1982: 91). It was a short step to take from this to the decision to try and overthrow, by whatever means necessary, legal or otherwise, movements identified with demands for change and a renegotiation of the relationship with the US.

Nowhere in the region were the consequences of containment so grave as in Guatemala. Guatemala, in fact, became a symbol of US intervention in response to change throughout the region during the Cold War period and the events of 1954 are central to the history of the Caribbean Basin. The personalist dictator, General Jorge Ubico, was forced to resign in 1944 by the determined opposition of the emerging middle class, university students, the small labour movement and reformist sectors of the army. Juan Jose Arévalo was elected president in 1945 and inaugurated a decade of moderate reforms. Replaced in 1950 by Jacobo Arbenz, the reforms deepened, especially in the countryside with the promulgation of an agrarian reform in 1952. Arbenz also legalized the small Communist Party, which was an important force in the growing labour movement, and tried to promote national control over external trade by building nationally owned roads and port infrastructure for the export of Guatemalan products. The reforms brought the government into a head-on collision with internal elites and external actors: the US government, alarmed by the legalization of the Communist Party; the powerful United Fruit Company, facing land expropriation and a loss of revenue from its monopoly over export facilities; and the landowning class, under threat politically and economically. Arbenz was toppled in a coup financed and organized by the State Department and the CIA and launched from Honduras, a close ally of the US in this period.

The coup, which was followed by the imposition of malleable Castillo Armas as President, has sometimes been used to demonstrate the power of multinational companies over US policy, because both the Secretary of State, John Foster Dulles, and Allen Dulles, head of the CIA, had links with United Fruit (Schlesinger and Kinzer 1983). Yet it might be more accurate to see a harmony of interest between Washington and the banana company. Both stood to gain from a demonstration of force. But for Washington, defeat of the 'Communists' and the removal of a critical government was the primordial motivation behind the intervention; and the incorporation of Guatemala into the inter-American military alliance, the TIAR, in 1955 was the symbol of its success. Success for United Fruit was only partial; though it won back previously expropriated land, the new deal signed with Castillo Armas included an increase in tax on company profits (Labarge 1960: 36).

The Cuban Revolution

A sea change occurred in US–Caribbean/Central American policy in the wake of the Cuban revolution. If we conceptualize a foreign policy agenda as simply a list in a descending order of priority, the region jumped from somewhere near the middle on the way down, to much nearer the top. Washington was convinced that the struggle against the Soviet Union had been displaced to the Third World. Because policy-makers remained locked in a bipolar vision of the world, indigenous factors in the revolution, and indeed in regional events generally, were accorded only secondary importance. As a result, the US responded to the revolutionary regime in Havana, not as a small state on the periphery of the world system trying to establish a more equitable social and economic system, but simply as a proxy of Moscow.

Once the Castro government had demonstrated its clear commitment to sweeping reform, which included nationalization of US-owned utilities, sugar plantations and mining interests, the US responded by drawing up plans to invade the island and overthrow the revolution. An invasion was duly mounted, with CIA-trained Cuban exiles at the head, in April 1961, landing at the Bay of Pigs. The invasion was a failure. Washington's attention then shifted from overthrowing Castro to trying to prevent revolution elsewhere in the region.

The success of the Cuban revolution and the apparent ease with which the old order was overthrown was the spark to a series of popular rebellions, primarily rural, throughout the region. Fearing the sudden collapse of its allies, the US designed a two-pronged response: a development model, through the Alliance for Progress; and a military counter-insurgency strategy, based on arming and training military forces, and if necessary, on preparedness to deploy US troops.

The military strategy was given the name 'flexible response'. It comprised both a reform of US–Latin American military relations overall and a net increase in outlay in the region, in particular for counter-insurgency hardware and riot control equipment. Robert MacNamara, Kennedy's Secretary of Defence, confirmed that the primary object of US military aid was to assist 'where necessary, in the continued development of indigenous military and paramilitary forces capable of providing, in conjunction with the police and other security forces, the needed domestic security' (Klare 1984: 87). The US Army Caribbean School in Panama in the Canal Zone was reorganized and renamed the US Army School of the Americas. It proved to be a major channel for the dissemination of anti-insurgency techniques. But where local armies still proved unable to defeat guerilla groups, a special US unit, the Green Berets, was created to be deployed anywhere throughout the continent.

The Alliance for Progress was unveiled in March 1961. Its aim was the promotion of moderate reform throughout Latin America, which would, it was thought, undercut any possibilities of revolution. It committed the US to spending 20,000 million dollars over a ten-year period (though in the end approximately half of that had been spent by 1969) in the development of a Food for Peace fund, in support of structural reforms aimed at economic growth – 2.5 per cent a year was the express aim – and in the creation of a Central American Common Market. In sum, it suggested that the US would look for new allies in the region: centrist, progressive groups, with an industrializing, democratic ideology.

Yet the Alliance failed in Central America and the Caribbean. It did not enable democratic, centrist groups to come to power. Why was this? Mainly because the policy rested on fallacious assumptions about regional politics. First, it presumed that credible liberal democratic forces existed, or at least that they could be created; second that these forces would be strong enough to win power electorally; third, it supposed that once in government they would be able to promote growth and reduce poverty; and fourth, that the military and the oligarchy would allow this process to take place. The policy ignored the social and economic entrenchment of the oligarchy in the region and the legacy of popular nationalism which was the result of a century of US exploitation.

Furthermore, the Alliance was based on ideas about 'development' in general rather than any real understanding of actual development processes in the region (though in most cases these were unconscious assumptions by US policy-makers). The theory of development which underlay the Alliance was similar to that of 'modernization', dominant in liberal US thinking in the late 1950s and 1960s. The region was thought to be fertile ground for communist intrusion because it was made up of 'traditional' societies struggling to get on the path to capitalist economic growth and a modern social order. Poverty, it was thought, erroneously presumed to be endemic in traditional societies, made worse by the consequences of partial modernization, coupled with elite instransigence to change, rendered oligarchical rule vulnerable to revolutionary guerilla movements. Development was therefore necessary to prevent revolution, and the deepening of capitalism, economic growth and a functioning liberal democracy were understood to be synonymous with development.

These ideas bear little relation to the reality of politics and regional development processes. Rather than the archaic survivors of a previous mode of production, the Central American oligarchies had become the vehicle for the penetration of capitalism in the countryside (Torres-Rivas 1987). The polarization of 'traditional' and 'modern' societies, inherent in the Alliance for Progress, ignored the capacity of agrarian elites to oversee agro-export diversification and industrialization without fundamentally altering the internal distribution of power or wealth: economic modernization without democratization. This process intensified with the establishment of the Central American Common Market, which stimulated production and created new possibilities for investment through the expansion of the regional market, the benefits of which were mainly reaped by the small local elite which controlled domestic capital and the transnational companies with local plants. The net result of the Alliance for Progress, therefore, was to strengthen oligarchic states and dictatorial rule, especially in Guatemala, El Salvador and Nicaragua, where the new rules of the game were cynically learned. As Torres-Rivas points out: 'the Alliance for Progress . . . meant the rise of governments profoundly repressive, but resulting from electoral consultations, respectful of the rotation of executive power, but within narrow military circles' (Torres-Rivas 1989: 82).

Acknowledgement of the failure of developmentalism and the primacy of the military response came in 1965, when intervention to uphold US hegemony was required once again: this time in the Dominican Republic. The local Armed Forces, despite their anti-insurgency training, proved unable to crush the protest movement which was gathering strength in Santo Domingo in support of the return of the democratically elected president, Juan Bosch, ousted in 1963. Alleging that the 'constitutionalist' movement, as it was known, was a front for communist infiltration, the US sent 23,000 marines to quell the uprising. In elections called a year later, the pro-US right-winger, Joaquin Balaguer, was installed.

From Carter to the Reagan Doctrine

After 1965, the threat of 'another Cuba' diminished, and with it Washington's interest in the region. It was not until the late 1970s that concerted interest was once more focused on the region. The 1970s witnessed an intense debate on the overall direction of US foreign policy in the wake of the Vietnam War, provoking open fissures in the foreign policy establishment for the first time. For some, the war was lost from a lack of commitment in Washington to winning; for others, the lesson from Vietnam was that no further erosion of US global power must be permitted; and for a third group, the war itself had been an error, and new ideological foundations for policy in the Third World had to be found. The shadow of Vietnam and the various 'lessons' which had been learned from the experience became major influences on the formation of regional policy in the late 1970s and 1980s.

President Carter (1976–80) was initially convinced that a new approach was needed. His strategy aimed at encouraging what were termed 'viable' democracies in the region, which in practice meant regimes that were not 'full' democracies, a euphemism for govern-ments which had resulted from the ballot box but which were repressive and dictatorial. It was thought in Washington that these governments, though somewhat unstable, were permeable to US influence: they could therefore be encouraged to take a slow road in the direction of a more complete democracy. This was the basis of the 'human rights' policy associated with Carter (Schoultz 1981).

One other change implicit in this approach was that it tended to break down policy in the region into a series of bilateral relations, in that some states were rewarded because their record on human rights was improving, while others were punished. The new policy was articulated in a confused and contradictory fashion, but it provided a rupture with the past, albeit a temporary one.

The main strand of policy-making rested on the imperative of finding and strengthening the centre ground. Yet events in El Salvador, Nicaragua, Honduras, Guatemala and Grenada illustrated how unrealistic and uninformed this policy was at that time. Carter underestimated the strength of both the left and right in the region. The dominant feature of regional politics in the 1970s was the development of popular movements, especially in Nicaragua and El Salvador, and a corresponding assertion of the power of the ultra-right. The Carter administration was unable to confront its erstwhile allies, the oligarchic and military elites in El Salvador and Guatemala, which had developed a considerable capacity for electoral mobilization after 1955; and in Honduras, rather than a new dynamic centre government which Carter hoped to see, the military took power in 1978 under General Policarpo Paz García.

The irrelevance of Carter's policies to the real struggles going on in the late 1970s was illustrated by the events of 1979. In that year, the dictatorship of Anastasio Somoza in Nicaragua collapsed and Carter was forced, reluctantly, to face the fact that no alternative other than the *Frente Sandinista de Liberación Nacional* (FSLN) could be found. Unenthusiastic at best about the FSLN, the revolution divided policy-makers, with some seeing no alternative but to work with them, and a more hardline faction developing around National Security Adviser Brezinski which was more interested in preventing a supposed Cuban penetration in the isthmus. In El Salvador, meanwhile, Carter cut assistance to the repressive military dictatorship under Romero, and in the midst of a wave of escalating government violence in October 1979, Romero was overthrown. The short-lived centrist regime which came to power collapsed in January 1980 when the civilian members of the junta resigned because of their powerlessness to halt the violence carried out by the security forces.

As doubts gathered in Washington about the efficacy of the human rights strategy, more ammunition for Carter's opponents was provided by the signing of the 1978 accords on the Panama

Canal, which established an end to US control over the Canal by the end of the century. And in addition to his 'failures' in the isthmus, critics pointed to his policies in the insular Caribbean. Decolonization by the British meant that the US now assumed 'responsibility' for the newly independent territories of the Commonwealth Caribbean. On the tiny island of Grenada, the New Jewel Movement established itself in power through a bloodless coup, and proceeded to improve relations with Cuba, and Washington looked on horrified as an airport was built on the island, partly with Cuban aid. Both Grenada and Panama were turned into important issues in the Republican candidate Ronald Reagan's campaign for the Presidency in 1980. Carter was accused of selling out US security interests and of sending signals to the Soviets of weakness and hegemonic decline.

Carter came under particularly severe attack from the new conservative wing of the Republican Party, who believed that the US government must signal greater toughness in the Third World. They were particularly influenced by the idea that the US would have won the Vietnam War if only there had been sufficient domestic commitment. Jean Kirkpatrick was to offer the most cogent of the new right analyses. She suggested that the US had 'lost' non-democratic, friendly regimes including Nicaragua in 1979, during Carter's presidency, because of a misunderstanding of 'traditional' societies. Somoza's dictatorship, she argued, was autocratic, but not totalitarian, essentially meaning that it was pro-US and anti-communist, and that it would have been have been possible to urge reform on the country (Kirkpatrick did not explain why the US had *not* urged reform on the Somozas in the past, or why, if they had, it had not been successful). Thus, under the guise of a sociological approach to change, Kirkpatrick offers an intellectual justification for a bipolar vision of the international system. Despite the spurious and a historical nature of her analysis, it would seem that she exercised a remarkable influence over policy-makers during Reagan's term of office (Schoultz 1987: 115). The Santa Fe Committee, from which some of Reagan's initial foreign policy team were drawn, adopted a similar line. Policy in the Caribbean Basin should be expressly subordinated to the global concerns of the US, it was argued, and an exclusively geopolitical and military focus on the Central American crisis was recommended. US policy from Kennedy onwards was criticized and, while nothing immediate could be done to unseat Castro, a second unfriendly regime in the area should not be tolerated.

The new right focus formed the ideological backdrop to the policies of the Reagan administration and to the Reagan Doctrine. The Doctrine meant, in principle, focusing on a global crusade against Soviet influence in the Third World. But, in practice, it signified a sustained attempt to dislodge new radical, unconsolidated regimes in the Caribbean Basin (Poitras 1988). In pursuit of this aim, Reagan relied on a military, rather than a political response. It led therefore to the low-intensity war which the US funded and fuelled in the region through the 1980s. The costs of the policy were high: US Congress voted 154.3 million dollars in military aid between 1983 and 1987 to be spent in Nicaragua alone; millions more were spent covertly as the Irangate scandal revealed. The economic costs and the psychological exhaustion resulting from the war were to be a major cause of the Sandinistas' defeat in the 1990 elections.

Meanwhile, the US increased both military assistance to El Salvador and the number of US military personnel in the country as part of a strategy to shore up the dictatorship against supposed Soviet–Cuban–Nicaraguan aggression. As a direct result of the decision to look for a military solution, debate in Washington about the causes of insurrection in the region, and in El Salvador in particular, was marginalized and the emphasis instead was simply on national security: whether there was Soviet penetration, and how much. Secretary of State Haig reduced at a stroke the complex struggles going on in the region to 'a Soviet priority target list, a hit list if you will, for the ultimate takeover of Central America' (Schoultz 1987: 65). The simplicity of the early Cold War years had returned, though this time it was applied to a region experiencing a daily reality of US-supported state terror.

During the early years of the 1980s, the US also built up forces in Honduras which became in effect a lynchpin for US anti-Sandinista strategy. More than 1,000 US soldiers were permanently stationed there, the number increasing to 5,000 or more whenever military manoeuvres were carried out. It was estimated in 1985 that the Reagan administration had spent 100 million dollars on joint manoeuvres since coming into office (*The Washington Post*, 24 February 1985). Honduras was also converted into a base for the *contras*, the anti-Sandinista counter-revolutionary forces. Estimates in the early 1980s indicate a presence of 7,000 *contras*, with the US operating as a source of logistical and psychological support (Casaus and Castillo 1990: 773). The purpose of the military build-up in Honduras was to strengthen the *contras* and at the same time to increase the isolation of the Sandinistas in Nicaragua. The same ideas were behind the manoeuvres in the Panama Canal zone in 1983, 1985 and 1986, and in the exercises which took place regularly through this period in the US base in Guatanamo, in Puerto Rico, the Gulf of Mexico and the Gulf of Florida.

The 1980s: US Hegemony Through Aid

The Reagan period also saw a dramatic increase in economic aid to the Caribbean Basin, though obviously only to allied governments, and Honduras and El Salvador in particular have been major beneficiaries (see Tables 4.1 and 4.2). Despite this economic assistance, per capita income fell in both countries throughout the 1980s.

Rather than bilateral aid, many US policy-makers argued that the US should be promoting private investment in the region. As a result the Caribbean Basin Initiative (CBI) was launched in 1983. Interestingly, for the first time, US policy addressed explicitly Central America, the Commonwealth Caribbean and the other Caribbean states in the same initiative. Countries were excluded from the programme for ideological reasons, not cultural. It marks the culmination of the US determination to exercise hegemonic control even over territories which were until recently British and which remain part of the Commonwealth. US concern with the Caribbean reflected both security and economic concerns, and CBI was designed not only to tie the region closer to the US but also to deal with some of the results of regional underdevelopment and poverty which were beginning to affect negatively US development: for example, regional out-migration to the US. From the Caribbean alone, it is estimated that around 80,000 Caribbean enter the US annually (Lewis 1990).

The emphasis on private capital as the motor of development for the region which characterized the programme was to continue under President Bush, and in 1990 the Customs and Trade Act was passed which made permanent the provisions in the original Reagan

Table 4.1   US assistance to Central America, 1980–6 (US$ million)

	1980	1981	1982	1983	1984	1985	1986
Costa Rica							
Military	0.0	0.3	2.1	2.6	9.2	9.2	2.7
Economic	14.0	13.3	120.6	212.4	177.9	208.0	187.3
Total	14.0	13.6	122.7	215.0	187.1	217.2	190.0
El Salvador							
Military	6.0	35.5	82.0	81.3	196.5	128.2	132.6
Economic	57.8	133.6	182.2	231.1	331.1	326.1	350.8
Total	63.8	169.1	264.2	312.4	527.6	454.3	483.4
Guatemala							
Military	0.0	0.0	0.0	0.0	0.0	0.3	10.3
Economic	11.1	16.6	23.9	17.6	33.3	73.8	77.2
Total	11.1	16.6	23.9	17.6	33.3	74.1	87.5
Honduras							
Military	4.0	8.9	31.3	37.3	77.5	62.5	88.2
Economic	51.0	33.9	78.0	101.2	209.0	138.9	157.9
Total	55.0	42.8	109.3	138.5	286.5	201.4	246.1
Total							
Military	10.0	44.4	115.4	121.2	283.2	200.2	233.8
Economic	133.9	197.4	404.7	562.3	751.3	746.8	773.2
Total	143.9	241.8	520.1	683.5	1034.5	947.0	1007.0

Source: Casaus and Castillo, 1990.

proposal. Bush justified this move by arguing in 1989 that the Caribbean Basin 'is an area of major strategic interest to the US' (SELA, *Trade Newsletter*, no. 26, 1989: 8). The initiative is significant, then, in that it demonstrates the importance assigned by the US to the region. Clearly the Caribbean Basin had taken shape as a separate area from that of 'Latin America' in the minds of US policy-makers. But although CBI was described as a major new development initiative, its benefits for the region, as we shall see, have been few. Rather it offers high profits to multinationals looking for cheap and convenient export platforms tied to the US. At best, CBI promotes investment in export promotion assembling plants and upholds a low-wage economy.

Table 4.2   Per capita income in Central America, 1980 and 1984 (US$)

	1980	1984
El Salvador	802	632
Costa Rica	1,766	1,466
Guatemala	1,345	1,162
Honduras	746	666
Nicaragua	1,063	1,089

Source: *The Washington Post*, 29 April 1984.

The main provision of CBI is the elimination of duties on most goods entering the US from any of the designated beneficiaries.[2] Overall, however, the successes of CBI have been few, if we analyse it from the point of view of the beneficiaries. A study carried out by the *Sistema Económico Latinoamericano* (SELA) indicates that exports to the US from CBI states declined between 1984 and 1990 by 13 per cent, only marginally better than Caribbean non-designated countries, whose imports to the US over the same period fell by 14.4 per cent (SELA 1992a: 29). The report concludes that

CBI has not made a significant impact on the development of Caribbean Basin countries and initial expectations concerning its potential positive effect . . . particularly as far as export trade is concerned, are far from being met . . . Export earnings are less than at the start of the programme . . . market shares have declined absolutely and relative to other developing areas, and the balance of trade picture with the US has reversed itself to the disadvantage of Caribbean Basin countries and continues to deteriorate. (SELA 1992: 71–2)

We look in more detail at the development implications of CBI in Chapter 5.

From Bush to Clinton: The End of the Cold War

Starting from the election of George Bush in 1988, US foreign policy has been dominated by the reconstruction and revival of US global power in line with the changes brought about by the collapse of the

USSR and the challenges to the US economy by the emergence of economic blocs (the European Union and Japan especially) outside US control. In terms of policy in the Caribbean Basin, this has meant a need to reassert hegemony without the easy justification of the Cold War. Policies have become pragmatic and apparently issue-related, with drugs and immigration from the Caribbean to the US the areas that come near the top of the agenda. The main ideological underpinning of US policy is increasingly that of supporting moves towards democratization. The Bush and Clinton administrations, however, have continued to understand democracy essentially within the limited framework of electoralism. None the less, the US policy statement condemning the coup overthrowing Jean-Bertrand Aristide and suspending Haiti's membership of CBI would have been unthinkable a decade earlier. And US support for the peace negotiations between the Cristiani government and the guerilla FMLN, also represents a break with Reagan's policy on El Salvador. Clearly, in the Caribbean Basin, as in the Latin American region as a whole, there is a shift in Washington from looking for military allies to a new understanding with civilian elites. But it is also true that Bush and Clinton have been able to afford a more democratic line on policy since they reaped the benefits of the Reagan years of high military spending and support for anti-insurgency wars which ousted the Sandinistas in Nicaragua, left the region economically devastated and exhausted the popular movements, thus lowering the revolutionary potential within the region. So how much has really changed?

Certainly Washington's determination to control the parameters of political possibilities in the region remains as strong as ever. Its influence in the economic and political planning of the region as a whole is undisputed. And the belief that US security remains vulnerable to events in the Caribbean Basin is still the dominant view in policy-making circles. US sensitivity to regional politics since the end of the Cold War was perhaps best illustrated in Washington's approach in Panama. Panamanian president, General Manuel Antonio Noriega, an erstwhile ally of Washington especially in the covert anti-Sandinista war, was by 1988 proving unreliable. He was insisting on fulfilment of the Panama Canal Treaty signed by Presidents Carter and Torrijos which would mean the Canal came under Panamanian control, and was pursuing an independent and nationalist line both internally inside Panama and with regard to external policies. Given Panama's extreme dependence on the US, this inevitably brought Noriega into direct conflict with Washington. A campaign was launched to overthrow him indirectly but failed, and President Bush eventually decided to commit troops in December 1989 in order to oust him. The invasion culminated with the capture of Noriega himself and his removal to stand trial in the US on narcotics charges.

Bush stressed four justifications for his action: first, the usual insistence that the invasion was necessary to protect US citizens in Panama, an argument used in Grenada in 1983 and the Dominican Republic in 1965; second, to offer support to the opposition to Noriega, described as the representatives of Panamanian democracy; third, the pursuit of a criminal indicted on drug trafficking inside the US, President Noriega himself; and fourth, the protection of the Canal, where 13,000 soldiers are permanently based. The Canal was less under threat from Noriega, however, as from the Accords signed by the US in 1979 and in particular Noriega's insistence that the Accords did not guarantee the continued existence of US military bases on Panamanian soil. As the 1999 deadline for US withdrawal drew closer, Bush, and Reagan before him, tried to look for more malleable interlocutors inside the country.

Panama serves as an extreme example of the dependence fostered in the Caribbean as a result of US expansionism in the region since the moment of Independence. It is impossible to understand Washington's relationship with Panama and the 1989 invasion without reference to the peculiar genesis of Panama as an independent state and its later history. Panama was once part of Colombia, but relative geographical isolation from the centre of Colombian production and politics led to the creation of a small independence movement at the end of the nineteenth century. The independence movement won an unexpected ally in the US who saw the territory as the ideal site for the planned trans-isthmian canal, but the movement found itself suffocated by US occupying troops as soon as the separation was achieved. As it turned out, the US troops were there to stay. Later, during the Second World War, Panama became the US headquarters and control centre for US–Latin American military relations and a vital link in maintaining US security from perceived threats south of the border. At the same time, its economy was distorted by its total dependence on the US dollar and its conversion into a financial paradise.

Just as important as the Canal itself for US security was the potential loss of the military headquarters known as South Command, based inside the Canal zone. In addition to land, air and sea forces located there, South Command comprises a 'special operations' unit, highly sophisticated technical and logistical equipment and a communications and exchange of information network with embassies throughout Latin American and the Caribbean. Along with the bases in Puerto Rico, South Command serves as the nerve centre for military operations throughout the region. In 1986, the ex-head of South Command operations was reported as saying that the US 'is prepared to return the Panama Canal even 10 years ahead of the date indicated in the treaty, providing the Panamanian nation agrees to prolong our military presence until 2025' (Casaus and Castillo 1990: 201). It was the US decision to retain control of Panama as a military base, therefore, perhaps even more than the desire to maintain control of the Canal and trans-isthmian trade which best explains the determination by Washington to overthrow Noriega, either by discrediting him internally and internationally for links with illegal narcotic trading, or through the economic sanctions which were imposed in 1989 and which reduced economic activity in the country by up to a half and created sufficient popular discontent to weaken Noriega's own appeals to Panamanian nationalism, or, eventually, through sending the troops in.

The Tools of Policy, or How Washington Gets What It Wants

Caribbean and Central American countries are inundated with advice and pressure from a multiplicity of US actors and agencies from the public and private sectors. In addition to the government departments such as the State Department, Defense and the Treasury, Congress, the National Security Council and the President's personal team of advisers may all have inputs into the formation of policies towards the region, and ambassadors and the embassy staff may influence policies in individual countries. At certain times, US public opinion might play a role in decision-making as might non-governmental actors such as multinational corporations and pressure groups. So there are a variety of groups who contribute to the formation of regional policies in Washington and who have different channels of influence over events in the region, or to put it another way, who offer different possibilities for the implementation of policy goals.

US influence rests on the economic vulnerability of the region and its relative diplomatic isolation which have created the conditions for an extreme form of dependence on Washington, underwritten by US domination of the international system after 1945. One way Washington can try and implement its policies is through bringing economic pressure to bear. US influence in the IMF, the World Bank, where the Presidency has always been in US hands, and the Inter-American Development Bank helps make sure that the region listens to US governments. Access to the US market for regional products can also be another form of economic pressure. Diplomatic pressure, for example in favour of elections, against or on behalf on political groupings inside a particular country through the Embassy, in the UN or in regional organizations, constitutes another well-used option. Pressure can also be brought to bear on governments through support for military factions or tampering with defence subsidies.

Washington's influence over regional politics is most visible when we analyse US responses to governments judged as 'unfriendly'. In attempting to bring 'unfriendly' governments into line, or overthrow them, Washington uses a whole range of levers ranging from economic, diplomatic and military pressure to undercover activity aimed at destabilization. Schoultz comments succinctly: 'since the end of World War II covert action by the Central Intelligence Agency has been among the most important means of implementing US policy. In every case where the record is available for public scrutiny US diplomatic and economic hostility . . . has always been accompanied by covert action' (Schoultz 1987: 244). In Guatemala in 1954, in the Dominican Republic in the early 1960s and in Panama and Nicaragua in the 1980s, covert action became a major tool of Washington's policy. In Cuba, the CIA have been involved in attempted assassinations of Castro and in failed invasion attempts, and even Costa Rica suffered covert CIA activity in 1989 when opposition groups hostile to President Oscar Arias received CIA funding.

The scale of US covert activity escalated to hitherto unknown heights in the 1980s as Reagan tries to overthrow the Sandinista government in Nicaragua, to prevent the *Frente Farabundo Martí para la Liberación Nacional* (FMLN) from coming to power in neighbouring El Salvador and to destabilize the government of Maurice Bishop in Grenada. According to Carlos Vilas, counter-revolutionary activity in Nicaragua alone, between 1980 and 1986, was responsible for the loss of production worth 3,600 million dollars and the loss of 17,500 lives directly (Vilas 1989). E.V.K. Fitzgerald's figure is lower at 370.7 million dollars plus 200 million dollars lost in approved development aid programmes blocked by Washington, but covers only the period up to 1984. It is more than a sufficient sum to damage severely a small economy such as that of Nicaragua (Fitzgerald 1987).

Less well documented, though just as effective, was undercover organizational, logistical and financial support for anti-communist death squads in El Salvador in the 1980s. Details were revealed at Congressional hearings in 1989 by an important ex-member of a death squad who later sought asylum in the US. And the testimony of the survivors of the massacre of the Jesuit priests at the University of San Salvador in 1989, published in the US and European presses, provides ample proof of FBI attempts to cover up evidence of US involvement. More bizarre even are the links which emerged between the CIA and the powerful cocaine cartel of Medellin, Colombia through which the CIA illegally bought and transported arms to the Nicaraguan *Contras* and later sold and distributed cocaine within the US in order to raise money for *contra* funding. Such activity is difficult to square with later statements from Washington describing cocaine dealers as 'public enemy number one'.

Finally we should remember that this battery of instruments have not only been used against 'revolutionary' regimes to bring them into line but have also been used against moderately reformist governments. Jamaica under Michael Manley in the 1970s found its biggest market for its most important export, bauxite, drastically cut after the passing of the Bauxite Production Levy Act of 1974, contributing directly to the economic chaos which led to the collapse of the government and with it the possibilities of redistributive reform. Costa Rica found itself pressured by the US in the wake of the 1980s debt crisis to accept contra bases inside the country, violating its traditional neutrality, and to participate in anti-Sandinista initiatives, including the construction of an air-strip which was used by the *Contras* from July 1985 to February 1986. This policy was only reversed definitively after the Irangate scandal of 1987 which made possible the emergence of a peace plan by Costa Rican president Oscar Arias.

Explaining US Policies

How can we explain the preponderant role the US has played in Central American and Caribbean history and its negative impact on the political and economic development of the region as a whole? And how are we to explain the enormous gap between the rhetoric of US policy, which assumes a developmentalist and democratic approach to the region, and the reality of the policies implemented? The policies implemented under Kennedy are a good illustration of the divergence between the aims of policy and the reality of their impact in the region. Kennedy came into office swearing to 'preserve and protect a world of diversity' yet invaded Cuba and went on to lay the foundations of counter-insurgency policies towards the region (Gaddis 1982: 201). Again, in the 1970s, President Carter championed a moral approach to foreign policy, only to end his term of office endorsing support for El Salvador's Armed Forces, responsible for the torture and murder of thousands of Salvadorean citizens. How are we to explain these apparent contradictions?

A variety of explanations of US policy in the Caribbean Basin have been offered. One of the most frequent explanatory models presumes that economic motivation triumphs over diplomatic considerations. The region is said to be an important supplier of primary materials, especially strategic minerals (e.g. bauxite from Jamaica, used in the production of aluminium) and of cheap labour, and constitutes a significant market for US goods. Indeed, so important is the Latin American region as a whole, that it has been suggested that the US has a 'strategic dependence' on Latin America (Muñoz 1980). US government is concerned about developments in the region because US multinational companies depend on operations there for a considerable percentage of their profits (Chomsky 1986).

This explanation contains some truth, especially when we use it to explain US policy at the beginning of the twentieth century. The first expansion of US capital outside national territory was into the

Caribbean. The Spanish–American war of 1898 which led to the seizure of Cuba and Puerto Rico stimulated US investment in sugar, infrastructure, finance and services. In recent times, US investment has diversified globally, making the Caribbean less important in relative terms, but still there was an estimated 23,000 million dollars invested in Central America as late as 1985 (Burbach 1986). Looking at the figures in detail, we discover that US investment is unevenly distributed throughout the region, with Guatemala, Costa Rica, Honduras and Panama being the most important countries of the isthmus. Yet recent US policy has concentrated on Nicaragua and El Salvador, both countries of less significance in investment terms. Nicaragua in particular has been at the centre of US interest in the mid-nineteenth century, the early twentieth and again in the 1980s, but is unimportant for US investment. And El Salvador, the key to Reagan's foreign policy in the 1980s and the recipient of most economic and military aid, is much less important than Guatemala for investment (Bermudez and Cavalla 1982: 48). So a purely economistic explanation of US foreign policy in the region is not wholly convincing.

Looking at policy after 1945, in particular, it has been suggested that Washington's Caribbean/Central American policies can only be understood within the logic of East–West confrontation and the Cold War. The US foreign policy establishment argued that conflict anywhere in the globe was essentially a fight between the 'free world' and communism and concluded that friendly governments must be maintained at all costs in the Caribbean Basin because of its location close to the US southern frontier. Policy was therefore determined not by a rational assessment of economic needs or security concerns but by superpower politics, where the US measures all its actions abroad in terms of how it will affect the balance of power between the superpowers. How the US regional policy would be received in Moscow became an important determinant of US external activity: the key question was whether it would indicate weakness or strength globally, rather than whether it would respond to US and Caribbean interests. This argument explains why the region continued to be thought of in Washington as of strategic importance, when in fact the region became less important for US security in an age of nuclear and inter-continental weapons: the US could not be seen to withdraw from a region which it has traditionally controlled for fear of seeming weak, which would have global repercussions. US policy therefore came to be based essentially on a fear of losing face.

A cold war mentality, then, led to the conviction that the US must bear the costs of empire (in the words of John Kennedy 'pay any price, bear any burden') in order to maintain hegemony in the region, not because the region warranted this attention in itself, but because it would directly affect the outcome of the East–West conflict. Even moderates in the foreign policy establishment found themselves caught up in the logic of this argument, leading to the contradiction which has lain at the heart of the double discourse towards the region constructed by liberal US thinkers. Many policy-makers in the Carter administration, for example, explicitly recognized that the real cause of instability in the region lay in the social and economic structures which prevented development and democracy, not in supposed Soviet penetration. Yet ultimately they were unable to transform the ideological bases which underlay policy decisions.

By the mid-1970s, a 'new realist' school of foreign policy had emerged, calling for a more rational response to US security needs in the Caribbean Basin, arguing that the traditional allies of the US were unstable and therefore unable to guarantee US long-term interests. At the same time, according to the new approach, new revolutionary governments needed trade, financial assistance and even investment. Therefore a pragmatic understanding was possible (Feinberg 1983; Fagen 1987). But the impact of this new school of thought was small. Throughout the 1980s, the dominant framework for analysing Washington's regional policy was a traditional understanding of security and geopolitics. In the Kissinger Report into the Central American crisis in 1984, only lip-service was paid to the notion that poverty and inequality is the key to insurrection in the region, and the principal cause of instability, as perceived by the Report, becomes the intromission of the Soviet Union and 'its client state', Cuba.

Policy-makers, then, have operated from an underlying belief since 1945 that US security is vulnerable to change in the Caribbean. The policies which have emerged from Washington have been shaped in accordance with that basic presumption more than from any objective analysis of the region. How policy-makers see the world and the place of the Caribbean within it in a general sense has been the main factor in shaping policy. At no time was this more evident that in the Reagan era. Policies reflected the ideological bases of Reaganism – anti-communism, defence of property, racism etc. – and were made 'on the basis of a surprising amount of mythology and misinformation' at the expense of any rational analysis of the regional situation (Whitehead 1988).

But how has the end of the Cold War affected Washington foreign policy mentalities and perceptions of the Caribbean region in particular? The fear of a concerted attack from the Soviet Union has evaporated. Cuba none the less remains to challenge the US. After the collapse of the Soviet Union, therefore, US attention in the region has specifically focused on the dangers which Cuba represents and an all-out attempt to unseat Castro through economic leverage and a tightening of the boycott through the Torricelli Amendment. Reversing the Cuban revolution and imposing calm on the Caribbean, the 'American Mediterranean', has become a number one priority. Elsewhere in the region, US interest has diminished, with the US returning to a policy of supporting formal democracies which have in practice little possibility for popular expression and less for popular participation.

In this situation, the most useful framework for analysis of Washington's policies might be a bureaucratic interpretation of policies. This means that policy is understood less as a result of ideological convictions and more as an outcome of negotiations, alliances and compromises between different foreign policy actors. Rosenberg, Whitehead, and Bermudez and Cavalla used this approach for explaining policies in the 1980s, and it is likely that in the more fragmented and ambiguous environment of policy-making in the 1990s that its importance will increase (Rosenberg 1989; Whitehead 1988; Bermudez and Cavalla 1982). Central America and the Caribbean will therefore continue to be the objects of pressure and influence from the US, but the content of policy and its outcome are slightly less easy to predict.

Relations with Western Europe: A Partial Alternative to the US?

The Caribbean Basin was shaped historically by European imperialism. Its political organizations, economy, racial composition and social structure are all fruit of a European presence and the consequences of Europe's past domination. But with the decline of European imperialism and the rise of US power, Europe's role in the region diminished as that of the US expanded. With the exception of the territories under British control, the years after 1945 were characterized by a separation of the Caribbean from European influence.

The 1970s and in particular the 1980s witnessed a revival of European interest in the region, through aid and development projects through institutional links forged by the European Union (EU – previously the European Community), through particular initiatives linking West European countries with Caribbean Basin states and through party political ties which linked Social Democratic or Christian Democratic parties in Western Europe with their counterparts in the Caribbean. At the time, some analysts began to talk of the development of a triangular relationship, linking the region to the US and to Western Europe. We look now at the ties between the Caribbean Basin and Western Europe and try to assess the importance of the relationship in the politics and development of the region.

The decline of Britain as a dominant world power and the fact that the international influence of the EU is for the most part confined to economic affairs, has led even the Commonwealth Caribbean to look to the US for leadership in security matters. While the first signs of this were the bases deals of 1940, this trend obviously accelerated with independence from Britain. The incorporation of the entire non-Communist Caribbean into the US area of influence culminated in the 1980s under Reagan with the granting of military assistance, aid packages and incorporation into the Caribbean Basin Initiative for Jamaica and the Eastern Caribbean. However, the EU continues to operate as an important trading partner for some Caribbean states and to offer a series of trade and aid possibilities for the 15 Caribbean states which are signatories to the Lomé Convention (Barbados, the Dominican Republic, Grenada, Guyana, Haiti, Jamaica, Suriname, Trinidad and Tobaga, Antigua and Barbuda, the Bahamas, Belize, Dominica, St Lucia, St Kitts and Nevis, St Vincent and the Grenadines). Until the present, four Lomé Conventions have been concluded, the first in 1975 and the latest, signed in 1989 but only ratified in 1991.

For the Caribbean signatories of the Lomé Convention, membership implies some trade advantages from the EU particularly in terms of access to European markets and a series of aid packages, which range from funds to stabilize primary commodities and minerals (STABEX and SYSMIN) to emergency aid. The Convention is therefore a package of trade and financial cooperation agreements, of which the most important are the sugar, banana and rum protocols, covering the traditional exports from the region which would have suffered even more intensely from the overall global decline in the prices of traditional commodities throughout the 1980s had the Convention not existed. Caribbean countries have received little benefit from the Stabex funds. But EU trade institutionalized through Lomé, has become vital to the region and has made it possible for the region to avoid an exclusive dependence on the US. By 1988, almost 20 per cent of the Caribbean Lomé members' exports were directed to the EU, worth 1,265 million dollars (SELA 1992B: 23). For some countries, especially the smallest of the Caribbean islands, the EU remains their most important trading partner: for St Lucia and St Vincent, the EU takes between 65–72 per cent of exports and for Grenada it is over 50 per cent (Table 4.3).

In spite of all of this, Lomé has been subject to many criticisms, the most important of which refer to its failure to stimulate export diversification in the beneficiary countries, the fact that EU markets remain closed in practice to the import of industrial and assembled goods and the context of dependency in which the relationship operates. Perhaps just as important, however, is the fact that the relationship is almost exclusively economic in content. Region-to-region, cultural and political links are limited, 'Britain is still regarded with affection in the Commonwealth Caribbean. But British governments are seen as being too weak or unwilling to play the old protective role. It is in that sense that the old British colonial loyalty is replaced by the new American neocolonial loyalty' (G. Lewis 1987: 138).

We can see from the nature of Lomé, that rather than perceiving the region as a geopolitical whole, as the US does, West European policies distinguish between the regional states which belong to the Lomé Convention, its ex-colonies, and Central America, which emerged from Spanish colonialism and later fell under the sphere of influence of the US. This rigid separation, which implied that EU links with the Spanish-speaking countries were minimal until the 1980s, has recently been questioned as we can see from the incorporation of the Dominican Republic in Lomé in 1989. The

Table 4.3   Lomé Caribbean trade with the EU and the world (selected countries) (US$ million)

Country		1985			1988		
		EU	%	World	EU	%	World
Dominican Rep.	X	92	12.4	743	151	8.9	1,697
	M	148	10.0	1,480	262	9.4	2,781
Grenada	X	12	54.5	22	19	55.5	34
	M	17	24.6	69	22	21.8	101
Haiti	X	59	13.1	449	46	10.7	428
	M	83	11.9	700	104	12.2	846
Jamaica	X	138	24.3	569	247	25.1	945
	M	118	10.3	1,144	229	13.7	1,673
St Lucia	X	52	89.7	58	100	70.9	141
	M	23	59.0	39	54	30.0	180

X = exports   M = imports.
Source: SELA 1992a.

EU also strengthened its diplomatic presence, albeit timidly, in the Central American mainland in the wake of the Central American crisis. Although that new relationship has some economic foundations, with around 20 per cent of Central American exports reaching the EU, the most important aspects of the relationship have been political.

In particular, Central America's quest for relative autonomy from the US was strengthened by the institutionalization of group-to-group dialogue between the EU and the Central American states within the San José process, which started in 1984. This has led to yearly mini-summits between EU representatives and foreign ministers of El Salvador, Guatemala, Nicaragua and Costa Rica. The EU consistently called throughout the 1980s for a negotiated peace to the conflicts in the isthmus, and rejected an imposed solution from the US despite some support from individual EU countries, including Britain. At the same time, the timid moves towards democratization were supported in Europe through the hosting of government–guerilla peace talks (e.g. between the Cerezo government of Guatemala and the *Unión Revolucionario Nacional Guatemalteco* (URNG) held in Spain) and the participation of EU observers in Central American elections, in Nicaragua in 1990 and El Salvador in 1994 for example. However, expectations about the potential mediating role of the EU in Central America and its willingness and capacity to balance out the US as part of a triangular relationship were on the whole overestimated in the 1980s. Lopez also noted that the economic benefits which the region received through the 1980s increased compared with the figures of the 1970s but were of limited impact for the development of the region (Lopez 1990). Tables 4.4 and 4.5 indicate that the EU lags far behind the US in trade and aid flows into the region. Without a substantial turnaround in this area, any further increase in political relations will be impossible.

Regional Integration

Cooperation and integration between the countries which make up the region have long been perceived as strategies which would strengthen regional economies and increase their bargaining power within the international system. Regional governments have recognized the value of cooperation, and external agencies concerned with development, for example the Economic Commission

Table 4.4 Financial flows to Central America according to region (US$ million)

Year	EU	Japan	US
1980	77.8	17.5	175
1981	83.1	16.8	183
1982	93.3	13.4	325
1983	88.1	24.2	550
1984	97.4	20.1	585
1985	122.6	21.5	735
1986	184.5	46.5	680
1987	231.0	51.6	838
1988	290.2	65.8	725

Source: Lopez, 1990.

Table 4.5   Central American exports by area (in percentages)

	1970	1979	1987
US	42	38	48
CACM	20	19	7
EU	19	26	20
Others	19	17	25
El Salvador			
US	21	29	44
CACM	31	22	16
EU	28	40	20
Others	20	9	20
Guatemala			
US	28	30	51
CACM	35	25	12
EU	20	21	17
Others	17	24	20
Honduras			
US	54	58	53
CACM	11	9	3
EU	22	21	21
Others	13	12	23
Nicaragua			
US	34	35	1
CACM	26	16	9
EU	20	27	33
Others	20	22	57

Source: Lopez, 1990.

for Latin America and the Caribbean (ECLAC), have consistently pushed for regional integration schemes as a means to development. The importance of expanding the mechanisms of regional coopera-tion was further stressed by the emergence of moves towards South–South dialogue and cooperation. The logic behind regional coopera-tion is more than obvious: it could help the countries of the region towards economic development (by deepening the industrialization process and expanding regional competitiveness). And international cooperation could help reduce dependence on the developed countries and pressurize for a reversal internationally in the terms of trade. All of these factors combined would strengthen the autonomy of the region in international affairs in general, and in particular in relation to the region's dealings with the US. Nye has indicated the importance of external factors in promoting efforts at integration: 'the way the regional decision makers perceive the nature of the external situation and their response to it is an important condition determining agreement on further integration. There are a variety of regional perceptions, such as a sense of external threat from a giant neighbour, loss of status . . . as a result of bipolarity, and simple demonstration effects' (Nye 1971: 84). Pushing regional states towards cooperation therefore is the threat from US, the big neighbour in the North, and an awareness that dealing with the US and other international powers would be easier if they could speak with one voice. However, in spite of the very positive reasons in favour of integration, the obstacles are enormous.

Feld and Boyd point out that in underdeveloped areas in general 'the development of cohesion and support for common institutions is difficult because of the divisive effects of cultural, ethnic and religious differences, the strength of historic antipathies, the small communication flows, the low levels of trade, and the degree to which each national leadership tends to be immersed in its own domestic support problems' (Feld and Boyd 1980). Central America and the Caribbean countries, in spite of sharing the objective characteristics of being small, agro-exporting economies on the periphery of the international system, and of being pulled together by the weight of US policy, belong to two different cultural universes. Ties between Central America and the Commonwealth Caribbean in particular are poor. Not only are trade flows between Central America and the Caribbean Community (CARICOM) negligible and were in fact on the decline through the 1980s, but there is an absence of technical or cultural collaboration which would serve as a base for deepening economic and diplomatic links. And more recently, there has also been competition between Central American states and Caribbean islands for markets abroad, as with the Central American insistence on their right to access to the EU market for bananas, a large part of which is reserved for the Lome signatories.

As a result, the mechanisms of regional cooperation which have emerged have been confined to Central America, on the one hand,

and the Commonwealth Caribbean on the other, with the Spanish-speaking Caribbean until very recently excluded completely from either process (see Table 4.6). Central American economic integration was seen as the way to provide a spurt for regional development through establishing a single internal market, leading to the creation of the Central American Common Market (CACM) in 1960. But although the CACM was to stimulate economic growth in the isthmus, it did not lead to *balanced* growth and in the long term deepened regional tensions. The crisis of the 1980s (debt, recession and civil war) weakened the economic relations between the Central American states, contributing to their economic decline in the period. But the crisis also brought a greater realization that development for Central America depends on cooperation between the states. Hence the Central American peace agreements have tried to establish a framework for diplomatic cooperation and fluid contacts and consultations between Central American states. In 1990 at a summit in Guatemala, the Central American states agreed to push the Central American dialogue beyond peace and security to cooperation for economic development through attempts to institute a common external tariff in 1992. Nevertheless, these contacts are still very much at an embryo stage and the collapse of the proposed Central American parliament, an initiative strongly supported by the EU, makes this cooperation less likely in the 1990s.

The Caribbean Community (CARICOM), formed in 1973, linking the English-speaking countries of the Caribbean, has proved rather more successful despite its limitations. It established a Common External Tariff, harmonization of fiscal incentives to industry, tax agreements and the formation of a Caribbean Investment Corporation. It aims at integration through the

Table 4.6   Exports between CACM and CARICOM: as percentage of total exports

	1960	1970	1980	1985	1989
CACM	7.0	26.0	24.4	13.7	12.6
CARICOM	3.9	4.2	6.4	8.3	7.9

Source: ECLA, *Anuario Estatistico de America Latina y el Caribe*, 1990.

establishment of a common market, primarily, although its under-lying goal is diplomatic and foreign policy coordination between the Commonwealth Caribbean with the aim of accentuating their presence within the international system generally and within the developing world. However CARICOM's effectiveness is reduced by a number of circumstances: for example, organizationally, its statutes require unanimity before any action can be undertaken and therefore limit the scope of action. More important, the formation of CARICOM has led to only moderate increases in trade between members because the production structure of CARICOM members is competitive. They produce a similar range of goods for export (Samuel 1990: 23).

It is evident therefore that much remains to be done before the region can negotiate with one voice. None the less, organizations such as SELA and ECLAC point to a resurgence of interest in regional integration as part of a strategy with increasing importance for the future in order to overcome development problems. As such, integration will be focused on economic issues and have much less direct impact on the region's role in the international system.

Conclusion

The countries which make up Central America and the insular Caribbean are all small societies, whose very existence today as independent states is part of a historical process that the developed world has controlled. They are therefore extremely vulnerable to external pressure. In this chapter we have analysed the influence the major external actor has played in the region, the all-pervasive US. By contrast to the US, even the EU, an important economic and diplomatic actor on the world scene, plays only a small role in shaping the destinies of the region. And there is no reason to suppose that the end of the Cold War will mark any significant change in the international relations of the region. In view of this what can the states of the region do? Some policy options include: regional cooperation; diversification of external relations; pressing for policies internationally which grant greater autonomy in trade and pricing policies to small producers and to primary producers; and adopting policies internally which tend towards more equitable development and thereby reduce the possibilities of outside interference in internal affairs. Like all options, these are only partial, but taken together they could represent a substantial movement towards greater autonomy and towards equitable development, both at the regional level and nationally, for the states which make up the area.

Notes

1. The phrase is that of Cole Blaiser, *The Hovering Giant: US Responses to Revolutionary Change*, University of Pittsburgh Press, 1976.
2. There were 21 countries in the original programme, including most of the British, Dutch and Spanish Caribbean islands, plus Haiti and the Central American isthmus, except Nicaragua and Grenada, who were excluded for political reasons. After the New Jewel Movement was overthrown and the Sandinistas were voted out of office, Nicaragua and Grenada were incorporated into CBI. Guyana was included in 1988, while Panama was suspended and then reincorporated in 1990. Haiti's membership was suspended after elected president Aristide was overthrown in 1990. Clearly membership is dependent on fulfilling implicit political conditions.

5

Regional Development

The aim of the chapter is to examine an important aspect of the contemporary crisis in the Caribbean Basin: the economic crisis. We look at the economic aspects of the Caribbean/Central American model of development from the 1880s to today, with its particular features of heavy external dependence, export orientation, agrarian capitalism, combined with weak industrial capitalism and regressive income distribution. We then explain why analysts concluded that it is exhausted and why governments in the 1990s have opted for transformation of the economic models.

We distinguish different phases in development in the region, and note the diversity of national experiences as well as overall trends. Three distinct periods in the construction of peripheral capitalism in the region are identified: dependence on agrarian exports; industrialization, both export-oriented and directed towards internal consumption; and the crisis of the 1980s. We also note the emergence of a fourth phase in regional political economy, as a result of the regional structural adjustment programmes, aimed at reactivating the economies based on a revived model of export development.

What is Development?

Before the 1950s, it was simply assumed that 'backward' naions, as they were referred to at the time within advanced capialist countries, would follow the path of 'developed' nations, the US and Britain in particular. Development was therefore implicitly equated with the given reality of Anglo-Saxon societies. Trade and the market were seen as key elements in bringing development about and it was thought that free trade would reduce the gap between poor and rich countries and, combined with thrift, saving and hard work, would end poverty. Belief in the market meant that an emphasis on exports and goods with a 'comparative advantage' for the world market went unquestioned in the Caribbean Basin. In the colonial Caribbean, where the running of the economy was in the hands of policy-makers who saw the function of the region as that of serving the needs of the metropolis, agrarian specialization remained inevitably the order of the day.

By the 1950s, it was obvious that these policies had created fragile economies in Central America and the Caribbean and indeed throughout the decolonized world, vulnerable to global fluctuations, and which enjoyed only limited sovereignty over decision-making. Some economists began to suggest that a new policy orientation, specifically designed for poorer countries, was required if development was to occur. This was the start of development theory and 'development economics'. In Latin America and the Caribbean, the UN's Economic Commission for Latin America (ECLA) played a vital role in pushing for a new approach to developent.

At the same time, the semantics of the word 'development' began to change. For orthodox economists, it had been almost synonymous with economic growth which had in turn meant the predominance of the market in the allocation of goods and services. In the 1950s, sociologists and economists began to suggest that development is not only a matter of economics but a total social process which would approximate 'underdeveloped' societies to the behavioural patterns and consumption standards of the US or Britain. This approach has generally been termed moderization, and it dominated development economics for more than a decade. Critics of modernization, however, argued that the colonized world cannot copy the US or Britain and must work out for itself a vision of the future, in accordance with a real assessment of the possibilities open to peripheral societies. Anthropologist Sidney Mintz commented:

The descriptions of 'development' and 'underdevelopment' are often based on too simplistic indicators. Thousands of miles of railroads per person, productivity per capita, consumption capacity per person, and literacy rates per thousand inhabitants, for example, are . . . indicators which lead us into rigid comparisons of one society compared to another . . . Using measures of this type, which reflect aspects of social, economic, political and industrial history of the West, implies an expectation that the development of other nations will follow the steps of a western model. . . . They are measures which do not always have any meaning for local conditions, historical or cultural. (Mintz 1991: 43)

These critiques led social scientists into analyses of the causes of underdevelopment, found alternatively in the structures of class and racial conflict in the colonized world, the operation of a 'world system', or a combination, or articulation, of external factors plus internal structures, as with the dependency school of analysis. Underlying these disparate ideas was a recognition that there is much more to development than simply growth; and that 'development' must take into account the real potential of a given society and its particular historical and cultural characteristics. Most development economists now would agree that a developed society must be able to guarantee for its members a family income sufficient to provide basic needs for all family members; employment; education; political participation; respect for gender and ethnic identity; the right to political participation; and the implementation of ecologically sustainable policies. In the 1970s, the UN Conference on Trade and Development (UNCTAD) went further, to argue that

the purposes of development should be not to develop things but to develop people. Human beings have basic needs: food, shelter, clothing, health and education. Any process of growth that does not lead to their fulfilment – or even worse, disrupts them – is a travesty of the idea of development. A growth process that benefits only the wealthiest minorities or even increases the disparities between and within countries is not development. It is exploitation. (UNCTAD doc. 74–10536; Brundenius 1984)

By the 1950s, industrialization was recommended as the policy most likely to lead to growth, increased social wellbeing and political democratization. However, industrialization was slow to take off in the region and limited in its scope. For small peripheral states, it could only ever have a limited impact. Partly as a consequence of the failure of development recipes from the 1960s and 1970s, there has been more recently a return to liberalism in the 1980s and 1990s in the Caribbean Basin, parallel in fact to the trend towards orthodox economics globally. Neoliberal policies since the 1980s have opened up regional economies and tried to roll back the entrepreneurial state but have failed to attack poverty or address the long-term problems of land use and job creation. At best, therefore, for the Caribbean Basin the new economic orthodoxy is a strategy which leads to uneven and impoverishing growth. None the less it has become once more the dominant policy-making paradigm throughout the region.

The Export Economy in Historical Perspective

In the Isthmus

In Chapter 1, we discussed how coffee and later bananas came to be the principal exports from Central America after 1880, linking the economies of the region to the international system. The reforms which turned land and labour into factors of production in the export economies were implemented by the local landowning classes, who were guided by a particular vision of 'development', in which the introduction of new technology – the railways – the expansion of trade and the availability of imported goods for consumption for the few who could buy them would 'civilize' countries regarded by their own elites as barbaric and backward. Undoubtedly, the liberal reforms of the late nineteenth century in Central America resulted in periods of macroeconomic growth. Export earnings, however, were concentrated in the hands of the oligarchies or in some cases in the coffers of the foreign companies – the banana companies, for example. Poverty, especially in the countryside, increased as a result of export-oriented development in almost all of Central America.

Bradford Burns has used the observations of the wife of the British Ambassador to El Salvador, Mrs Henry Foote, and other travellers to the country in the mid nineteenth century, before the coffee boom, to demonstrate the effects of export development there. Mrs Foote noted in the mid-1850s that Salvadorean peasants enjoyed a ready supply of food and access to land in a situation of relative social and economic equality. She wrote: 'what strikes me most arriving from Europe is the absence of all extreme poverty' (Bradford Burns 1988: 174). At the time of Mrs Foote's travels, El Salvador remained in large measure a subsistence economy, in which the Indian communities, then a quarter of the population, inhabited the most fertile stretches of land. By 1930, however, coffee production had shaped Salvadorean society into a very different mould. Land concentration had occurred to such a degree that only approximately 8.2 per cent of the population could be classified as landowners.[1] As a result, society was polarized between the very rich and the (landless) poor. A US observer noted in 1931: '30 or 40 families own nearly everything in the country. They live in almost regal splendour with many attendants, send their children to Europe or the US to be educated and spend their money lavishly (on themselves). The rest of the population has practically nothing. These poor people work for a few cents a day and exist as best they can' (Bradford Burns 1988: 191). This perceptive American observer had spotted another feature of export development in El Salvador and indeed the region: the tendency of the numerically very small owners of the means of production to spend the profits generated from exports on luxury consumption rather than on reinvestment.

This pattern of development brought landlessness early to El Salvador. But El Salvador constituted the most extreme example in Central America. In Honduras, where coffee was not planted until after the Second World War, land was till then plentiful and relatively cheap, and the oligarchy quite weak. In Costa Rica, though no significant diversification occurred beyond coffee and bananas, export-led growth had less dramatic consequences for land and labour, partly because of the fact that there was no shortage of new land to be brought under cultivation. It was also due more fundamentally to the fact that the Costa Rican coffee elite commanded fewer economic and political resources than elsewhere in the region and did not exert exclusive control over the state. Significantly, small landowners were not eradicated in Costa Rica. In Nicaragua, coffee growers constituted only a part of the oligarchic elite, sharing power with pre-colonial cattle-farmers, and enjoying only limited influence over the crucial stage of coffee processing; while in Guatemala, coffee production was based on large estates, with coffee growers enjoying seignorial rights over labour, but without the benefits of capitalist rationalization and technology, with processing and exports largely in the hands of German immigrants. In all four countries, the power of the oligarchy, though substantial, was to some degree restricted in comparison with El Salvador. Only in El Salvador did the coffee oligarchy enjoy virtually unrestricted political power through economic specialization and integration of coffee production from the estate to the export stage. According to Paige, the differing ways the elite organized coffee production established the frameworks in which national politics were shaped and account for the differing political systems which emerged in the twentieth century (Paige 1987).

Even in Costa Rica, where the social and political consequences of export development were somewhat attenuated, the influence of export agriculture over state policy was excessive and had detrimental consequences in the long term throughout the region. Damage was sustained on three fronts. First, export specialization created economic vulnerability. At least 70 per cent of the region's export earnings were in coffee and bananas, and for El Salvador and Guatemala this figure was over 90 per cent. Yet coffee exports had peaked by the 1920s in almost all the area, and even earlier in Costa Rica (1898) and Guatemala and Nicaragua (1906–7). None the less coffee production remained privileged in terms of state policy because a bias against diversification of the economy had been built into the system which sustained export agriculture in spite of the decline in the value of exports (Bulmer-Thomas 1987). Credit, for example, was difficult to obtain for products other than coffee. As a result, dependence was fostered on a product in which the export value was steadily declining.

Dependence on coffee and bananas created other problems as well. They were luxury goods, whose consumption was limited to the rich countries in Western Europe and the US; market concentration, therefore, was an integral feature of the export model. This intensified after 1929, when market dependence on the US at the expense of Europe increased. And export crops enjoyed privileged access to the best land in the region, so land used to produce food for the internal market was continually cut back. Food price rises and food imports were the result. This tendency was accentuated by the fact that farmers would switch to coffee whenever possible not simply for economic reasons but because growing coffee was the key to social and political prestige.

Politically, the export model sustained the hegemony of the oligarchy until 1929 and in some cases the influence of foreign companies over the state. Oligarchic domination and/or state subordination to foreign interests and export specialization were mutually dependent upon each other. But once the economic frailty of the model had been exposed after 1929, it was threatened by popular organizations mobilizing to demand political change. Its retention after this date required an increasing reliance on state repression, for example during the banana strikes in Honduras in the 1920s, or the massacre of Salvadorean peasants by the army in 1932. Even in Costa Rica, *caudillismo* became the political order of the day in the 1930s under Leon Cortés (1932–40). None the less, the control over the state exercised by the oligarchy and the partial recovery of the international prices of Central American exports by the middle of the decade meant that the model went unchanged until the 1950s.

According to Bulmer-Thomas, the period following the Second World War constituted a 'lost opportunity' for development prospects, when the chance to correct the deficiencies in the system were not taken up (Bulmer-Thomas 1987: 106–7). Oligarchic domination meant that agriculture for domestic consumption continued to lose ground to export crops, food prices maintained an upward trend, poverty deepened and external vulnerability went unchanged. The main difference in pre- and post-war production lay in the development of new crops for the export market to complement coffee and fruit production and in the technification of export production. However, the benefits of the changes were as narrowly distributed as before.

In Guatemala, a transformation in the way goods were produced was attempted in the brief period of reform which opened in 1944 and deepened after the election of Jacobo Arbenz, but it was brought to an abrupt end in 1954 by a CIA-backed coup. Arbenz had tried to renegotiate the country's relationship with the United Fruit Company, the most important banana company inside Guatemala, and to reform relations between labour and capital. Only in Costa Rica was the political context of the export economy transformed in any lasting way in the wake of the civil war in 1948. The differences between Costa Rica and its neighbours became more marked as the 1950s progressed following the implementation of a series of reforms which established the bases for a participative society in which welfare and education became main concerns of the state.

In the Insular Caribbean

In the insular Caribbean the political context of the development of the mature export economy was very different from that of the Central American states. In Central America, export economies were established at the peak of European imperialism and economic influence, whereas the export orientation was imprinted on the insular Caribbean much earlier, during seventeenth-century mercantilism. The twin forces of colonialism and the establishment of a global economy created the modern Caribbean and led directly to the export economy, based internally on the plantation and slavery, establishing the Caribbean as a sub-sector of the world capitalist system. Overseas tropical extensions of the European economies, their role was exclusively to satisfy European consumerism. As a result, Caribbean political economy was shaped by the demands of the metropolis. Analysts of the plantation economy draw attention to its capitalist nature despite the use of unfree labour – for example in questions of labour discipline, of capital investment and of accumulation (Best 1968; Beckford 1972).

Early integration into the capitalist system and product specialization were the fundamentals of the original model of development in the insular Caribbean. Although eighteenth-century exports from Caribbean plantations to Europe were various, including tobacco, spices etc., sugar production more than any other crop shaped economic development.[2] It remained the principal export from the region until after 1929. In Jamaica, slavery and sugar flourished until the nineteenth century when the transformation of Britain into the leading industrial economy ended the slave trade (1807) and slavery (1834) and free trade was introduced. Sugar production began its long decline throughout the British Caribbean as a result.

Contributing factors to the decline were increased competition from Brazil and later Cuba and the shrinking of the European market for cane because of the expansion of the sugar-beet industry within Europe. The reorganization of sugar following the introduction of wage-labour relations and the importing of new sources of cheap labour from other parts of the British Empire temporarily revived the industry after 1880, when the larger islands such as Jamaica and Trinidad also experienced some agricultural diversification, for example, into bananas which were controlled by foreign companies. But a major consequence of the changes was the development of a marginal peasant economy.

In Haiti, independence led to the decline of sugar production and the formation of a subsistence peasantry. Attempts to find a new export crop in the nineteenth century, for example coffee, failed partly because of the absence of an landless labour force. In the Spanish Caribbean, sugar arrived later than elsewhere in the region. But by the end of the nineteenth century the political economy of Cuba, which became the leading sugar producer in the region, had been transformed. Sugar expansion also brought the island into a close relationship with the US although politically it remained under Spanish control. A similar process, though much less intense, can be identified in the Dominican Republic and Puerto Rico, where sugar coexisted alongside precapitalist production and subsistence agriculture (Cassá 1979: 124). By the end of the nineteenth century, therefore, large-scale sugar production using modern technology and based on capitalist relations of production was limited to the Spanish Caribbean, especially Cuba and Puerto Rico producing for the US market.

Sugar brought impoverishment to the peasantry of the Spanish Caribbean. It expanded rapidly in Puerto Rico after the Spanish-American war of 1898 which led to occupation by the US. The situation which followed was described by a US official, Harold Ickes, in 1935 in the following way:

> Puerto Rico has been a victim of a laisez faire economy which has led to the rise of absent sugar corporations, which have acquired much land which previously belonged to small independent farmers, who have been reduced as a result to economic servitude. Although the inclusion of Puerto Rico inside our tariff barriers has been very beneficial to the share-holders of these companies, the benefits have not been passed on to the mass of Puerto Ricans . . . Today there is greater misery, poverty and unemployment in Puerto Rico than at any other moment of its history. (Dietz 1986: 150)

Sugar production created export economies with similar limitations to the coffee and banana economies of Central America. The distortions imposed on the insular Caribbean by export development mirrored the structural problems of the Central American economies in the following ways: export-led growth fostered external dependence in terms of investment and markets; investment was concentrated almost exclusively in the export sector, which became the only 'modern' sector of the economy in terms of technology and relations of production; good land was absorbed by the plantation, restricting domestic food production; economic infrastructure was created to service the export sector, limiting the possibilities of internal development; and it led to increasing dependence on food imports. Imported food was responsible for a seventh of all imports in Haiti and a quarter in Grenada. This remains a debilitating feature of Caribbean economies today (Table 5.1).

In terms of class formation within the export economy, however, there were significant differences from Central America. Whereas export development in Central America consolidated oligarchic domination, the plantation economy created a weak local dominant class. Plantation owners, who were at the top of the pyramid of power and prestige locally, were often absent, leaving the management of the estates to the overseers and the exercise of political domination to the metropolitan state. As a result, national identity was weak. Nation-building and independence never became major concerns of the local dominant class. Consequently, in the British Caribbean metropolitan-based interests remained dominant until Independence. Export-oriented colonialism limited the power of the

Table 5.1   Food imports as percentage of total imports (selected countries)

Country	1980–90	1980–84	1985–89	1990
Grenada	25.6	27.4	24.7	25.6
Jamaica	16.1	17.1	13.9	–
Montserrat	16.6	21.0	20.0	19.8
St Lucia	20.4	21.3	20.0	21.9
Trinidad and Tobago	17.4	16.7	18.4	16.5

Source: *Statistical Profile of CARICOM*, The West Indian Commission, 1992.

local elite while at the same time forcing it culturally and politically into the colonial mould. And in Haiti, the Dominican Republic, Cuba and Puerto Rico, the influence of the US over the export sector of the economies and the subordination of the local dominant class to US interests by 1900 limited possibilities for development alternatives outside the export model in a similar way.

The depression of the 1930s exposed the vulnerabilities of export development throughout the region. Government responses were multiple, however, because of the fragmented political geography of the region. In Puerto Rico and the Dominican Republic, the depression led to a drastic cut in wages and lay-offs in the sugar industry to maintain profitability. Unemployment in Puerto Rico, high since 1900 when the expansion of modern sugar plantations reduced land available for subsistence farming, reached 50 per cent (Pantojas 1990). In the long term, the collapse of the plantation economy in Puerto Rico led to the development of an alternative strategy of industrialization tied to the US market. In the British Caribbean, hardship was already severe before 1929 because of economic decline. Massive popular demonstrations occurred in Jamaica and Trinidad during the Depression, culminating in the establishment of martial law by the British government. The Kingston Riots, as they became known, were followed by a Commission of Enquiry in 1938 set up by the British government. It revealed poverty and marginalization on a scale unimagined in Westminster. The recession had increased unemployment and lowered wages, making labour in the British Caribbean even cheaper than in Puerto Rico or Cuba. In spite of the evident collapse of the export economy in the British Caribbean, however, the lack of interest on the part of the British government in Caribbean development froze policy in the established pattern of economic decline and poverty.

Following the Second World War, as Britain debated the merits and demerits of decolonization, the Moyne Commission proposed in 1945 agricultural modernization and the establishment of new export industries as the means to revitalize local economies. But in the absence of major inflows of state investment to promote diversification, emigration became one of the few options to escape certain poverty. Britain and the US were the preferred destinations of most emigrants, though many also left to live in the Dominican Republic and Cuba, where banana and sugar production continued to generate some employment opportunities. In Haiti, emigration, especially to the neighbouring Dominican Republic, also intensified after 1930. Resentment of the Haitian immigrants was to cause a massacre of migrant workers inside the Dominican Republic in 1937. By the 1930s, therefore, we can see that emigration had became an integral feature of Caribbean development.

Capitalist Modernization, Industrialization and Integration

For the Caribbean Basin, the impact of the transitional period in the international economy (1929–45) was limited and its legacy was rather a change in patterns of external linkages. Contacts declined with Europe, and the US secured its position as the major investor and international broker in the region. For the colonial Caribbean, the decline of European powers meant deepening economic decay. Within the Caribbean Basin, only Puerto Rico experienced industrialization on any scale before 1960.

But development strategies within Latin America and the Caribbean as a whole were undergoing a period of upheaval and change. During the 1930s, some of the larger Latin American countries had strengthened their industrial sector, partly in response to the 'external shock' following 1929, a process which was intensified by the economic isolation thrust upon them by the Second World War. Aimed at replacing goods which until then had been imported, this process was known as import substituting industrialization (ISI). By the 1950s, the influential team of economists based at the UN's Economic Commission for Latin America (ECLA) was advising industrialization as a new development strategy for the whole region, including Central America and the Caribbean. Industrialization was slow to get off the ground, however. First, because it required a fairly substantial internal market and small states were limited by their size and the fact that only a tiny percent of the population enjoyed sufficient financial resources to become consumers of internally produced goods. Second, industrialization, especially ISI, could not be implemented while export interests remained dominant in economic policy-making, whether controlled locally or from the metropolis.

Until the mid-1950s, then, economic modernization in the region meant simply greater efficiency in agricultural production and the development of new exports. One of the most important of the new exports was bauxite, used in the manufacturing of aluminium, which assumed a strategic importance for the defence industry, in particular during and after the Second World War. By the 1950s, the US multinational companies who controlled production and processing globally, began to invest in processing plants throughout the Caribbean – Jamaica, Suriname and Guyana especially. By the 1960s, bauxite and aluminium exports amounted to 60 per cent of Jamaica's total exports (Zunder 1986). In the Dominican Republic, meanwhile, the dictatorship of Rafael Trujillo, who came to power in 1930 on the back of the economic crisis, concentrated on modernizing the sugar industry, much of it under his personal control.

In Central America, high post-war prices for primary products assured the retention of export agriculture until the mid-1950s. When high prices ended, there were two alternatives: either profitability could be increased to be set against falls in price, or production could be diversified. In El Salvador the coffee oligarchy decided to make exports more profitable by reducing wages. But new export crops were also introduced, in El Salvador and throughout the isthmus: cotton, wood, cocoa and sugar. Cotton was by far the most important, creating a new and distinct sector of the agrarian bourgeoisie. Later, cattle-raising, which had been introduced by the Spanish to provide for internal consumption, expanded production for export, until the region became the third most important source of beef exports from Latin America. Consequently, by the end of the 1960s, land for domestic agriculture had declined still further, despite moderate land reform everywhere except El Salvador, and the cost of food and dependence on food imports had increased.

By 1960, the exhaustion of development models which relied upon the export of primary goods was evident. Throughout the Caribbean and Central America, attention turned to industrialization. We can identify three models of industrialization in the region. Only one envisaged that manufactured goods would replace agrarian exports as the major source of foreign exchange. Elsewhere, the new development model was grafted onto the old (Bulmer-Thomas 1987: 187). Industrialization, therefore, came to offer growth without structural change, a process which ECLA called 'additive development', meaning that the ceiling for industrial growth was low and its social and political impact reduced (ECLA *Bases de una política de reactivación y desarollo* 1985; Gorostiaga and Marchetti 1988).

Industrialization in a Colonial Economy: Puerto Rico

Puerto Rican history was transformed by the Spanish-American War of 1898. Henceforth its development was conditioned almost exclusively by colonial ties with the US, separating it from the rest of the Caribbean. As a result of the relationship with the US, industrialization occurred here before the rest of the region.

The US occupation marks the beginning of the modernization of the economic base of the island. At the same time the occupation created the ideological crisis of Puerto Rican nationalism out of which 'Operation Bootstrap', as the industrialization programme was known, was born. The decline in the traditional agrarian exports – coffee, tobacco and sugar – in the 1930s, caused high unemployment and provoked the crisis which led to the start of the industrial transformation which took off in the 1950s. 'Operation Bootstrap' was an industrial promotion programme based on attracting US capital to the island in light manufacturing and assembling sectors, especially textiles. The main draw was the island's sizable reserves of cheap labour. The Puerto Rican state, subordinate to Washington but strengthened after 1945 by negotiation of 'Associated Statehood' under President Muñoz Marin, actively promoted the new policy. Industrialization went hand in hand with some increases in autonomy for the island, made possible by the Great Depression and, later, Washington's absorption in the Second World War. The Federal Government in the US meanwhile saw a reduction in unemployment as the main advantage of the programme. But ironically, rather than increasing autonomy or even leading to independence, industrial promotion deepened Puerto Rico's dependence on US markets and capital and created employment vulnerable to changes in the global economy.

A package of incentives was established for industries that decided to open up plants on the island. Attractions for investors included the provision of crucial infrastructure at subsidized rates by the Puerto Rican state. Parastatal agencies were set up specifically for the purpose of administering and servicing the programme, the Economic Development Agency (known as

Formento, a shortened version of its Spanish title) being the most important. Tax incentives were also conceded to investors, which has allowed US manufacturers to repatriate profits generated in Puerto Rico back to the US tax-free. And goods manufactured or assembled on the island were given duty-free access to the US market. In sum, investors were offered the advantages of a low-wage, low-tax off-shore economy, but with the added benefit of not paying import duties on goods entering the US since the island was constitutionally a part of the mainland. The Puerto Rican state also regulated the labour force to guarantee industrial peace. It ensured basic welfare rights and encouraged labour moderation in wage demands through informal control over labour unions as part of the ideology of 'developmentalism' which meant, in effect, the need to maintain a favourable climate for foreign investment. As a result, by 1978, 34.1 per cent of US investment in Latin America was located in Puerto Rico (Bonilla and Campos 1981).

Within the terms in which it had been conceived, the model worked moderately well until the 1970s, though it was never able to reduce unemployment below 12 per cent and relied on continual migration of Puerto Ricans to the US as a safety-valve. Although the model undoubtedly favoured foreign investment, it also created some opportunities for local capitalists, initially encouraged by *Formento* (Dietz 1986). And the model turned the island into a showpiece of US policy for the region, demonstrating in the eyes of some economists and politicians the possibilities for growth in poor countries if economic expansion is linked to the markets of the developed economies. For other more critical observers, the experiment led to a loss of sovereignty and only functioned due to cheap labour, particularly female, and the establishment of a large pool of unemployed who keep wages low (Safa 1986).

After 1972, competition from the export economies of South East Asia reduced the island's share of the US textile market. This was aggravated by the decision to apply US minimum wages on the island, which meant that it was increasingly undercut as a cheap labour economy.[3] The result was recession in Puerto Rico and a sharp increase in unemployment which reached 20 per cent by the late 1970s. The Puerto Rican government responded by concentrating on attracting high-tech industries with higher productivity (pharmaceuticals, petrochemicals, electronics) and financial investments and services rather than the traditional labour-intensive garment industry. These sectors generate high profits and benefit most from the island's corporate tax exemption. However, they also deepen the problem of external control over development in Puerto Rico because their points of contact with the local economy are much fewer.

Although these policies paid off in terms of economic growth by the 1980s, the newer capital-intensive industries have generated far too few new jobs to replace the ones lost. By 1985, unemployment had risen to 22.4 per cent and emigration to the US continued. In fact, the exhaustion of the model was visible from the mid-1970s, since when increasing subsidies from US federal government have become necessary to finance welfare and social services on the island. At the same time, larger amounts of capital were repatriated to the mainland than ever. Throughout the 1980s, the structural crisis of the island's economy deepened. The high-tech focus has led to fewer backward and forward linkages with the local economy, intensified the problem of unemployment and worsened the state's fiscal crisis, increasing dependence on external financial markets (Cabán 1990).

Taken together, these problems have undermined the stability of the colonial model of development, leading to breakdowns in the system of industrial relations and an increase in labour militancy from the 1970s. The colonial pact itself has been put in doubt by calls for integration into the mainland economy, from the US in order to reduce welfare subsidies and food stamps which had become a structural feature of the economy by the 1980s, and from sectors of the island's bourgeoisie, grouped in the New Progressive Party (PNP). The current model of colonial industrialization is recognized as exhausted on all sides of the spectrum politically within Puerto Rican politics, though the island's financial dependence on the US and the US military presence in Puerto Rico ensure that the colonial model is kept alive.

Industrialization by Invitation

To some extent based on the Puerto Rican model, the British Caribbean adopted policies of industrialization in the 1960s which came to be known as 'industrialization by invitation'. The idea was first put forward by West Indian economist W. Arthur Lewis who provided the basic framework for the policy. Lewis recommended industrialization at the end of the 1940s and in the early 1950s as the only policy option open which would diversify the productive base of the economies and create jobs (Lewis 1950). His interpretation of the Caribbean was based upon the idea of a 'dual economy': he envisaged the development of a dominant urban economic sector alongside a subsistence rural economy. The articulation between the two was to be the supply of labour which could be drawn from the rural to the urban sector. This unlimited supply of labour constituted the region's chief advantage within the terms of the model, partly because it would guarantee low wage costs for investors. The policy was based on the recognition that the British Caribbean offered the same sort of advantages to manufacturers as Puerto Rico, cheap labour in particular. Governments were therefore recommended to adopt a similar pro-active strategy of attracting foreign investment, through tax exemption, etc. Given the small size of the internal market and the need to generate new sources of foreign exchange because of the decline of agriculture, industries were to be mainly aimed at the export market.

Lewis's analysis that the traditional economies based on agriculture were unproductive was undoubtedly correct. This was the main weakness of the economies of the English Caribbean. Agriculture for domestic consumption was inefficient for historical reasons: emphasis on the plantation sector and neglect by the government of other kinds of farming. Agriculture, as a result, could not provide a livelihood for all the rural inhabitants, many of whom were thus condemned to bare subsistence. But the recipe Lewis offered contained the seeds of future problems – especially in its failure to generate employment. This became clear after the strategy was implemented in Jamaica and Trinidad where the policies were found to rest, in reality, on the existence of a pool of unemployed people as a means of assuring low labour costs for investing industries. For Lewis, high unemployment became simply a feature that Caribbean societies would have to come to terms with (Sankatsing 1990).

Although industrialization policies were seen as providing employment in the cities for some of the rural labour surplus, it was also recognized that these policies alone would not solve the problems of un- and under-employment. As a result, alongside industrialization, migration was to be encouraged in order to act as a 'safety-valve' for 'excess labour'. Hence the model brought considerable demographic change and with it problems of social dislocation and alienation as migrations of two kinds took place: from the countryside to the cities or to new industrial estates where jobs could be found; and within and beyond the Caribbean for the unemployed in search of work. This strategy, with its emphasis on migration, foreign capital and export assembling, was at the heart of policy-making in the region in the 1960s and 1970s.

Jamaica, independent in 1962 and one of the largest of the Caribbean islands with a population of over 2 million, became one of the testing grounds for 'industrialization by invitation'. Foreign investment had been important to the Jamaican economy before industrialization thanks to bauxite and, to a lesser degree, sugar production, controlled by the British company, Tate & Lyle. But it diversified in the 1960s, under government encouragement, into manufacturing, tourism, banks, insurance companies and communications. Some opportunities were also created for local capital, especially in manufacturing, though these were not great. It is difficult to calculate accurately the importance of local investment because 'the distinction between a family firm and the branch plant of a foreign company was hard to discern in practice' (Payne 1988a: 16).

The strategy undoubtedly brought economic growth – up to 8 per cent between 1958 and 1970. But it also intensified the country's already skewed and uneven pattern of development. Real income fell for the poorest 40 per cent of the population through the period. The state, despite encouraging industrialization, did little or nothing to alleviate the social costs attendant on it. Since there were no investments in housing programmes, for example, shanty-towns quickly mushroomed around the city, where living conditions were particularly desperate. At the same time, manufacturing generated fewer jobs than envisaged because of its capital-intensive nature, deepening still further un- and under-employment and generating an expanding urban informal economy in which wages barely ensured survival. And rather than strengthening the autonomy of the state, the model tended to weaken it *vis-à-vis* foreign capital. Local bourgeois groups remained content to play subordinate roles to foreign capital. In fact, it was probably naive to have expected local bourgeois groups to challenge colonial arrangements in view of the fact that most had accumulated capital through import-export trade and in general working with the British, and had long collaborated with foreign investors. At the same time, domestic agriculture continued to stagnate, leading to increasing poverty in the countryside and ever higher food import bills. Dissatisfied with the failure of post-independence policies, the poor of Kingston erupted into riots in 1968, the torch to which was the dismissal of radical professor, Dr Walter Rodney, from the University of the West Indies. The open economy was to be modified by Michael Manley and the state to play a much more dynamic role in the economy between 1972 and 1980.

Industrialization Through Integration

In Central America industrialization took off in the 1960s and was designed to supply manufactured goods for a newly created regional market. Economic integration within the isthmus, which had been recommended by ECLA in the mid-1950s, was a necessary first stage and was seen as the way to overcome the limitations in size of the national markets which had proved one of the biggest obstacles to industrial development in the past. A Central American Common Market (CACM) was therefore established in 1960, with El Salvador, Nicaragua, Honduras, Guatemala and Costa Rica as members. Panama, with a service economy tied to the US, remained outside.

The US supported the creation of CACM from the first and came to exercise a decisive influence on the way the Market operated. Security concerns in the wake of the Cuban revolution were the main reason for US interest. Economic motivation was also important – Central America was conceived as an untapped market for manufacturing companies. American pressure led to the abandoning of ECLA's original model of integration in which regional planning bodies would determine the nature and location of new industries, and instead a more liberal approach to trade and investment was adopted which allowed foreign investment virtually a free hand in determining production and location (Perez-Bringoli 1989a: 140). At the same time US influence over the new regional organizations was established because of the region's increasing dependence on US aid. As a result, 'some of the regional institutions [operated] like foreign enclaves' (Bulmer-Thomas 1987: 177).

The 1960s were years of overall growth, due to the increase in manufacturing and intra-zonal trade which the CACM promoted, and to export diversification. Intraregional trade grew from 6.5 per cent of total trade in 1960 to 26.1 per cent by 1971. But growth masked the serious flaws in the way Central America pursued industrialization, which became apparent by the late 1970s. The main problems stemmed from the fact that industrialization took place in an unchanged political and economic environment. So as a result, industrialization generated little revenue for the member states because of the failure to tax foreign investment, deepening the fiscal problems of the region. This was so even in Costa Rica, where the state tended to borrow in order to finance expenditure. In addition, the reforms made little or no impact on elite political behaviour. Rather than encouraging a democratization of politics to admit excluded groups into the state, industrialization coincided with the establishment of military dictatorships in three of the Central American states – El Salvador (1961), Guatemala (1963) and Honduras (1963) – and the continuation of the family dictatorship of the Somozas in Nicaragua, where Anastasio Somoza came to power in 1967. As a result, the industrialization process did little or nothing to alleviate the unequal distribution of income in the region, limiting the size of the market and restricting growth.

US influence over industrialization was also excessive. It accounted for nearly half of all intra-regional trade and helped weaken local capital everywhere except Costa Rica, and contributed to its remaining subordinate to export interests within the state. Small local firms were most important in Costa Rica, Honduras and El Salvador. Industrial linkages were limited as a result, and manufacturing concentrated essentially on consumer goods, in which the processed food sector was particularly important. Capital and intermediate goods were imported, generally from the US, increasing dependence on the US market. And finally, disparities within the region meant that growth was unevenly distributed within the CACM. New industries, and especially foreign investment, tended to concentrate in those areas where population was densest and where salaries were lowest. El Salvador and Guatemala benefited most, while Costa Rica and Honduras, where labour organizations were strongest, benefited the least.

The first indication that there were serious problems inside the CACM came with signs of Honduran dissatisfaction in the mid-1960s. Importing more goods from other members of the Common

Market than it was able to export, the economy was in deficit to other members every year from 1965 to 1970. Since the deficit had to be paid in US dollars, this meant using foreign reserves. In the first six months of 1969, Honduras' deficit with El Salvador alone was 5 million dollars. Honduras was to leave the CACM in 1970, bringing to a close the first phase of integration. These problems were the background to the 'football war' between Honduras and El Salvador in 1969.[4]

Industrial growth slowed down with the end of the 'easy phase of industrialization', which occurred when the internal market for consumer goods reached a point of saturation. The rise in international oil prices after 1974 and the internal dissension within the CACM over economic strategy deepened the problem. At the same time, dependence on agrarian exports had increased considerably by the early 1970s. Unfortunately, almost simultaneously (1977–83) the terms of trade declined for traditional export products by about 40 per cent. By the late 1970s economic growth, either through industrial output or through agriculture, was failing. Integration could not protect the CACM members from the negative effects of a decline in the prices of traditional exports because it had not lessened the external vulnerability of the economies. Given the external dependence common to all members of the CACM, by the height of the crisis in the mid-1980s, interdependence within the isthmus had become a mechanism for transmitting recession.

Recession and the Descent into Regional Crisis: the 1980s

In the early 1980s, the most serious economic recession of the twentieth century hit the Caribbean Basin. In one sense it was provoked by short-term factors – global recession, falling prices for exports and a rise in international interest rates coupled with a fall in investment. But the crisis was also due to the fact that, by the 1980s, the regional development model was only sustained by external funding and that model was close to structural exhaustion. This was the fundamental cause of the crisis to which the collapse of the CACM, in the case of Central America, was an important contributing factor. The onset of economic crisis was accompanied in nearly all cases by capital flight and decapitalization of national economies, and in some cases by a process of disintegration of the state. At the same time, the decline in the terms of trade had encouraged governments to borrow in the previous decade, so that servicing the international debt, though small by Latin American standards, became a major problem after 1982.

In the insular Caribbean, Jamaica, the Dominican Republic and Puerto Rico were the worst affected. Foreign investment, the main source of capital in the region, had slowed down through the 1970s, with disinvestment occurring in Jamaica and Trinidad and Tobago. Prices for the region's main exports fell – sugar (which went down 32 per cent between 1980 and 1985), alumina, bauxite and coffee – reducing foreign exchange earnings and lowering the capacity to import (Deere *et al.* 1990). Food production also declined dramatically in these countries through the 1980s, increasing the need for food imports and deepening the problems with the external sector. In Central America, where the recession followed almost three decades of steady growth, real per capita income dropped 33 per cent. The costs were unevenly spread across society, however, intensifying in particular the hardship facing the poor.

The economic crisis was exacerbated in El Salvador, Nicaragua and Guatemala by the costs of war and state repression; and by the fact that the hegemony of the dominant class was put in doubt. In these countries, the most dramatic consequences of the collapse of the model were the impoverishment and destruction of rural communities, the collapse of living standards and employment in the cities, and the eruption of the 'Central American crisis' – the militarization and internationalization of the conflicts internal to the three countries. Across Central America and the insular Caribbean, falls in living standards were most acute for the poor, for ethnic minorities and for women. As living standards declined, popular protests were organized, but met with a violent response from the state, as in the Dominican Republic in 1984 and 1988. In Jamaica, the Dominican Republic and Puerto Rico, unemployment figures registered all-time highs of 30 per cent, a phenomenal 50 per cent, and 23.4 per cent respectively in 1983, the worst year of the crisis. Research into health care during the 1980s indicated rising mortality for newborn babies and mothers in the Dominican Republic and Haiti (Whiteford 1991).

Deepening poverty had proved to be as much a structural feature of the Caribbean model of development as the growth which characterized the region until the late 1970s. It failed to create employment, relied on cheap urban labour and in some cases a pool of unemployed, exhibited an in-built tendency towards reducing land use for food production and expanding export agriculture, leading to impoverishment in the countryside, and concentrated income. The economic crisis, therefore, contributed to the delegitimization of the state in the region. But it was not the cause. The validity of the development model was brought into question as a result of the fact that it depended on the exclusion of a majority of the population in the region. Industrialization alongside the expansion of export-agriculture had transformed economic production, but the poor – in class and ethnic terms – were excluded from the benefits. In fact, the rural poor in particular turned out to be a major casualty in the development process. The causes of the insurgencies which emerged in Guatemala and El Salvador, for example, lie in the operation of the development model in the post-war period, not in the recession with which the revolutionary movements are contiguous, but where a particularly heavy cost was paid by the rural communities who lost access to land. Only in Costa Rica, where economic policy benefited the middle sectors and public employees rather than simply the top 20 per cent of the population and where the welfare services operated as a form of income redistribution, did the state remain legitimate through the years of growth and through the crisis.

Responses to the Crisis: Capitalist Reform and Structural Adjustment

Government responses to the development crisis of the 1980s varied. In some parts of the region, there were attempts to implement new models of development – Nicaragua and to some extent Grenada. Cuba was largely protected from the crisis until the end of the decade by its special relationship with the Soviet Union. Elsewhere, governments addressed primarily the immediate crisis and attempted to put capitalism in the region onto a more viable footing through the introduction of policies designed to reduce balance of payments problems and alleviate the fiscal crises which emerged in the 1980s. In some cases the reforms have been aimed simultaneously to reduce or remove the challenge from politicized popular sectors – in Jamaica, for example.

Various factors pushed Caribbean Basin states in the direction of a new orientation in economic policy (or a return to an old one) of liberalism and export-led development. Firstly, the balance of payments crises, exacerbated in some cases by external debt – the case of Costa Rica and Jamaica for example – increased the leverage of international agencies who traditionally favour laissez-faire economics, such as the IMF over policy-making. Secondly, falling prices for traditional exports meant governments had to seek new and more varied sources of foreign exchange through loans or investment, though the latter in particular was difficult to attract in the midst of an international recession on the scale of 1982–88, especially without opening the economy. Thirdly, the economic problems facing those governments which had tried to pursue growth with equity policies, Nicaragua especially, contributed in a general sense to the belief in the region that there were no workable policy alternatives. The US, whose interest in the region as a whole increased in the 1980s, also pushed for a liberal approach to development and offered funding as an inducement. And finally, the trend towards democratization in the Latin American and Caribbean regional as a whole brought with it a tendency to equate democracy with the market.

Economic liberalization has generally been accompanied by the implementation of structural adjustment programmes and the signing of stabilization agreements with the IMF which are designed to counter balance-of-payments problems so that affected economies can continue to import, to facilitate export expansion and to assure private capital of the will of the government to embark on liberalizing reform. Stabilization policies include reduction in import controls, the liberalization of foreign exchange policies, the devaluation of national currency, anti-inflation programmes based on credit restriction, reduction in state expenditure, wage controls and the ending of price controls. Though adjustment programmes may or may not create conditions for growth – the evidence globally would appear to be contradictory – they have consistently been associated with a decline in labour's share of national income (Pastor 1987). That is, their social impact is very negative indeed. Cuts in social services, removal of minimum price controls, lower wages and higher unemployment inevitably hit poorest families hardest. The costs of stabilization in the Dominican Republic in 1984 led not only to rises in the costs of basic necessities, including bread, baby milk and medicines, but also to crises in public hospitals as medical instruments ran out (Murphey 1987). In addition, in the insular Caribbean at least, the evidence also points to stabilization programmes compounding the economic crisis.

More than simply changing the role of the state and stabilizing the economy, structural adjustment programmes in the region aim at increasing integration into the global economy. They challenge the concept of state-led development with a belief that the private sector and foreign capital, given the 'correct environment', can produce development. Policies are therefore shaped to encourage private investors, especially foreign capital. Investment is encouraged in particular in non-traditional sectors of the economy, in new export industries, mainly 'off-shore' or assembling plants with goods destined for export to the US or even Europe. Tax concessions, low labour costs, tight labour control and the creation of free trade zones are associated policies. In the Caribbean, in particular, tourism is also a focus of new investment. For the Dominican Republic and Jamaica, where exports fell dramatically in the late 1980s, the tourist industry has become the only area where expansion has occurred.

Since the introduction of liberal development programmes, oriented towards growth rather than redistribution, economies have tended to stabilize, though overall increases in GDP have been low and have not been sufficient to make up for the dismal economic performances of the 1980s (see Tables 5.2 and 5.3). But

Table 5.2   Annual growth of GDP (selected countries)

	1965–80 (*annual % growth*)	*1980–90* (*annual % growth*)
Costa Rica	3.3	0.6
Grenada	0.1	5.1
Panama	2.8	−2.0
Jamaica	−0.1	−0.4
Dominican Republic	3.8	−0.4
El Salvador	1.5	−0.6
Nicaragua	0.7	—
Honduras	1.1	−1.2
Haiti	0.9	−2.3

Source: UN, *Human Development Report*, 1993.

there are other development issues which are not addressed and which are made worse by structural adjustment. These include inequitable income distribution. Structural adjustment has reduced popular consumption and further concentrated income in high income groups. It has failed to address the problems resulting from the reduction of real wages in the region throughout the decade. This is leading to an increase in the poverty experienced by the poor, especially by poor women and children. At the same time it leads to a transformation of the labour market, reducing employment possibilities and leading to an increase in the size of the informal sector. Approximately 29 per cent of all employment is now within the informal sector. The increase in hardship has intensified the trend in emigration, affecting the poor and skilled and professional workers. In the insular Caribbean, where emigration has traditionally operated as an escape valve for economic pressures, migratory flows are occurring within the region, for example Haitians to the Dominican Republic, and out-migration to the US, usually illegally. In Central America, where it is difficult to separate economic and political motivation in cases of displacement and emigration, the numbers of displaced people and refugees reached new levels in the mid to late 1980s.

Liberal policies are designed to encourage foreign investment but have on occasion contributed to outflows of capital seeking more

Table 5.3   GDP growth, 1990 and 1991 (selected countries)

	1990 (%)	1991 (%)
Cuba	1.0	—
Haiti	−0.6	−1.5
Jamaica	3.8	2.0
Dominican Republic	−4.8	0.0
Panama	5.1	5.0
Costa Rica	3.2	1.0
El Salvador	3.4	3.0
Guatemala	3.3	3.0
Honduras	−0.1	1.0
Nicaragua	0.1	1.0
Trinidad and Tobago	1.3	1.5

Source: ECLAC, *Annual Report*, 1992.

secure investments, The distribution of investment within the region has also been affected, as foreign capital has moved into those parts of the Caribbean where investment is most profitable, stimulating competition within the region for scarce capital inputs. At the same time opening the economy has weakened local capital *vis-à-vis* foreign capital which tends to have a greater share of export-oriented industries. This trend is especially marked in the insular Caribbean, where export industrialization was always emphasized over import substituting industrialization (ISI), but where nonetheless there was a significant ISI component in the 1970s. Part of the problem lies in finding new export industries which offer stable prices and secure markets, which the policies are explicitly designed to stimulate. In the absence of other viable exports, it is not surprising that illegal narcotics have recently become an important 'non-traditional' export from the Caribbean to the US. For instance, 60–80 per cent of cocaine entering the US comes through the Caribbean Basin. Marijuana for the US market is also supplied from Jamaica and Guatemala. The value of illegal drugs to the Jamaican economy has been variously estimated at between one and two billion dollars in the late 1980s and it constitutes the third most important export in terms of foreign exchange (Griffith 1992; Serbin 1990). The problems resulting from the growing importance of narcotics inside the economies of the region have been documented, some of the most significant being increasing violence and social instability; a weakening of the authority of the state and possible disintegration; concentration of resources outside the control of the state; and the possibility of conflicts internationally.

External Assistance for Liberalization: The Caribbean Basin Initiative

Liberal economic reform in the region rests upon promoting closer integration between the Caribbean Basin and the global economy. External funding plays an integral part in assisting the process of integration. We now examine the most ambitious programme of financing liberal reforms in the area in the 1980s: the US government's Caribbean Basin Initiative (CBI). In particular, we focus on a controversial theme: whether the programme has contributed to development needs in the region.

In accordance with the renewed interest in the Caribbean Basin by the Reagan administration, the CBI was launched in 1982, and put into operation following Congressional approval in 1983. In order to have a clear understanding of its role in the political economy of the region, we must bear in mind the context in which it was created: recessionary economies, structural adjustment programmes and 'denationalization' of the Caribbean states. Washington tried to promote growth as part of a strategy of maintaining control over the region; but there were other reasons behind CBI, including the need to buoy up the United States' own economy, facing threats from Japan, Asia and the European Union, through extending its opportunities in Central America and the Caribbean.

Looking beyond the rhetoric of the proposal, the CBI offers only limited assistance to the region. Its most important components are credits for private companies investing in the region, guaranteed through the Export-Import Bank; the elimination of tariffs on most, though not all, products from the region entering the US for 12 years, textiles and clothing being the most significant items excluded; and 350 million dollars in economic assistance for the beneficiaries of the Initiative. The impact of the Initiative was weakened by the fact that 350 million dollars is a tiny sum when compared with the needs of the region – and in practice, most assistance was reserved for El Salvador, Costa Rica and Jamaica; and also by the fact that around 60 per cent of the region's products already entered the US market duty-free.

CBI is most beneficial to multinational companies interested in the 'screwdriver' assembling plants which were the most important component of industrialization programmes in the regions by the 1970s – electronics, pharmaceuticals etc. – who will benefit from unrestricted access to the US market. Comparisons with Puerto Rico, where this policy has been practised for a long time, suggest that intensifying assembling-style industrialization will be as negative in the medium term for the rest of the Caribbean Basin. Deere concludes from her study of the operation of the programme that it has had no impact on the economic crisis in the region as a whole because the export industries it promotes do not create backward or forward linkages in the local economies or local demand for materials, services or goods (Deere 1990). Rather the US has benefited most since it has been able to establish positive trade balances with the region. It is contributory evidence of the failure of liberal economics to respond to development needs within the region.

CBI has not only affected models of development in beneficiary countries. It has had a knock-on effect in Puerto Rico, though the island is not one of the beneficiaries of the Plan. Fearing increased competition for off-shore investment from CBI beneficiaries, Puerto Rico responded with a programme to encourage the creation of joint ventures, twinning arrangements and production sharing between Puerto Rico and CBI beneficiary states. The aim was to transform the island into a broker within the Caribbean for US investment. The programme was supported by the US government to the extent that Section 936 of the US tax code, which allows US manufacturers to repatriate profits tax-free, was extended to include these joint ventures. The new twin plants combine the cheapest labour of the Caribbean Basin (the Dominican Republic for example) with the tax breaks that only the island offers. By 1987, 50 companies had twinning arrangements between Puerto Rico and other Caribbean states, of which 28 were with the Dominican Republic, the closest neighbour to Puerto Rico in the area. However, these policies have been unable to reverse the trend in Puerto Rico towards economic slow-down, rising poverty and increasing out-migration.

The US has been concerned to 'favour' those states adopting structural adjustment policies with privileged access to CBI investment. Jamaica was chosen as a CBI showpiece and amply illustrates the consequences of the approach. Chosen for overwhelmingly political reasons to do with the conservative orientation of the incoming Jamaican president in 1980, Edward Seaga, Jamaica was also quick to adopt structural adjustment and negotiate with the IMF. Seaga became a firm supporter of President Reagan's policies in the region and was regarded in Washington as an anti-communist crusader, having just defeated Michael Manley, suspected in the 1970s of harbouring socialist intentions for Jamaican development. Apart from benefiting from CBI, Jamaica was therefore also a privileged recipient of other forms of US aid. For example, Seaga negotiated a 108 per cent increase in the island's quota of textiles, outside the rubric of CBI, destined for the US market.

What has been the impact of CBI and the new relationship with the US for Jamaica? CBI became effective in the midst of the structural adjustment programme which included deregulation, the dismantling of import controls and lowering the value of the Jamaican currency. The result of the policies together was to increase the weight of foreign enterprises in the economy over local capital. Local manufactures lost markets to cheaper imports and, especially in textiles, the most dynamic sector of Jamaica's export industries, foreign-owned firms expanded to take up the opportunities for export. Manufacturing had expanded to employ 12.8 per cent of the labour force by 1987. But the social costs of the model have been high – increasing unemployment, poverty, malnutrition etc. At the same time, Jamaican sovereignty has been further undermined and its vulnerability increased as the main centres of decision-making for its economy have shifted outside the country. Jamaica is suffering from a process of 'economic recolonization' according to Jamaican economist, Carl Stone (Payne 1988b).

The impact of CBI in terms of countering the recession in the depressed economies of the region in the 1980s has therefore been small. This can be measured by the fact that in those countries where it was most felt, in Costa Rica, Jamaica and the Dominican Republic, economic recovery, even understood simply in terms of macroeconomic growth, did not occur. GDP per capita grew marginally in these countries in 1984–9, between 0.35 per cent and 1.3 per cent per annum. But if the idea was to favour US investment abroad and to offer a patina of concern about development and poverty in a policy otherwise characterized by an obsession with security, then it was undoubtedly rather more successful. CBI remains a symbol of White House 'good intentions', and its most important purpose may indeed have been propaganda in a charged international and regional climate.

Case Studies of the Crisis: Costa Rica: From the Entrepreneurial State to Structural Adjustment

In Costa Rica, the most negative features of the regional model of development have been mitigated by the actions of the state since the civil war of 1948. Although the civil war was a decisive defeat for the left, organized around the figure of Manuel Mora Valverde and the *Partido Vanguardia Popular* (PVP), the post-1948 state assumed the role of mediating social conflicts and reducing class polarization. Education and health services were extended and a system of pensions and welfare benefits was created which marked the country out as exceptional in the region. These policies, although they came under severe threat during the 1980s and were much reduced, softened the impact of the crisis. None the less, even in Costa Rica, the combination of recession and structural adjustment hit the rural and urban poor hardest and bit into the consuming power of the white-collar middle class. It also brought into question the viability of Costa Rica's own variant of the regional development model, where the state acted as a major axis of capital accumulation.

Until the mid-1950s coffee and bananas were responsible for nearly 90 per cent of Costa Rica's exports. But following Costa Rica's incorporation into the Central American Common Market in 1963, the country experienced a period of industrial growth, complimented by agricultural diversification. Industrialization was stimulated by integration and the creation of a regional market; by the emergence of a small internal market in Costa Rica itself, made up especially of urban middle sector groups; and by state intervention which acted especially in two areas: infrastructure and credit, following the nationalization of the banks. Between 1960 and 1970 the role of foreign capital changed dramatically, moving out of bananas and into ISI regional industries until foreign capital in industry began to outweigh local capital (Franco and Leon 1984). The economic transformation of the country was accompanied by a change in social structure as urbanization increased. By the 1960s, the country was characterized by the relative size of the tertiary sector and in particular the number of people employed by the state.

The role of the state grew steadily through the 1970s. The *Partido de Liberación Nacional* (PLN), a party with an important following in the bureaucracy, had stimulated the expansion of the state to compensate for the shift in foreign investment to agroindustry and the growing problems with the Central American Common Market (CACM). Growth in the state sector, which occurred particularly under President Daniel Oduber (1974–8) led to Costa Rica earning the title 'the entrepreneurial state'. The creation of the *Corporación Costaricense de Desarrollo* (CODESA), which financed mixed companies, offered loans to industry and was particularly active in key industries like energy and fertilizers, was a symbol of the new extended role of the state, the dynamism of which was a reflection of the absence of an entrepreneurial class with sufficient economic power to make policy, a legacy of the export agrarian model of development. At the same time, the state continued to finance welfare policies which have elevated living standards in Costa Rica far beyond that of its neighbours in the region. By the 1970s, welfare services covered 80 per cent of basic needs.

However, this style of development had various problems which became evident by the 1980s. Like everywhere else in the region, industrialization was dependent upon imported technology, heavy industry, capital and oil; regional and internal demand was quickly saturated, limiting growth; and the costs of funding state-led development meant an increasing tendency to borrow. Costa Rica became the regional state facing the most serious debt crisis in the 1980s. 'Under Oduber, the public sector debt tripled, while the proportion owed to private banks . . . rose from 22 per cent in 1970 to 53 per cent in 1979' and by 1982, the external debt had reached 3.5 billion dollars (Roddick 1988: 195).

In 1982, the incoming government of Luis Alberto Monge, facing internal chaos, high inflation (81.7 per cent per annum) and the suspension of debt payments, decided on stabilization of the economy and US aid as the way out. Costa Rica, important strategically for Reagan in the isthmus because of its long democratic history, became one of the principal recipients of US aid in the 1980s. Total US aid to Costa Rica rose from 15.8 billion dollars in 1981 to 202.9 billion dollars in 1986 (Rivera Urrutia, Sojo and Lopez 1986: 58). By 1985, 35.7 per cent of Costa Rica's budget came from US assistance (Dunkerley 1988: 636). The aid was conditional on the adoption of a structural adjustment programme which was to shrink the size of the state and cut into the welfare politics which had characterized Costa Rica after 1948. The result was to increase poverty and un- and under-employment. The reduction of price subsidies led to food price increases of 100 per cent in 1982 and wages were consistently held below the rate of inflation. Privatization of CODESA's industries began in 1985. Possibilities for growth, meanwhile, were limited by the difficulties of servicing the external debt. In 1988 the cost of servicing the total debt of 4,530 million dollars was 715 million dollars, 58.9 per cent of export earnings. This situation continued until 1989, when Costa Rica reached agreement with its debtors, and was incorporated into the Brady Plan for debt reduction.

It is true that the social costs of structural adjustment were somewhat softened in Costa Rica compared to the rest of the region. Nevertheless, poorest groups bore the hardest burden. Open unemployment increased in the mid-1980s and the size of the informal economy in San José rose to the unprecedented level of 23 per cent of total employment (Pollack and Uloff 1985). The decline in real wages as structural adjustment got under way led to public sector strikes in 1988 and 1989 and protests by farmers who produced for the internal market, because of the government's prioritization of cash crops in order to earn foreign exchange.

In the long term, the crisis brought state-led development to an end. Privatization, in the absence of a strong entrepreneurial class, has meant the growth of US influence over the economy, threatening Costa Rica's traditional neutrality in international affairs. And the growth of non-traditional exports (cut flowers, vegetable oils, exotic fruits, African palm) from 15 per cent to 40 per cent of exports, many of which are exported to the US under the CBI, has cut into agricultural production for domestic consumption. The costs, therefore, in terms of increasing social inequality, declining national autonomy and security and increasing dependence on outside capital have been high and will be felt for many years to come.

Case Studies of the Crisis: The Dominican Republic

The economic crisis in the Dominican Republic has been much sharper than in Costa Rica. This is a result of development patterns historically since the sugar boom and in particular since the Trujillo dictatorship, and to the way the crisis of the 1980s was handled.

Whereas the 1929 depression in Puerto Rico had led to the subordination of sugar to industrial promotion, in the Dominican Republic sugar survived and the Trujillo dictatorship was able to bring about some considerable expansion of production in the 1950s supplying the US market. This was accompanied by some small expansion in ISI industrialization. Economic uncertainty and political turmoil, however, intensified by the US invasion in 1965, brought to an end the timid attempts by the Dominican state to promote industrialization and diversification. At the same time, the invasion focused attention on the expansion of US multinationals in the country; Gulf and Western in particular expanded its holdings through the 1970s in traditional and non-traditional agriculture and expanded into industrial and tertiary sectors.

State promotion of industrialization did not occur until the 1970s. Between 1968 and 1977 manufacturing employment more than doubled. Although aimed principally at supplying the internal market and dominated by local capitalists, around 25 per cent of all employment in manufacturing was located in the export sector, mainly in free trade zones, where US capital was dominant, which began to expand in the mid-1970s. Between 1975 and 1980, remitted profits from the Dominican Republic to the US quintupled from 7 million dollars to 35 million dollars (Bray 1987: 87). None the less, sugar remained the single most important foreign exchange earner, with sales to the US alone responsible for 20 per cent of total foreign exchange in the mid-1980s. The economy remained primarily agrarian, with only 12.6 per cent of the population in total engaged in manufacturing.

The crisis of the 1980s hit the Dominican Republic particularly hard. Between 1975 and 1980, the external debt tripled as the country was forced to borrow to offset oil price rises. The rise in interest rates after 1982 meant that 48 per cent of all goods and services produced in the country went to service the debt. At the same time, the price of sugar fell with the recession, by 32 per cent, with disastrous consequences for a country which relied on foreign trade for over half of all government income. Finally, the cut in the sugar quota for the US market – sales to the US alone represented 20 per cent of all foreign exchange – brought the country to the brink of collapse. The predictable result was the signing of a stand-by agreement with the IMF in 1983, structural adjustment and the promotion of non-traditional exports especially from free trade zones under the aegis of foreign capital.

The first round of policies included devaluation of the Dominican peso, and the removal of price controls leading to rising inflation with increases in the costs of basic foodstuffs and medicines by 200 per cent and 300 per cent. Popular protests against the measures which called for an end to negotiations with the IMF met with police repression and left 80 people dead and 300 injured. An ever more severe austerity programme was introduced in 1985, notwithstanding. Since then the country has been able to service its debt at least in part, foreign investment has increased by the rate of up to 80 million dollars a year and contraction of the economy has stabilized, with the economy even experiencing some growth. But stabilization has masked two problems: the 'solution' has been socially regressive; and the underlying vulnerability of the economy remains unchanged. The Dominican Republic's debt remains a problem too, with the country in arrears to commercial banks (SELA 1991c). Research undertaken by Deere *et al.* demonstrates clearly how structural adjustment has led to increases in poverty and increases in the number of poor in the Dominican Republic (Deere *et al.* 1990: 51–84). In particular, the burden has fallen heaviest on poor women and children, in the lowest paid jobs, who have increased their participation in the labour force as men have withdrawn or been excluded. Their situation has been made worse by food price rises and falls in public expenditure.

The priorities of government policy since 1983 have been diversification and reinsertion in the international economy through foreign investment and reform of the state. Carlos Morales Troncoso, vice-president during the late 1980s and previously an executive for Gulf and Western, explained, 'our government has assigned a top priority to encouraging both foreign and local capital . . . we are doing all we can to improve investment incentives and streamline the bureaucracy to cut red tape' (*The Wall Street Journal*, 22 June 1987). Although these reforms are aimed at export diversification, the economy remains vulnerable: investment in free trade zones, where most of the growth has taken place, is easily dismantled if conditions deteriorate; it creates relatively few jobs – 70,000 in 1988; fosters a low-paid workforce; and generates few linkages to the local economy. This vulnerability has been intensified by concentration on the export sector to the detriment of production for internal consumption, especially in food production. The fall in the production of rice, milk, corn and even sugar – in 1990 some $15,000 was spent on importing sugar from Brazil – is indicative of a policy of government neglect. Any growth in such circumstances is bound to be uneven and impoverishing.

Conclusion

Development policies in Central America and the Caribbean have historically been subject to the demands for agrarian exports to advanced regions. This has shaped the external sector and the possibilities for planning and reform internally. Development has also been subject as a result to international demand and the cycles of the international economy. But within these overall limitations national development patterns have varied.

The 1980s witnessed a profound restructuring of the regional economies in the wake of the global economic crisis, the exhaustion of the industrialization strategies of the 1960 and 1970s, the fall in the prices of primary products and the increased interest on the part of the US in the region. The new development focus, with a greater reliance on the market and increased attempts at competitiveness, is stabilizing the region but with considerable social costs, including out-migration, the expansion of the informal economy, and marginalization.

What does this experience tell us about development processes overall in the region? Regional development remains a problem to which the solution has yet to be found. The different strategies for capitalist growth which have been implemented (various forms of industrialization, export agriculture, liberalism) have enjoyed only partial and temporary success. The region remains dependent and vulnerable and some groups have become significantly poorer and have faced severe repression as a result of the development process. Why is this?

The advocates of the new liberalism via structural adjustment insist that the causes of the failure to develop can be located in a lack of entrepreneurship, an over-extended state and excessive protectionism leading to inefficiency and maladministration. But structural adjustment policies ignore specific regional problems: for example economies which, in some cases, lack – for geographic or historical reasons – an export sector beyond commodities of declining value such as sugar. They also fail to address the problem of external dependency, acute in a region fragmented in geographical, historical, ethnic and linguistic terms, and located on the fringes of the US mainland. And, perhaps most important, they fail to take into account the politics of the region. Development in Central America and the Caribbean cannot be brought about simply through selecting the right 'technical' recipes. It is a *political* problem. Development strategies have been chosen over time because they have been beneficial to maintaining the economic and political power of elites. The overall impact of these policies may have been negative in the medium to long term for the nation as a whole; but that was not a consideration uppermost in the minds of elite policy-makers. Development patterns cannot be changed therefore until there is a redistribution of power internally. This is why democratization in the region, of which there are the first timid signs, *could* be positive for development, if it leads to a genuinely pluralistic polity. A transformation of the political environment is the only path to development policies in which meeting basic needs, including political participation, is as important in designing policies as searching for economic growth.

Notes

1. The figure refers to land ownership, not use. Various forms of tenancy meant that peasants still had access to land, a situation which was itself later threatened by the expansion of export agriculture. By the 1960s, 40 per cent of Salvadorean peasants had access to no land at all. Land hunger was greatest in El Salvador because of the absence of a land frontier and the widespread practice of large landowners of restricting access to land in order to create a landless class in the countryside and therefore secure for themselves an adequate labour supply in the coffee plantations.
2. Sugar, introduced in the eighteenth century, was quickly displaced from some islands where conditions were not suitable – Grenada, Tobago, Dominica, for example. Other crops, of less importance economically, replaced them and land holdings remained less concentrated as a result.
3. This did not mean that wages in Puerto Rico rose to the levels of the US. Wages in the US are rarely paid at the minimum level, so with average wages in the US at $6.54 an hour, in Puerto Rico the average wage was $3.58. The differential had narrowed, however, from 1950 when the average US wage was $1.50 an hour and in Puerto Rico was $0.42 (Dietz 1986: 266).
4. The 'football war' had less to do with football and far more to do with Honduras' attempt to expel the Salvadorean peasants and labourers living in Honduras. Many had found themselves landless as a result of the expansion of export agriculture in the 1950s and 1960s; others had gone to work in the banana plantations. It was estimated that 300,000 Salvadoreans lived in Honduras in 1969.

6

Revolution: Cuba, Nicaragua and Grenada

So far, we have looked at the politics and economics of the region in those societies which have tried to promote growth and development within capitalism. In this chapter, we examine how regimes which have attempted to promote development through different forms of socialist development have fared. For revolutionary regimes, winning power is only the first step on the path to the creation of a better society. The real battle, that to produce egalitarian development, is only then about to start. Fidel Castro, President of Cuba since the revolution, commented on the tenth anniversary of the Cuban revolution: 'many people thought, on the first of January 1959, that they had entered the world of the rich. But the world they had entered in reality was one of opportunity – to create, amid the underdevelopment, the poverty, ignorance and misery, wealth and welfare in the future' (Fagen 1986: 87).

The revolutionary regimes we deal with in this chapter have all been described as 'socialist'. But this label is not very accurate for two reasons. Firstly, these regimes resemble hardly at all the Soviet-style regimes of Eastern Europe which many observers associate with socialism. And even if we look at them from a theoretical Marxist perspective, it is difficult to see them as 'socialist'. Marx had envisaged that socialist revolutions would occur in the most economically advanced parts of the globe. When revolutions occur on the periphery of the capitalist system, the socio-economic and political conditions within which Marx thought socialism would be built are absent. For example, new social and economic relations must be created in societies which display none of the material abundance which Marx had originally thought to be an essential precondition for revolution, but which suffer instead from material poverty. And the new revolutionary regime must also build a new kind of social base, given that the proletariat, which Marx thought of as the revolutionary class, is weak or absent. It is clear, then, that revolutions in the Caribbean cannot be understood if we analyse them from the standpoint of what revolutionary socialism *should* be.

Revolution in the Caribbean Basin

Successful revolutions in the region are the result of overwhelming popular demands and organization for national control over resources, government and decision-making. That is, they are concerned with building a sovereign nation-state via the implementation of socialist development policies. National liberation, because of the region's colonial past, is usually seen as the first stage towards a more developed and egalitarian society. The revolution, therefore, is being made by and for 'the people' rather than any clearly defined or articulated class. For Castro, the 'people' was made up of all those Cubans who 'desired a better, fairer country in dignity'; and for Daniel Ortega, leader of the Sandinista revolution, 'the workers, the peasants, soldiers, artisans, intellectuals and professionals, women, children and all patriotic Nicarguans' made up the Nicaraguan people. Though this broad social base endows the incoming revolutionary regime with widespread support, it also indicates a potential problem in policymaking – how to identify those sectors of 'the people' who are the subject of the revolution, and who should benefit most from the distribution of scarce resources in the post-revolution period? We have to remember that while revolutions promise more efficient and rational production, and a more equal distribution of material wealth, the possibilities of reforms are limited by the poverty and resource-limitations which characterize Caribbean and Central American societies.

A common strategy for revolutionary regimes is to adopt a 'basic-needs' approach to development and resource allocation. This means the adoption of national development plans and policies [which] included explicitly as a priority objective the promotion of employment and the satisfaction of the basic needs of [the] country's population . . . . they include certain minimum requirements of a family for private consumption: adequate food, shelter and clothing as well as certain household equipment, and furniture . . . essential services provided by and for the community at large, such as safe drinking water, public transport and health, educational and cultural facilities. (Brundenius 1984: 79)

These policies have the advantage of redistributing resources in society more equitably without threatening capital accumulation or leading to indebtedness. But they will almost inevitably antagonize a consumer-minded bourgeoisie, which will resent the taxation and the import-restrictions the policies imply. And the strategy may also be threatened by pressure from social groups who wish to see 'populist' economic policies which satisfy immediate demands for higher consumption.

Alongside commitments to radical economic transformation, revolutions offer political change by altering the power relations between classes in society. Democracy, understood not as a system of competing political parties but as access to government by the mass of society and popular influence in government decisions, has usually operated as a motivating force during the years of struggle before the revolution, and the new regime must find ways of channelling demands for participation. There are, inevitably, limitations to their success: for example, there is always the problem of how to increase participation without creating a bureaucratic and unwieldy political system; and how to triumph over the problem of creating a participatory and democratic society where no political tradition of democracy exists. And all revolutions in Central America and the Caribbean also face the challenge of balancing security needs with demands to create an open and free society. This can become an acute dilemma if the revolution has external enemies.

The problems, then, can be summed up succinctly – how to produce growth and pursue redistribution of goods, services and political power in a peripheral economy, while at the same time trying to neutralize external hostility. In order to try and fulfil these goals, revolutionary regimes must make tough policy decisions in three vital areas: economic and development policies; the question of power within the revolutionary society; and external relations. In the rest of the chapter, we analyse policies in these areas under the revolutionary governments of Cuba, Nicaragua and Grenada.

Participation and Power in Revolutionary Regimes

The goal of revolutionary regimes can be summed up as equitable development. This means creating the conditions for real equality in political, economic and cultural terms. Even economics is subordinate to the demands of politics here. Revolutions put an end to personalist, dictatorial and elitist regimes and promise broad popular access to government and participation in decision-making. The revolutionary regimes of Cuba, Nicaragua and Grenada inherited profoundly anti-democratic political structures from the past. How did they go about broadening channels for participation? And were they able to overcome the classical dilemma of revolutionary regimes, caught between the demands for a system of participatory democracy, tied to the revolution, and representative democracy, on which much-needed Western aid is often contingent, but which suggests ultimately that the revolution is reversible?

Cuba

The Communist Party is the only political party in Cuba and is regarded as the leading force in society. The collapse of communist regimes of the Soviet Union (USSR) and the Eastern bloc has had no direct reformist impact on Cuban political structures. Under the revolutionary constitution, the party represents the will of the Cuban people. Party decisions are made in accordance with the principle of democratic centralism and are binding on party members. But though clearly the most important, the party is not the only officially acknowledged political force in Cuba, because the administration and mass organizations created by the revolutions also exercise some input in decision-making. And since 1990, in particular, a small internal opposition has developed, though with little influence beyond elitist cultural circles.

This structure, which bears the imprint of Soviet influence, took some time to appear. The revolution was made by an ideologically disparate group, the 26th of July Movement, which only later allied with the Communist Party. Moreover, during the early years of the revolution, mass mobilization was encouraged and decision-making through popular organizations was attempted, especially through the Committees for the Defence of the Revolution (CDRs), created initially to repel the attacks by Cuban emigrés and the US in 1962. Mobilization was seen as the key to popular democracy because of the prevailing view among the revolutionaries that a socialist transformation – towards which the Cubans were explicitly committed – depended as much on changing people as changing the material bases of society; the revolution had to create a 'New Man', in the words of the leading thinker of the revolution, Che Guevara. Gradually, however, as the 1960s progressed, the CDRs lost real power and became simply neighbourhood associations, coordinating and implementing policy decisions taken elsewhere. And even during the 1960s, mobilization remained under the control of the state, partly because the tradition of popular organizations before 1959 was weak.

Party hegemony at the expense of the popular organizations increased during the 1970s and was enshrined in the constitution of 1976. Mass participation was to continue through the Organizations of People's Power (OPPs), but their real influence was limited. Their functions include enforcing regulations from superior state bodies, participating in the judicial system, evaluating some reports from the executive committees of the party, and participating in national defence and internal order. Their independence from the Communist Party is, in practice, also limited, because dual membership is standard, although no one is formally required to be a member of the Communist Party for election to the OPPs.

The tensions between the goals of popular representation, explicitly endorsed by the revolution on coming to power, and the need for rational, efficient decision-making, planning and party control have never been resolved in Cuba. The initial spirit of participation of 1959 and 1960 was gradually worn away by the need to defend the revolution from outside aggression, and assure internal security from the hostility of the US. At the same time, the attractions of aspects of the Soviet political model increased as the economic ties between Cuba and the USSR strengthened. Yet despite the similarities with the USSR, the system always remained more open and with a greater degree of popular legitimation than the political system of the USSR. Personal leadership, especially that of Fidel Castro, whose charisma has dimmed after more than thirty years in power but who still commands respect on the island, remains one of the most significant features of the political system. And the system is also more flexible than the Soviet polity was. The mass organizations, especially the Confederation of Cuban Workers and the Federation of Cuban Women, have remained active and labour in particular was revitalized during the 1980s. According to some observers of the revolution – before the 1990s – 'the subculture of local democracy is strong', evidenced in the vigorous debates which have been reported to take place in the neighbourhood and the workplace (Azicri 1988: 111). But a fear of manipulation of opposition from outside has made dissent difficult and organized opposition impossible. It would be difficult to sustain the idea that Cuba is a totalitarian society, despite the total absence of liberal democratic features in the political system. But the political system rests on party control and personal charisma, both of which limit real participation in public life. It remains to be seen how the post-Castro political system will take shape, since the structures created by the revolution are unlikely to outlast Castro's term in office.

Nicaragua

Influenced only partially by marxism and perhaps with the Cuban experience in mind, the *Frente Sandinista de Liberación Nacional* (FSLN) was careful to avoid centralist and bureaucratic political models. Instead, the new political system attempted to combine participation with representation. How did the Sandinistas go about achieving this?

On the simplest level, the answer is that it was through the hegemonic role of the FSLN within the state and the establishment of grass-roots movements in society. The main instrument of mass participation and popular democracy during the ten years of the revolution were the Sandinista mass organizations, which served in different degrees to link the state, controlled by the FSLN, to society. The main organizations were the *Central Sandinista de Trabajadores* (Union of Sandinista Workers – CST), the *Asociación de Trabajadores del Campo* (Association of Rural Workers – ATC), the *Union Nacional de Agricultores y Ganaderos* (National Union of Farmers and Ranchers – UNAG), *Asociación de Mujeres Nicaraguenses Luisa Amanda Espinosa* (Association of Nicaraguan Women – AMNLAE) and the *Comités de Defensa Sandinista* (Sandinista Defence Committees – CDS). Although the organizations grouped together significant numbers of people, their influence was on the whole limited to conveying policy downwards. Only UNAG retained relative independence from the state. For some organizations, especially the CDS and the ATC, this meant a fall in militants from the mid-1980s. UNAG, meanwhile, the most independent, grew in numbers. As in Cuba, then, the most important popular organizations were linked to the governing party, though the links were looser and more diffuse.

In marked contrast to the Cuban system, however, the Sandinistas not only tried to promote participation through party-directed popular organization, but also tried to encourage a representative democracy, establishing formal mechanisms for general elections and a party system. In this way, the Sandinistas have played a fundamental role in constructing a broad and open political space after the revolution where none had been allowed to form earlier. Over 86 per cent of Nicaraguan citizens turned out to vote in 1990. General elections were held in 1984, won by the Sandinistas led by Daniel Ortega, and in February 1990, when the Sandinistas lost power to a broad opposition front, *Union Nacional de Oposición* (UNO). The reliance on elections marked an important shift within *Sandinismo*. We can measure the increase in electoralism within government strategy by comparing the 1984 elections with the those of 1990. In 1984, the revolution, legitimated still in fact by the 1979 insurrection, called elections in order to make clear, internally and externally, popular support for the revolution. By 1990, the revolution was competing electorally for power. The Sandinistas had moved away from the idea of institutionalization through popular participation towards accepting a competitive party system.

This new strategy was not adopted without internal tensions within the FSLN. While the 'tercerista' faction of the movement, around Daniel and Humberto Ortega and Sergio Ramirez, was responsible for designing and supporting the electoral strategy, others, for example Bayardo Arce and Tomás Borge, resisted the drift towards the institutionalization of a competitive party system.

They rejected the idea that Western political models are applicable to Nicaragua, especially in view of the war and the *contra* funding from the US. They also opposed what they saw as international pressure deciding the pace and timing of Nicaragua's elections – the 1990 elections were brought forward in accordance with the wishes of the opposition who threatened to boycott any elections held later. In spite of the electoral defeat, however, the Sandinistas remain influential inside the country. They won 42 per cent of votes for the National Assembly, compared to almost 55 per cent for UNO, and they constitute the single largest party. The Armed Forces remain under the control of the Sandinistas, though the Chamorro government is committed to reform in this area. Dissension within UNO, a multi-party coalition, increasingly turned the government of Violeta Chamorro towards pragmatic collaboration with the Sandinistas within the National Assembly. The electoral defeat of the Sandinistas therefore was not a complete defeat for the revolution nor was it a reversal to the pre-1979 situation.

Grenada

The revolution of 1979 was a reaction against the Westminster model of politics imposed on newly independent ex-British colonies in the Caribbean. Along with other radical and nationalist groups in the Caribbean (for example Black Power movements or the New World Group), the New Jewel Movement (NJM) had questioned the viability of the Westminster model for Caribbean societies since its formation. The NJM manifesto of 1973 described the system as 'only taking the people into account for a few seconds every five years, when citizens make a cross on their ballot paper' (Whitehead 1990: 350). Independent studies of the operation of the Westminster system in the Caribbean have in fact confirmed that it tends to function to guarantee over-representation for majority parties and reduce to a minimum the size of the parliamentary opposition. The real limitations of the system in Grenada, however, lay beyond the formal structures. The island's social system was rigidly constructed and operated as a guarantor for the retention of the privileges of the minority and the political culture was deferential and authoritarian, the legacy of a plantation economy and a colonial society. The island's weak civil society was simply unprepared and unable to control the excess of the post-independence regime of Eric Gairy, in which personal aggrandizement, clientelism, pay-offs and pragmatism played important roles. The participatory democracy that the People's Revolutionary Government (PRG) tried to put in the place of the Westminster system was therefore intended to transform Grenada's political culture as much as the mechanisms of representation.

Community groups had been prominent in the anti-Gairy protests of the early 1970s. These were an important formative influence on the New Jewel Movement (NJM), the main party within the PRG, which took on board the demands for broad popular political consultations through popular assemblies and workers' councils. Prime Minister Maurice Bishop and other leaders of the PRG insisted that decentralized decision-making formed part of the Grenadian popular culture, in marked contrast to the elitism and neo-colonialism of Westminster politics (Thorndike 1990). Once in power, therefore, the PRG tried to create a new political system through mass organizations: increasing the powers of parish councils, and encouraging the formation of youth movements, women's organizations and cooperatives. The Village Coordinating Bureaux, at the apex of the system, represented the attempt by the NJM to channel popular participation in favour of the government.

Political culture, however, is not transformed overnight; and it is not surprising that the four years of the revolution were a time of experimentation and innovation. And, in a scenario with certain similarities with the revolutions in Nicaragua and Cuba, there were undoubtedly limitations on the degree to which the PRG was prepared to preside over a process of popular participation and consultation in conditions where it was not assured of support. There was some tension between the ideal of participation and the revolution's need for internal control. The democratic centralism of the NJM and the centralization of decision-making in the hands of the Central Committee militated against the introduction of non-party and grass-roots participation. By the end of 1983, the NJM was concerned by the fall in levels of participation, but had not implemented any effective reform before the revolution collapsed amid internal divisions and the US invasion.

Development Policies

The Caribbean Basin is poor and underdeveloped. Revolutions cannot change that reality; they cannot work miracles; and the policies of revolutionary regimes must be evaluated in this light. Many basic features of the economy remain unchanged and the international system continues to determine the limits of development policies. Small peripheral economies which depended upon producing primary goods before the revolution will continue to do so afterwards, for the same reasons as before – the need to accumulate capital, the difficulties of export diversification, the absence of technology and markets, and at times the lack of a sufficiently skilled internal labour force able to produce more sophisticated goods. Revolutionary regimes continue to face the problems which affect all the economies of the region: dependence upon two or three export products of fluctuating value, unemployment and under-employment, especially seasonal, poor infrastructure etc.

However, though the structural problems remain the same, policies are now made in a changed environment, internally and externally. On the debit side, the three revolutions we are dealing with have faced external hostility, which can lead to withdrawal of investment, the closing of markets abroad, an end to aid or credit and economic blockade. At the same time, they encounter internally long-supressed demands for welfare and higher incomes. The need to respond to internal pressures to raise living standards may stimulate internal demand for new products which, if they have to be imported especially, will almost certainly contribute to inflation. Yet revolutionary governments will have more trouble controlling the economy because they will have rejected some of the traditional tools for doing so: for example, inflation control through demand reduction. On the positive side, revolutions offer the possibility of implementing some positive changes in ownership and production. This may act as a stimulus to growth in the short term. And in those cases where a predatory dictatorial regime is overthrown, considerable assets may fall into the hands of the state. These can be used to create the nucleus of a new sector within the economy, whether state-owned or resold or redistributed. The export sector and in particular the internal use made of the foreign exchange generated through exports is also an important difference between pre and post revolutionary economies.

Economic Policy-Making in Cuba

Cuba was the first country in the region to attempt a transition to socialism. Though sugar and external vulnerability continued to shape the political economy of the island, until the mid-1980s the island was regarded as a showpiece of socialist planning and its development policies served as examples of what peripheral societies *can* achieve in the areas of health, education and the eradication of gross inequalities. Since then, the loss of external support with the collapse of the Soviet Union has seriously undermined the island's economic performance. Soviet aid to Cuba was calculated as up to a million dollars a day in the 1970s and its removal has had a catastrophic effect on economic performance. Just as important as the loss of aid, is the loss of oil which Cuba imported cheaply from the USSR; like most of the region, with the exception of Trinidad and Tobago, Cuba is completely dependent on importing energy. As a result, Cuba's economy slowed by 80 per cent after 1991, when the loss of Soviet assistance began to bite. The subsequent economic collapse has brought into question the validity of Cuba's development programme. Notwithstanding, the reforms implemented remain important examples of the possibilities and limitations of revolutionary change on the periphery.

Following the revolution, Cuba's leaders decided that a radical change was needed in the economic base of the island. Rather than continuing to promote growth through export agriculture, they decided to pursue development through industrialization. Strengthening Cuba's industrial base became the central goal of policy-making in the early 1960s. One of the objectives of the nationalization of foreign-owned utilities which occurred almost immediately following Castro coming to power, was to stimulate the capitalization of the economy and encourage import-substituting industrialization. Yet the revolutionaries failed in this task and were forced to turn back to agriculture. Why did this happen? In fact, the drive for industrialization was thwarted from the beginning by the effects of the US blockade, which closed Cuba off from much-needed machinery, spare parts loans, etc. And there were serious problems later in the 1960s in adapting Cuban manufacturing to Soviet machinery. There were also severe structural limitations – the small size of the internal market, for example. At the same time, investments in industry proved negative for the economy as a whole because they distracted attention away from sugar, with a consequent fall in production in the early 1960s and a shortage of foreign exchange.

The failure of industrialization prompted a return to sugar. It was a decision taken reluctantly since sugar had distorted the Cuban economy; for example, despite its strategic importance, it generated relatively few jobs, and then only irregularly and with unstable wages, fixed as they were to the international price of sugar. According to the 1953 census, around 60 per cent of the population was engaged in non-agricultural activities. Culturally and psychologically too there was a rejection of the crop most associated with imperialism and slavery. But by 1964, when the industrialization drives and diversification in food crops led to a severe drop in exports causing balance of payments problems, the central role of sugar in the economy was accepted. After all, sugar accounted for 80 per cent of all exports. The task ahead, therefore, was to produce sugar outside the plantation economy, which was swept away by the revolution, diversify markets (60 per cent of sugar produced before 1960 went to the US) and use the export revenue earned to promote economic diversification.

The structure of sugar production and its relationship with other agricultural crops was completely changed by a series of agrarian reforms. The large plantations had led to poverty and land concentration in the countryside, leaving only a small number of small peasants in possession of family or subsistence farms. Food production was therefore low and credit was difficult to obtain for non-sugar farmers. As a result, food was imported, amounting to 145 million dollars in 1958 alone. Legislation passed between 1959 and 1963 destroyed the plantation by determining that all estates over 67 hectares be expropriated. Some land was distributed to sharecroppers and tenant farmers but most of the expropriated holdings were transformed into collective farms. After the reforms were completed, collectivized agriculture accounted for 80 per cent of agricultural land in contrast to 12 per cent for cooperatives and 8 per cent for privately owned farms (Mesa-Lago 1981). A combination of political and economic reasons had led to the decision to collectivize rather than redistribute. Large estates were thought at the time to have a greater potential output; and there was little pressure for land redistribution from below. Also, the agrarian reform was part of a total plan for rural development which included building schools, hospitals and new housing. This tipped the scales in favour of large estates which could offer a rational use of labour for construction and for the sugar economy.

In 1965, therefore, there was a major reorientation of economic policy. Emphasis was henceforth placed on increasing sugar output through state planning and investment. Cuba set targets for maximizing output without any reference to international demand and prices for the product. Although the 1970 target of 10 million tonnes was not met, by the end of the 1980s, 7.5 million tonnes of sugar annually was being produced. As a result, Cuba remains the world's largest exporter of raw sugar, the second largest producer of raw sugar and the third leading producer of sugar cane. Sugar still accounts for 80 per cent of total exports. If dependence on sugar remained the central feature of the Cuban economy, what therefore did the revolution change?

First, the way sugar is produced was greatly modified. Modernization and technification of harvesting and processing have largely meant the elimination of manual labour. In the mid-1980s, manual cane-cutters numbered less than 80,000. Second, output increased and land left idle on pre-1959 large estates was brought under cultivation. Third, with the destruction of the sugar oligarchy, the benefits of revenue from sugar have been more evenly distributed and workers have benefited from regular employment and stable incomes. And finally, from the early 1960s until the end of the 1980s, Cuba established a unique trading relationship with the USSR and the trading bloc it controlled, COMECON, which assured markets for Cuban sugar and therefore avoided for two-and-a-half decades the vulnerabilities of selling on the international market.

Even during the time that Cuba was assured of privileged access to Soviet and Eastern bloc markets, however, the island was unable to avoid completely the consequences of falls in world demand for sugar, with a consequent decline in prices. This trend intensified between 1984 and 1987 especially. More importantly, Cuba was locked into producing for a few countries, the USSR and the Eastern European states, whose decision to buy Cuban sugar was not a result of market demands. Therefore, the collapse of the

Eastern bloc socialist states has meant an end to Cuba's special deals – especially sugar for oil – and exposed Cuban sugar to the vagaries of international demand for a product whose price is falling as demand declines due to sugar substitutes and changes in European and US eating patterns. So while concentrating on sugar seemed a good idea in the 1960s and 1970s, the wisdom of that decision today is more questionable.

Agriculture currently employs about 20 per cent of the workforce. As well as sugar, Cuba produces small amounts of coffee, potatoes, rice, dairy foods, livestock and fish, and tobacco and citrus fruits, which formed part of a drive to diversify exports in the 1980s, a policy of limited success until 1989. Some of these products were produced within the small private sector, which achieved a higher output per hectare than the state sector. However, the Cuban regime has only ever expressed a marginal interest in encouraging the private sector in agriculture. Government initiatives to stimulate the private sector and encourage a limited internal market in agricultural goods, which began in the late 1970s, came to an end by the mid-1980s. Decisions about the role of the private sector in the economy have been motivated less by production levels and more by the ideological perceptions of policy-makers and international alliances. But in any case, encouraging the private sector would have had only a peripheral effect on Cuban agriculture because sugar remained the mainstay of the export sector; it is this fact which has led to Cuba's present-day vulnerability. Overall, the revolution led to better and more efficient production, to better health and safety and improved living standards for sugar workers, but it has not ended the island's dependence on one crop, the value of which is determined by external demand.

Cuba returned to sugar in the 1960s without completely abandoning industrialization as a complementary strategy. During the 1970s, industrial planning once again became an important objective. This time, however, industrialization was linked to the agricultural needs of the economy: for example, emphasis was placed on producing agricultural machinery and processing agricultural products. Rather than replacing agriculture, industry was now meant to complement it. By the mid-1980s, the industrial sector employed around 45 per cent of the economically active population and accounted for around 43 per cent of Cuba's gross social product. The early 1980s also witnessed the expansion of some heavy industrial plants, such as steel, and the growth of light industry producing consumer goods. Possibilities for further expansion proved limited, however, because growth was determined by Soviet aid, investment and oil. So by 1987 growth was slowing and by 1989 the falls in output were huge. Once again, Cuba's development was curtailed by external vulnerability.

The privileged relationship between Cuba and the USSR ended in 1990–1, but, so far, commercial ties have survived. An agreement signed in 1991 meant that Russia imports sugar at around the price established in the Lomé Convention, less than earlier agreements and less than the costs of sugar production inside Russia. Nickel and citrus fruits are priced in the agreement according to the international market. The loss of oil proved most detrimental to Cuba and in 1992 a further agreement was signed offering oil to Cuba for sugar. Other agreements were signed with the remaining countries of the *Confederation of Independent States* (CIS) with Cuban exports priced at world market prices. The greatest vulnerability resulting from the loss of the agreements, however, is not the fall in prices as such but the collapse of the trading system in which Cuba operated and the absence of another structure in which the island can function.

The revolution's greatest success has been in the struggle against poverty. Welfare spending was a government priority through the 1960s and 1970s. Even in the early 1980s, when a combination of external debt, low sugar prices and increasing oil prices laid the foundations for Cuba's current problems, welfare spending was maintained. The resources generated by sugar were consistently used to allow the state to intervene on behalf of those sectors which were benefiting least from the pre-1959 market economy. However, government spending was shaped by the need to satisfy basic rights – health, housing etc. – rather than consumption. Improvements in the quality of life in Cuba were startling. Ninety-four per cent of all workers were brought into the state sector, which meant a guaranteed income, health care, unemployment benefit and a state pension. Life expectancy rose to 71.8 years. Infant mortality fell to 19.6 per thousand live births, comparable to Costa Rica, and the availability of hospital beds and doctors was higher than in Costa Rica by the late 1980s (Mesa-Lago and Diaz-Briquets 1988). Illiteracy, which was officially 24 per cent before the revolution but estimated at 50 per cent in the poorest provinces, was reduced to

4 per cent by 1979. An estimated 10,000 schools were built in 1959 alone. Land speculation was ended and vacant lots of land were sold for houses, while households also benefited from low-cost loans and energy tariffs. The Economic Commission for Latin America (ECLA) concluded that the social reforms improved the living standards not only of the poorest but also of middle income groups (Mesa-Lago and Diaz-Briquets 1988). However, by the beginning of the 1990s, the loss of international support and the tightening of the US blockade through the Torricelli Amendment were proving disastrous for Cuba, with severe reductions in living standards, food and petrol rationing and an increase in preventable diseases associated with poverty and undernourishment.

The Economic Policies of Revolutionary Nicaragua

While the economic policies of revolutionary Cuba were circumscribed by the weight of history and by sugar, on the one hand, and international relations and the Cold War on the other, Sandinista economic policies were caught between the need for economic reconstruction and a war economy, and dependence on export agricultural products in which Nicaragua exercised no comparative advantage of any sort. In contrast to Cuba, the Sandinistas chose to promote a mixed economy, though the revolutionary government retained a similar commitment to boosting living standards. As we shall see, however, their successes were considerably less.

Unlike the 26th of July Movement in Cuba, the Sandinistas came to power after a long and destructive war. Material damage was sustained in the course of the revolutionary insurrection in the order of 520 million dollars, and just as important, the harvest of 1979–80, which would have generated much-needed foreign exchange, was severely damaged. GDP had fallen in 1979 by 30 per cent in relation to 1977. But the war had only exacerbated the problems of an economy which was one of the most sluggish in the region. The dictator Somoza had increased the external debt and the public sector deficit in his final years which intensified the problems of underdevelopment. At the same time, the Sandinistas came to power on the eve of the worst recession in Latin America since the 1930s, and were soon to find themselves facing a US-backed military threat from the counter-revolutionaries, the '*Contras*'.

The economic policies of the revolution must therefore be assessed within the context of these unprecedented difficulties.

The first measures adopted by the revolutionary Junta on coming to power in 1979 were directed at economic reactivation. The aim was to recover the productivity levels existing prior to the final insurrection. In this limited sense, the policies were successful. GDP rose by 4.5 per cent in 1980 and 5.4 per cent in 1981. Inflation went down from 48 per cent to 23 per cent between 1979 and 1982. But as export prices fell in the early 1980s, the government began to create a new framework for production, based on the principles of agrarian reform and the mixed economy. This new, more radical, orientation was possible because of the divisions in the revolutionary Junta. In 1980 the *Frente Sandinista de Liberación Nacional* (FSLN) established control over the government, alienating the moderate forces which had originally supported the revolution.

The key to the new economic policy was the mixed economy. The FSLN adopted this strategy because, ideologically, the Sandinistas rejected the idea of a monolithic centralizing state; and also for the practical reason that it appeared to offer the best guarantees for increasing production with a minimum of disruption through reorganization. The role envisaged for the state was two-fold: to restructure the economy so as to reduce dependence on exporting primary goods; and to redistribute income in favour of low income groups. Creating a state sector in the economy, known as the *Area de Propiedad Popular*, was initially easier than might have been anticipated because of the substantial personal holdings of the Somoza family and their close collaborators, which were expropriated in July 1979. This was followed by the nationalization of the financial system and foreign trade, thereby bringing domestic and foreign currency flows under state control, and then by the nationalization of forestry and fishing industries. By 1980, the state sector accounted for 18 per cent of total agricultural production and 100 per cent of mining, banking and insurance (Ruccio 1987). In 1982, transport and distribution of basic goods were brought into the state sector and the basic contours of the state holdings were completed, totalling around 40 per cent of GDP.

It was clear from the start that industrialization was not a viable strategy for the revolution in Nicaragua. The FSLN inherited a small and weak industrial base, mainly assembling goods for the home market. Although the urban population was relatively large, it was engaged mostly in commerce and services. Therefore, although the Sandinistas took some industrial holdings into the state sector, industry was never regarded as priority. Instead, the overall economic strategy stressed agriculture, especially the external sector. Combined with the difficulties of obtaining spare parts because of the US blockade, credit problems, deinvestment and a slump in consumer spending, industrial production contracted through the 1980s. Industry's contribution to GDP fell from 23.4 per cent in 1978 to 15.8 per cent in 1988.

Agriculture, then, remained the main economic activity of the country and, significantly, the agro-export sector (coffee, sugar, bananas, cotton and cattle) remained outside the state. None the less, the Sandinistas did promote agrarian reform, redistributing in total more than one million hectares of land. The aim of the reform was to increase production for internal consumption. The policies were relatively successful in that food production increased, unlike production for export, at least in the early years of the revolution (Table 6.1). There were three stages to the reform: 1979–81, when the main emphasis was on collective agriculture, 1981–4, when

Table 6.1   Agricultural production in Nicaragua, 1977/78 and 1981/82

	1977/8	*1981/2*
Export crops		
Cotton	100	55
Coffee	100	112
Sugar cane	100	106
Bananas	100	73
Cattle	100	70
Domestic		
Corn	100	104
Beans	100	119
Rice	100	182
Pigs	100	158
Chickens	100	268
Eggs	100	348
Cooking oil	100	143
Pasteurized milk	100	187

Source: Dunkerley, 1988: 302.

cooperatives were encouraged, and 1985–90, when attention was paid to the needs of small peasant farmers. The Sandinistas' relationship with the landless labourers and poor peasants who make up 70 per cent of Nicaragua's rural dwellers, was at times contradictory and undirected, with the government curbing land invasions by peasants demanding access to land, especially up to 1981. This was because the government expressly committed itself to maintaining the export sector. Vilas suggests it was also a reflection of the social base of *Sandinismo* which was essentially urban, with links to the rural poor much weaker (Vilas 1989).

The first agrarian reform collectivized the holdings of the Somoza family, amounting to around 18 per cent of agricultural land. It also included a package of incentives for large and medium-sized farmers to increase output, including low taxes and cheap credit. The second reform, dating from 1981, led to the formation of agrarian cooperatives, which was more in line with the peasant demands. In order to provide land for the cooperatives, abandoned, idle and under-utilized land was expropriated, though efficiently farmed land in private hands remained untouched. The new cooperatives were given preferential access to credit with the aim of stimulating grain and food production for internal consumption. The reform of 1985 signified, however, a change in focus because it concentrated on the promotion of individual peasant farms over collectives. The policy shift was motivated by practical reasons: the *Contra* war had displaced over a quarter of million peasants, who now needed new land so as not to increase the numbers of unemployed in the cities. The reform also responded to land hunger in the richest provinces (Masaya, Carazo, Granada and Rivas) where little land was underutilized or idle. In 1985, a reformed sector of 5,000 hectares was created by expropriating large landowners who were offered land in Leon in exchange. The law still recognized private property, though, but only where owners accepted their responsibility to produce as efficiently as possible (Table 6.2). None the less it marked a clear commitment on the part of the government to a gradual reduction in large private holdings in favour of medium and small farmers.

The sweep of the agrarian reform was limited by the government's decision to keep the export sector in private hands, reflecting Sandinista commitment to the mixed economy. As the revolution progressed and the political situation inside the country polarized,

Table 6.2   Land ownership in Nicaragua (% of land owned)

Owner	1978	1981	1984	1986
Large private	35	18	13	11
Medium private	46	43	43	43
Small private*	18	19	25	28
State	0	20	19	18

*includes cooperatives.

Note: Large estates are classified as those over 500mz or 350 hectares; medium as between 50 and 500mz, and small as under 50 mz.

Source: Close, 1988: 98.

this was to prove the Achilles' heel in the government's development policies. Unlike the mixed economy of Western Europe, which operates in a context in which the owners of property enjoy unrestricted political rights, the Sandinista mixed economy was based on the exclusion of the bourgeoisie from political power. Yet the economic policies depended for success upon the collaboration of private capital. Political and social policies were to be more radical than economic policies, with the result that the Sandinistas failed to allay the fears of the bourgeoisie or to allow them political power, while trying to reassure them that their right to accumulate capital would remain essentially untouched (Weeks 1987b). The FSLN assumed that private capital would continue to invest and produce, and with this in mind, policy – on taxation for example – was cautious. Producers, especially in the agro-export sector, were given preferential access to dollars and credit. Sandinista plans for economic growth depended on the agrarian sector to provide the bulk of the country's exports and foreign exchange. Yet the policy failed and by the mid-1980s the bourgeoisie was de-investing. Weeks sustains that the policy was untenable from the beginning, for political reasons, in that Nicaragua's propertied classes were excessively dependent culturally on the US and engaged in competition with the Sandinistas not for profit but rather for power and control of the state (Weeks 1987). Certainly it is interesting to note that Sandinista relations with multinational companies (Exxon, Royal Dutch Shell and Texaco in particular) were less conflictive than with domestic producers, indicating that the economic conditions of production allowed for private profits.

The failure of the private sector to respond to Sandinista incentives lies at the heart of the collapse of Nicaragua's economy in the 1980s (coupled of course with the costs of the war). It contributed to the massive balance of payments deficit which built up at the end of the 1980s. The Sandinistas continued to try and encourage private production by economic inducements. In order to avoid squeezing high income groups, therefore, the government raised credit abroad. This meant increasing foreign indebtedness, with the result that Nicaragua achieved the distinction of having the highest debt in Central America. Consequently there was a shift to austerity policies after 1985, to the detriment of the short-term interests of a variety of social groups, many of which were Sandinista supporters, increasing tensions between the state and society.

One area which was outside the control of the market was the satisfaction of basic needs. FSLN policy included the introduction of a 'social wage', that is non-cash social benefits, social services, health and education in particular, and the introduction of food subsidies. After 1979, the government extended pension and social security rights to cover twice as many people as in 1979. But these policies were affected, severely in some cases, by the shift to austerity. In addition, the revolution had been unable to solve some of Nicaragua's social and economic problems because the pressing demands of the war combined with the recession of the 1980s turned government attention towards survival. Urban unemployment never fell below 20 per cent, the informal sector remained large, with informal workers for the most part unprotected by the new legislation and conditions of work uncontrolled.

The austerity measures – reduction of state investment, wage increase freezes, devaluation, etc. – were intensified after 1986 but were unable to stem the precipitous decline of the economy in the face of US hostility, civil war and de-investment. The costs of the US-backed war in particular were too great to be mitigated by government policy. In 1988 Nicaragua was close to economic collapse, with inflation running at 36,000 per cent, an unserviced external debt, an absence of new credit, and plummeting exports. Unemployment rose, especially in urban areas, and basic necessities were in short supply. Industrial production fell by 20 per cent in 1989. Peace was the only route to economic stability; in February 1990, Violeta Chamorro was elected into office on behalf of the *Union Nacional de Oposición* (UNO) because of a belief that the

Sandinistas were unable to negotiate an end to the *Contra* war. In sum, then, how can we account for the collapse of the Sandinista economy? While the price of the war and US aggression can scarcely be exaggerated, we must also recognize as causal factors the poor economic base which the new regime inherited, the recession of the 1980s, and errors in economic strategy, which led the regime to promote a mixed economy which was unable to guarantee even the maintenance of 1979 levels of production. Were there alternatives? Hardly any at all. Whatever theoretical options the Sandinistas could have chosen, the implementation of an alternative economic strategy required external backing, which in the 1980s was unavailable.

The Economic Policies of Revolutionary Grenada

The revolution of 1979 on the tiny island of Grenada brought the People's Revolutionary Government (PRG) to power, dominated by the New Jewel Movement (NJM). Jewel stood for Joint Endeavour for Welfare, Education and Liberation, which were the stated goals of the revolutionary movement. The island has a population of less than 100,000 and possessed one of the lowest per capita incomes of the region. Unemployment was around 20 per cent and emigration was high, running at a rate of 2.5 per cent a year. None the less, the economy was not, strictly speaking, in a critical situation. The 1970s had witnessed a slow process of growth and the economy was rather more diversified than other Caribbean islands, with nutmeg, cocoa and bananas representing the main exports. And despite large numbers of small and uneconomic holdings in the countryside, there was little evidence of widespread land hunger or of a radical peasantry pushing for reform. Together, these factors, so different from Cuba or Nicaragua, account for the fact that the PRG presided over a process of reform of capitalist economic structures, rather than attempting to introduce a socialist model of political economy. US hostility to the revolution did not mean particularly harsh treatment from international lending agencies, in contrast to Nicaragua. In fact, the IMF approved a loan to Grenada just months before the US invasion in 1983 toppled the divided revolutionary government.

The starting point for the design of PRG economic policy was the need to relieve poverty on the island. According to Prime Minister

Maurice Bishop, the causes of poverty in Grenada lay not in the smallness of the economy, but rather in the island's dependence. Formally independent from Britain in 1974, the island's economy remained dependent upon the powerful capitalist states which controlled Grenada's exports and determined the prices of imports – food, agricultural inputs and manufactures. Policy was therefore aimed at increasing food output, diversifying imports, promoting some industrial development and creating a 'new' kind of tourism, to reduce the island's dependence. In all of these areas, the state was envisaged playing an important role.

As in Nicaragua, the role of the state was central to policy-making within the overall context of a mixed economy. But, in Nicaragua, the mixed economy was still viewed by the Sandinistas as the first step to a transition to socialism, whereas the approach of the PRG was overtly populist (Thorndike 1985). Bishop explicitly acknowledged the reformist nature of government policies. He argued that the revolution was 'national-democratic, anti–imperialist', and not 'socialist'. 'It is obvious that we do not have a socialist revolution', he added, 'and it is precisely due to (1) the low level of development of the productive process . . . and (2) our working class is small and too underdeveloped politically' (Whitehead 1990: 356). The more orthodox left in the NJM was dissatisfied with the reformist nature of government policies and the issue was to become one of the major factors in the internal divisions within the Central Committee of the NJM which led to the revolution's collapse and created the conditions for the US invasion. In Grenada, ideological conflict, rather than economic collapse, laid the foundations for the defeat of the revolution.

Nevertheless, despite internal party criticism, Bishop persisted with the mixed economy approach. According to Bishop's major policy speech, the *Line of March* of 1982, the state sector, most of which had been inherited from the previous Gairy government, was to be dominant, but was to operate on competitive lines and was to be compatible with the small bourgeoisie. In 1979, before the PRG reforms, the state owned 10 per cent of land, which was used to grow export crops, and 50 per cent of all public utilities. The PRG increased the size of the public sector through the nationalization of the four major banks, took more land into state ownership to bring the figure to 25 per cent of land, nationalized the properties of the deposed leader Eric Gairy, and bought and refurbished the Holiday Inn, to be the prototype of the new tourist industry.

The role of the state was to reorganize economic activity through planning, improve production techniques and to take charge of marketing produce. The state was also to finance projects of economic reconstruction which required high levels of investment – tourist infrastructure and the ill-fated new airport, which aroused the suspicions and resentment of the US because of Cuban participation in the project, fell into this category. The idea was less that the state would dominate the economy as that it would impose a rationale and a culture of efficiency within the economy. Bishop outlined a series of five-year plans for state activity in the *Line of March* : the first was to push the island from primary exports and tourism, to mechanization and industrialization of agriculture, to the final stage of economic diversification. Of course, none of these proposals could be implemented because of the 1983 invasion.

The four-and-a-half years that the revolution lasted are too few to analyse the economic policies in any definitive way. We should note the activities of the Marketing and National Importing Board as a success in controlling the process of basic commodities, including drugs and hospital supplies, fertilizers, powdered milk and cooking oil (Thorndyke 1985). Politically, however, the very success of the state in this area increased the antagonism of the private sector, whose profits were low in 1980 and 1981. The PRG tried to respond to the needs of private enterprise and introduced further economic incentives for private industry. This policy appeared to be successful, with private activity growing more dynamic in 1982. But the upturn was only partial and not sufficient to guarantee anything more than passive acceptance on the part of the business community towards the government. This became clear in the attitudes of private capital towards the US invasion. And not all public sector bodies were as efficient as the Marketing and National Importing Board. The PRG acknowledged that most state industries were undercapitalized and lost money and that the small industries set up by the government generated net losses. This is not surprising in the first stage of a major economic reorganization. How the revolution would have addressed these problems in the long term is, unfortunately, a matter of only conjecture.

It is interesting to note that, given the fact that land concentration is high on the island, the land issue was never particularly important for the PRG, in contrast to both Nicaragua and Cuba. Few demands were made by the rural population on the government. Rather than transforming the structures of production, therefore, the PRG concentrated on raising the production levels of export crops. One way was through bringing idle land into cultivation. The Land Utilization Act allowed for the expropriation of idle land and its redistribution through the Land Reform Commission to unemployed young people who were interested in setting themselves up as small farmers. Not surprisingly, with little formal training in agriculture or management, the productivity of this reformed sector was poor.

Like Nicaragua, the Grenadian export economy suffered considerably from the fall in commodity prices in the early 1980s. While the government successfully pushed up the output of nutmeg, for example, during 1980–3, from 3.35 million pounds to 5.34 million pounds, export earnings from nutmeg remained almost the same: 3.16 million dollars in 1980 to 3.25 million dollars in 1983. Cocoa was also affected by a fall in international prices. But on the positive side, production for internal consumption increased and self-sufficiency in food production rose from 69.4 per cent to 72.5 per cent. And the small-scale development projects that the PRG backed – for example, small rural cooperatives – offered a real alternative in terms of meeting people's needs for basic necessities and employment. Although they generated small profits, they constituted an important development initiative for local communities. The director of one small women's fruit cooperative defended cooperative farming in the following way:

> you're saying to farmers that you're creating an alternative for farmers to produce things that do not have to be exported . . . they have an alternative to foreign exchange with money being put directly into the pockets of the very small farmers . . . you don't have to walk into a rural community and put down a massive industrial plant . . . you can . . . allow people to take decisions and make decisions and discuss their own problems and find solutions. (Deere *et al.* 1990: 111)

As in Cuba and Nicaragua, the PRG committed itself to raising living standards, and in the short time the revolution survived, its achievements were remarkable (Payne, Sutton and Thorndyke

1984). The policies to improve living standards were underpinned by a conviction that poverty fostered dependency, which operated as an obstacle to development and encouraged emigration. Education was the first priority, absorbing 22 per cent of the 1982–3 budget, followed by health, which accounted for 14 per cent. The idea behind the educational reforms was not simply to increase access to formal education but to transform cultural assumptions implicit in the system in a way which would increase national dignity. For example, Creole, spoken by many Grenadians especially in the countryside, was recognized alongside English in schools. The importance of adult education was also stressed.

The revolution also expressed strong support for policies that would reduce gender inequalities. The PRG went further than either Nicaragua or Cuba in this area, and created a separate Ministry for Women which was prominent in trying to extend job opportunities and create infrastructure – daycare, etc. – which would enable poor women to enter the formal labour force. Maternity leave was created for the first time in 1980. Behind the different approach to gender issues on Grenada lies a very different social and cultural reality: women in Grenada have long assumed the roles of principal earners in the family unit due to the prevalence of female-headed families and male emigration.

Given Grenada's small industrial base, manufacturing under the PRG was bound to remain weak. Private investment was low, and fell during the period of PRG government. Yet the PRG was unwilling for political reasons to increase production through an expansion of the state sector for fear of attracting more international hostility than already existed. The exception to this was to be the tourist industry which the PRG decided to push strongly. Considerable hopes were placed on expanding the economy through increasing receipts from tourism. Unfortunately, income from tourism fell steadily throughout the period. This occurred for a number of reasons. First, though the PRG decided to prioritize the industry, many political leaders displayed an ambivalent attitude towards an industry which, beyond all doubt, reinforced a series of negative stereotypes about Caribbean culture and was vividly indicative of the dependence of the island on the spending power of North Americans and Europeans. Bad publicity about the revolution in the US made the situation worse and led to a fall in the number of US visitors. But the real problem was that tourism in

Grenada was less competitive than in other islands such as St Lucia because of poor infrastructure on the island. This led to the decision to build a new airport so tourists could arrive directly. The project required international funding which was provided in part by Cuba, the revolution's most important ally. This collaboration brought the PRG into a head-on conflict with Washington, who argued that the airport would be used by the Cubans for military purposes and therefore constituted a threat to US security. It was to serve as the justification behind the invasion.

Revolutions and External Relations

Cuba, Nicaragua and Grenada are small, vulnerable societies whose history has been shaped by the needs of great powers. Today their economies depend upon external trade in primary commodities. Their export sectors have become specialized over time in accordance with the external linkages. Both external cooperation and a new pattern of foreign relations were therefore perceived as fundamental for the success of the revolutions in all three cases.

Creating a new pattern of external relations has in all three cases meant conflict with the US. The reasons for this are many. Revolutions bring into question the political, economic and cultural hegemony of the US in the region, and it is only to be expected that the US will resist any decline in its influence in the Caribbean. The external relations of revolutionary regimes must therefore seek to limit the potential damage done by US hostility as well as try to use aid from abroad, where it can be obtained, to foster equitable development. Cuba, Nicaragua and Grenada sought, at least in the first instance, to construct 'peripheral autonomy' (Jaguaribe 1979). This refers to the process by which states which lie within a geographical area that the US has defined as vital for its own national security none the less try and establish autonomous external relations. In their search for peripheral autonomy, the three revolutions sought support in different degrees from the USSR until its disappearance, and from Western Europe, Latin America and the Non-Aligned Movement. The difficulties of this task were increased by the international climate of the period 1960–90. The Cold War determined the contours of the international system and the three states were vulnerable to the pressures of superpower politics.

Cuba

Cuba was the first revolutionary state in the Americas; the revolution occurred at the height of the Cold War. Cuba's external relations have been decided by these two facts. Despite an early attempt to court support from Washington, including visits from Castro to the US in the months following the successful march on Havana, in April and May 1959, relations with the US soured quickly. By the summer of 1960, the US had eliminated Cuba's sugar quota, a prelude to the general economic embargo which was to follow, and Castro had expropriated all US property on the island, to be followed by the nationalization of the economy in October 1960. The US broke off diplomatic relations in January 1961 and attempted to overthrow Castro in the infamous Bay of Pigs invasion in that year. The attempt failed, but illustrated the vulnerability of the revolution and prompted further radicalization, with Castro declaring himself Marxist-Leninist in December 1961, leading to closer ties between the island and the USSR. Soviet support at this point probably guaranteed the survival of the regime, but made the revolution dependent on Soviet assistance.

Soviet aid, especially in the economic field, was slower to materialize than is often realized. The results of Cuba's 'moral incentive' approach to economic planning had proved disappointing, symbolized by the failure of the attempt to harvest 10 million tons of sugar in 1970, and this fact formed the backdrop to closer ties which were based on Cuban accommodation to Soviet-style development. It was not really until the second decade of the revolution that Cuba adopted the Soviet system of planning, followed by the first five-year plan in 1975. Cuba was admitted to the Council for Mutual Economic Assistance (COMECON) in 1972, which led to an intensification of trade with Eastern bloc countries. Despite rising output throughout the 1970s and early 1980s, integration into the Eastern bloc did not prove a perfect solution for the island. Economic development was hampered by the incompatibility of Soviet spare parts and machinery with the existing economic infrastructure and by the fact that Cuba was awarded low priority in trade terms by COMECON. Partly to offset these difficulties, Cuba tried to diversify its trade by building links with Western Europe and Japan.

The effects of Cuba's relationship with the USSR has been the source of intense debate, particularly the question of whether it can be termed a 'dependent' relationship. The centre of the debate was the significance of the Cuban–Soviet agreements. The agreements covered loans, trade credits, and technical assistance, and promised markets for sugar and nickel. It is difficult to establish exactly how much the agreements cost the USSR partly because the debate about dependency and 'sovietization' became charged with ideological vehemence. One-sided views were common in the 1970s and 1980s on both sides of the debate (F. Fitzgerald 1978; Binns and Gonzalez 1980; MacEwan 1981).

According to Leogrande, Cuba remained dependent on the USSR, though to a lesser degree than it had been on the US before the revolution (Leogrande 1979). On the other hand, Brundenius dismissed the notion that dependency can be measured on a sliding scale and argued that Cuba's relationship with the USSR was not dependent at all because it was not exploitative, the core meaning of the term. He concluded that there was a reduction in trade dependency after 1970 and pointed to the diversification of the Cuban economy which took place with Soviet assistance (Brundenius 1984). The USSR also bought Cuban sugar in guaranteed quantities and at assured prices, while paying in convertible currency for sugar bought outside the agreement. Cuba was also sometimes able to sell sugar from the Soviet quota on the open market when prices were higher than in the agreement. The relationship undoubtedly saved Cuba from the vulnerability which would have otherwise resulted from selling sugar at unstable international prices during this period.

On the other hand, the negative aspects of the relationship cannot be ignored. Apart from encouraging a political model of central control and one-party dominance, the deal also had some negative side-effects economically. It perpetuated reliance on sugar through to the present day, though international demand has been steadily contracting since the 1960s because of increases in global production, especially from within Europe, and the rise of sugar substitutes. For Mesa-Lago, integration into COMECON constrained Cuban development and he warned somewhat prophetically that 'the USSR has the capacity to cut supply off to the island of virtually all oil, most capital, foodstuffs and raw materials, about one-third of basic capital and intermediate goods and probably all weaponry' (Mesa-Lago 1981).

What measures could Cuba have taken in the past to improve the situation the island is in today? Diversify external relations beyond the USSR and COMECON is the obvious answer, but Cuba *tried* to promote closer ties with countries beyond the Eastern bloc and the result was overall a failure. The US blockade was observed by most Western countries until the 1970s, and Cuba's pro-Europe policies, including offering trading agreements and looking for credit and the creation of mixed enterprises between the Cuban state and private European capital, have been of very limited impact. Cuba has complained since the 1980s of the European Union's protectionism and of the fact that the members of Lomé receive preferential access to European markets in detriment to other developing countries.

A second strategy was to try and rebuild bridges with Latin America, broken by the support of the Organization of American States (OAS) for the US position following the Cuban revolution. In 1986, Cuba became an observer in the *Asociación Latinoamericana de Integración* (Latin American Integration Association – ALADI) and throughout the 1980s ties deepened with Latin America. Cuba tried to reduce its oil dependency on the USSR by importing petroleum from Venezuela and Mexico in 1978, 1983 and 1991, though the agreements were for a very small percentage of Cuba's needs. It could be argued, therefore, that the limitations on Cuban development, now painfully evident, are less the result of sovietization, and rather the structural limitations which result from being a small agro-exporting peripheral state, exacerbated by a fall in international demand for the main exchange-earning commodity, and intensified by oil dependence. The real criticism of Cuba's foreign policy since the revolution is that it masked these problems without solving them. The relationship with the USSR allowed the Cuban leadership to avoid facing the most pressing problems of underdevelopment but at the expense of leaving unchanged Cuba's market concentration.

Nicaragua

The external relations of Nicaragua after 1979 were determined by the decision of the revolutionary government to diversify diplomatic and commercial relations, partly as the key to economic growth and partly to reduce dependence on the US; and the reassertion of US hegemony under President Reagan in the early 1980s, which was to culminate in the *Contra* war, financed from Washington against the revolution. Nicaraguan foreign policy thus aimed at constructing a viable pattern of economic and political external relations in a war situation with the idea of limiting the impact of the war on the economy as far as possible. Sandinista foreign policy became in the process, in the words of the Sandinista *comandante*, Tomás Borge, 'an instrument of survival' (Yopo 1987). The Sandinistas emphasized external diversification, which was in fact the only possible strategy after the US blockade was decreed. In particular, they needed new markets, alternative sources of military supplies, industrial and technological goods, credit and diplomatic support. The Sandinistas sought to intensify relations with Western Europe, the Eastern bloc countries, Japan and the rest of Latin America and the Caribbean. They were, however, to be only partially successful.

The core problem was vehement opposition from the US. The Sandinistas had inherited an economy particularly dependent on the US which made diversification in some areas of the economy difficult in the short term. And diversification of external markets could not in any case counterbalance the impact of US hostility and of the US-financed war, the impact of which is difficult to exaggerate. The most direct effects were felt at the macroeconomic level: the loss of primary products, the collapse of forestry, fishing and mining, the impossibility of picking coffee harvests and of maintaining viable agricultural enterprises in the areas affected by the fighting. To all of this, we have to add the costs of direct structural damage, of the financial aggression on the part of the US which blocked international loans, of the trade embargo decreed in 1985 and the impact of having to prioritize defence spending over social reform inside Nicaragua in order to fight the war. The US also mined Nicaraguan ports in 1984, an act which was condemned by the International Court of Justice in the Hague. By 1989, the contra war was absorbing 50 per cent of government expenditure. According to some estimates, had it not been for the war, the Nicaraguan economy would have functioned with a healthy rate of growth and without serious imbalances throughout the 1980s (E. V. K. Fitzgerald 1987).

In Western Europe, where Nicaragua had placed most hopes and where the size of the European Union (EU) market created greatest expectations, the response to Nicaragua was mixed. West European aid to the revolution peaked in 1981 and thereafter declined, though the EU continued to support dialogue and a negotiated solution to the wars in Central America throughout the 1980s. After 1981 especially, European assistance was patchy. Credits and loans from Western Europe constituted only 11.6 per cent of the total of Nicaraguan multilateral and bilateral finance between 1979 and 1985, a figure surpassed by credits from other Latin American/ Caribbean countries who provided collectively 23.1 per cent during the same period, despite the continental recession (Stahler-Sholk 1987). Nevertheless, by 1988, 70 per cent of economic aid to Nicaragua was being provided by Eastern Europe. West European–Nicaraguan trade presented a slightly happier picture, with Europe taking 55 per cent of Nicaraguan exports up to 1986 and 90 of her coffee exports, with Spain, West Germany and France figuring as particularly important trading partners.

West European military assistance followed a similar pattern. In the early years of the revolution, European sympathies meant that Europe became an important supplier of arms; in 1981, for example, France sold the Sandinistas 15 million dollars worth of armaments. By 1985, Western Europe was reluctant to continue this policy, partly due to US pressure against the policy which was by now intense, and partly because of the shift rightwards in European politics, which meant that European governments were more prepared to accept that view that it was the radicalization of the Nicaraguan revolution which was provoking the Central American crisis.

Economic links were established also with Latin American countries, some of whom provided important diplomatic legitimation for the revolution. The Contadora group (Panama, Mexico, Venezuela and Colombia) with the *Grupo de Apoyo* (Brazil, Argentina, Uruguay and Peru) insisted on the need to solve the Central American crisis through diplomatic means without extra-regional (that is, the US) interference, which was important for Nicaragua. Mexico and Venezuela provided oil on concessionary terms, Venezuela up to 1982 and Mexico until 1984, reportedly stopping as a result of IMF pressure (Stahler-Sholk 1987). Relations with Cuba were also close, with economic aid totalling 286 million dollars during 1979–82. Cuba also provided industrial aid, development assistance, especially in the fields of health and education, and military aid until 1988. There was some response too from other countries. Libya provided a one-off loan of 100 million dollars in 1981, and trade links were established with Algeria, Iran and Japan. Cotton found a major outlet in Japan. Cotton sold to Japan increased from 38 per cent of total Nicaraguan cotton sold abroad in 1978 to 44 per cent in 1982 to 60 per cent in 1985.

As economic cooperation from Western Europe and Latin America waned in the mid-1980s, Nicaragua was forced to lean more and more on the Eastern bloc countries. A repeat of the aid package on the scale of Soviet assistance to Cuba, however, was never a possibility, nor indeed an aim of Nicaraguan policy. Nevertheless, after 1985, oil was provided almost exclusively from the USSR. Imports and development projects, including the setting up of textile factories and a deep-water harbour project on the Atlantic coast, increased after 1985. Soviet military aid, the most contentious area of cooperation, became more significant in the absence of supplies from Western Europe and the intensification of the *Contra* war. By 1989, the total of Soviet economic and military aid was estimated at 3,000 million dollars. But there is no evidence to suggest that this aid increased Soviet influence over internal political models or other areas of foreign policy.

Revolutionary Nicaragua tried to limit the damage that US hostility wreaked on her development prospects by pursuing diversification of external linkages. In contrast to Cuba, which became more and more integrated into an alternative trading bloc, Nicaragua tried to foster relations with Western Europe, Latin America, Japan and non-aligned countries. Up until 1985, the policy was relatively successful, but in the second half of the revolution, the combined effects of US pressure on allied governments and the stepping up of the *Contra* war substantially weakened Nicaragua's productive base while external aid from Western countries dropped significantly. These events serve to emphasize the difficulties which face societies which embark upon the task of constructing alternative development patterns in the region.

Grenada

Independent only since 1974, small and poor, Grenada has been dependent on external economic and military aid since its independence from Britain. Not surprisingly, in view of its size and history, its dependence is even more marked than that of Nicaragua or Cuba. For the People's Revolutionary Government (PRG), therefore, the management of external relations was of utmost importance. One analyst described the attempted transition in Grenada as 'socialism through external aid', such was the significance conceded to external cooperation (Pryor 1990). The New Jewel movement (NJM) argued that Grenada's underdevelopment could only be fully overcome within the context of a new system of international relations, conceding greater power and autonomy to primary-producing nations, but that, meanwhile, policies such as a non-aligned foreign policy, diversification of external markets, aid and imports should alleviate dependence. A close relationship with Cuba was of central importance to Grenada's revolutionary strategy, both as a regional ally and as an example of what could be achieved socially through the adoption of socialist policies. The PRG also tried, with noticeably less success, to court the support of the USSR. None the less, the US continued to assert that Grenada was on the road to 'becoming the second Soviet proxy in the Caribbean' (Payne 1990).

Cuba provided the most steady support, regionally and otherwise, to the Grenadian revolution. Aid from Cuba increased steadily during 1979–83. It included technical assistance in agriculture, education, health care and military support. By 1983 it was estimated at 500 dollars per capita – though with a population of only 100,000, this was not a huge amount (Whitehead 1990). The planned new airport in Port Salinas was only possible because of an agreement with Cuba to contribute 40 million dollars to the project, approximately half its total cost. Cuban advisers played an important role on the island, with 800 present when the US invaded. Not surprisingly, Cuba came to be seen by the PRG as its lifeline, especially in view of the hostility towards the revolution expressed by Washington after the election of President Reagan in 1980.

Unlike the FSLN, which successfully courted support for non-intervention from Latin American countries, the PRG was unable to assure itself of the support even of its closest neighbours in the Commonwealth Caribbean. Although the government moderated somewhat the ideological content of its discourse, with a view to neutralizing the opposition of regional governments, the other member states of CARICOM, whether for reasons of ideology or because of US pressure and the temptations of the Caribbean Basin Initiative (CBI) programme, did not offer regional solidarity to the PRG and rather supported the US invasion. Indeed, troops from Barbados and Jamaica actually participated in the invasion.

The experience of Grenada illustrates the limitations imposed from outside on policy-making by revolutionary governments in the region. Not large or important enough to attract any significant investment or diplomatic support from Western Europe and too radical to command the acceptance of the rest of CARICOM, the invasion of the island made little impact internationally. It did no damage to US–European relations even though Grenada is a member of the British Commonwealth. At the same time, Grenada discovered that the USSR was not prepared to back a second revolutionary state in the Caribbean. Cuba, its only real ally, and itself the victim of external aggression, was of course powerless to protect the PRG from invasion, especially after the murder of Maurice Bishop. More even than Nicaragua and Cuba, the room for manoeuvre in Grenada was always limited in the extreme.

Conclusion

The findings of this chapter paint a very sombre picture of the possibilities for radical change and transformation in the region. The three revolutions we have looked at have experienced external opposition and found real difficulties in designing alternative development programmes. Only Cuba partially escaped these problems – for a time – by tying its fortunes overwhelmingly to the USSR. In Nicaragua, where the collapse of the revolutionary economy was most severe, output declined, there were capital shortages, lack of investment, hyperinflation and shortages of basic necessities. Why did this happen? Are the policies adopted misguided and inadequate? Does the answer lie in the external vulnerability of these regimes? To sum up, we can identify four major reasons for the overall disappointing economic performance of revolutionary regimes in the region: first, the problems inherent in a transition from a capitalist system to production, to different forms of socialism; second, the difficulties of pursuing development and growth in small peripheral economies, where economic policies have been articulated historically in the interests of external forces, and which are subject to broad fluctuations in the international prices of their exports; third, the problems which arise from the internal opposition of the displaced political and economic elite, leading in some cases to counter-revolution; and finally, the difficulties of managing external relations, meaning trade, investment and aid, and relations with the US. Given the weight of these problems, it is perhaps less surprising that Cuba, Nicaragua and Grenada encountered such severe problems in constructing the new societies that they aimed at and more surprising that they achieved some limited successes in vital areas such as redistribution, health and education.

Revolutionary change and building socialism are not seen at the moment as the way forward to development and prosperity in the region, partly due to a general disorientation of the left throughout the region, as a result of domestic defeat and the collapse of the USSR. Cuba, Nicaragua and Grenada are not perceived by other states as models to follow. This is not only because of their association with Eastern bloc socialism or with economic collapse but also because all three revolutions failed to develop a political system which is participatory, democratic and internationally acceptable. This, along with economic development, is the challenge for the region's progressive movements in the future.

Conclusion: Is the Crisis Over?

In this book we have analysed the political and economic development, since the deepening of capitalism in the 1880s, of the countries which make up most of the Caribbean Basin (Central America and the insular Caribbean). We have discussed the legacy of the past on development patterns and examined the different development policies (export agriculture; models of industrialization; assembling for export etc.) that states have adopted to try and promote growth. We have also looked at the way radical alternatives in political economy – in Cuba, Nicaragua and Grenada – have operated. But throughout the region, whether governments adopted capitalist development models or tried to promote various forms of socialist planning, growth has been partial, unstable or skewed.

Even during the period of expansion in the 1960s and early 1970s, economic development was uneven, led to income concentration and contributed in many cases to social and political conflict. Throughout, we have noted the relationship between economic policies and political systems. That is, we have seen clearly that economic decisions are also political. Poverty in the region, therefore, has much to do with political conflict – with class and ethnicity as the main cleavages of national conflicts. All of this suggests that development, if it is to be sustainable and lead to equitable growth, must also include political reforms which redistribute power. But redistribution of power internally is not enough to promote development in the long term: changes internationally are required, which liberate the region from external dependence and excessive vulnerability. We have therefore located the causes of underdevelopment in the region in a combination of internal political factors which have allowed elites to plan development strategies exclusively in their own narrow class (and sometimes ethnic) interest and the force of history which has left the region on the periphery of the international system.

We have also emphasized the structural limitations of these small economies, highly vulnerable to external factors which have conditioned economics and politics. During the 1980s, most countries experienced recession and a deterioration in their socio-economic conditions *whatever* policies governments chose to implement. As a response to the recession, over the last few years, we have seen a new policy orientation emerge, based on liberalization of trade, export production and fiscal austerity. So far, these policies have slowed macroeconomic decline, but have not produced development in human terms.

What about the future? The countries of the region, as they go into the twenty-first century, face a series of crises which prevent the people of the region realizing their potential. Unless these problems are addressed, the region will continue to face deepening poverty for most of the population, *whatever* the macroeconomic situation, and thus potential political instability. This might take the shape of changeovers in governments; a militarization of politics; problems of insecurity and violence in cities; oppression of ethnic minorities; and localized conflicts.

There are three main aspects to the contemporary crisis: first, we can talk of a regional development crisis; second, a crisis within the political systems; and third, the external vulnerability of the region.

The 1980s have been called the 'lost decade' for all developing countries throughout the world. The international recession, falls in the prices of primary commodities, debt, conflict, the militarization of politics etc. all led to dramatic falls in per capita income, in foreign trade, in investment, employment, consumption and living standards. The rise in international interest rates, coupled with the fall in value of regional exports, meant that servicing the debt, for the members of the Central American Common Market for example, represented almost 40 per cent of exports by 1988. The negative tendencies of the 1980s remain the backdrop to policy-making today, and although the average rate of growth regionally has improved since 1991, the *Sistema Economico Latinamericano* (SELA) estimates an average of only 2 per cent annual growth until the mid-1990s at least. World Bank estimates predict growth for the 1990s at 1.3–2.0 per cent (SELA 1991a: 33; World Bank 1991: 3). Given rises in the population size, this means in effect a drop in the per capita product and 'the prospect of greater poverty, increased unemployment, sacrifices in consumption, a continued contraction in investment . . . the blocking of opportunities for progress in health and education, the persistence of environmental deterioration, and still further abandonment of policies for promoting welfare and social development' (SELA 1991a: 33). The point we are making here is that the sharp recession of the 1980s has ended but the development crisis, though it is no longer quite as fashionable to talk about it, has not gone away.

Regional governments, encouraged by international agencies, are currently embarking on a major reform of economic policies, one of the aims of which is to acquire new sources of capital investment. The new orientation includes export promotion; the development of 'non-traditional' industries and exports; and deregulation and reform of the state. As part of a drive to increase regional export performance, governments have adopted measures to promote liberalization of trade. With only a few exceptions (for example Costa Rica), the results so far in terms of increases in exports have been meagre and the social costs high.

The World Bank report of 1992, *Global Economic Prospects and the Developing Countries*, explains why there are legitimate reasons to doubt the success of the region's export performance. Without significant trade liberalization on the part of developed countries, trade liberalization by the developing countries will mean 'terms of trade losses because (as with primary commodities) the relative price of their manufacturing exports would decline' (World Bank 1992: 23). Additionally, in a global atmosphere of increased competitiveness between developing economies, Central America and the Caribbean is not well placed to compete. The industrial performance of the region is low and its percentage of global trade in industrial goods falling (SELA 1991b). As a result, the region continues to depend on primary exports for most of its foreign exchange.

The UN has concluded that the only way to see stable and sustainable development occur throughout the underdeveloped world as a whole is through a reform of the international system, given that the 'rules' of international exchange are unfair and benefit the developed countries to the detriment of the periphery. Within this overall framework, the poorest groups within peripheral societies pay the highest price. The changes recommended by the UN include reform of IMF policy, especially in terms of loans policy which at the moment reduces consumption and slows growth; reform of GATT in such a way as would weaken the protectionism of developed countries and open up markets for peripheral countries in agriculture and manufacturing especially; the introduction of regulatory mechanisms over multinational companies; reform of international aid policies; and a more equitable distribution of decision-making internationally to reflect the fact that over 70 per cent of the world's population live in underdeveloped countries while only 12 per cent live in the rich, industrialized countries which make up the 'Group of Seven' (US, Britain, Canada, Japan, France, Germany, Italy) (UN 1992: 168–75). Unfortunately, whatever internal policies the countries of the region adopt and whatever the nature of the political regime, until such a time as changes in this direction occur, it is unlikely that Central America and the Caribbean will experiences any permanent process of sustainable or equitable development.

For a region so dependent on external factors, then, the international environment is particularly important. How has Central America and the Caribbean been affected by the massive global transformation which is currently taking place in the international system? The end of the Cold War has meant an end to systemic polarization based on ideological antagonism and instead has brought a new emphasis on economic considerations and trade competition. This in turn is prompting the formation of large trading blocs – the completion of the internal market within the European Union and the formation of the North American Free Trade Association (NAFTA) between the US, Canada and Mexico, with the possibility of later cooperation with other 'big' Latin American economies, such as Venezuela and Chile. On the one hand, the end of superpower conflict could conceivably mean greater pluralism – in political models, choice of trading partners etc. – for the region, but it is unlikely that it will lead to greater autonomy for the states of the region.

The tendency towards regional blocs could be particularly detrimental for Central America and the Caribbean countries, which may find themselves excluded from their main export markets or at the very least facing sharper competition. CAR-ICOM members have already been identified as the principal losers of the completion of the European Union market (Stevens 1991). Worthy of note, too, is the fact the US remains as influential today in policy-making throughout the region as ever. But though the degree of influence over internal and external affairs remains almost unaltered, the issues in US–Caribbean relations have shifted somewhat. No longer dominated by the Cold War and the 'threat of another Cuba', relations with the US are now principally about trade, investment, democratization, narcotics and immigration. One effect of these changes within the international system at the regional level may be to stimulate moves towards integration. But whether regional integration can deal with the social and economic problems facing the region – including the demands for equitable and sustainable economic development – is more doubtful.

What of the political changes in the region? Paradoxically for some observers, the 1980s, while ushering in a development crisis on an unprecedented scale, also brought a trend towards greater political democratization. For the first time, the Spanish-speaking countries of the region appeared to be moving towards civilian governments, legitimated in elections and through party competition, a process which was already established in the English-speaking Caribbean. Only Haiti, where military dictatorship followed the overthrow of Aristide, and Cuba, where a one-party system remains in force, are the exceptions to this trend. None the less, democracy is fragile in the region, and at times merely cosmetic. For example, it is difficult to see Guatemala, where human rights abuses continue unchecked and uninvestigated by the state, in the same light as the consolidated democracy of Costa Rica or even Jamaica. And the new democracies have been installed in countries where huge social inequalities persist and where it is unlikely in the short term that these problems will be addressed in any meaningful way. We come back to this issue below. Let us just note here that democratization will always be difficult as long as the excessive power which the Armed Forces enjoy in many countries of the region remains unreformed. One indication of the power of the Armed Forces is military spending, and in Table C.1 we can see that it remains high, in Central America especially.

Democratization and the Region's Future

Latin America evinced an early tendency towards what appears to have since become a global trend: democratization. To what extent

Table C.1   Military spending (selected countries)

	Military budget as % of GDP		Military budget as % of social spending*	
	1960	*1990*	*1977*	*1990*
Costa Rica	1.2	0.5	8	4
Panama	0.1	2.5	10	23
Jamaica	–	–	8	9
Cuba	5.1	10.0	41	118
Dominican Rep.	5.0	0.8	55	25
El Salvador	1.1	2.9	37	121
Nicaragua	1.9	28.3	57	318
Guatemala	0.9	1.2	47	87
Haiti	2.4	1.5	93	45

*Calculated on the basis of the budget for health and education.
Source: UN, *Human Development Report*, 1993.

can we see that trend taking root in the sub-region of Latin America, in Central America and the Caribbean? And what difference does it make to the development prospects of the region? These are important questions to raise, not just because democratization is a vital issue for the internal politics of the region but also because many international actors are now demanding the implementation of measures tending towards democratization before releasing funds or offering cooperation. International policies towards this region, which remains locked in a dependent relationship with the advanced countries, rest on a policy agenda, now and for the immediate future, in which democratization occupies a prominent position. Nowhere has this become more evident than in Haiti, where the US, the European Union and the Organization of American States (OAS) have called for the reinstating of President Aristide from the start of the military coup which ousted him in 1991 and have implemented an economic embargo against the country to try and bring about political change. That the embargo has bitten into Haiti's already depressed economy is evident from the fact that before Aristide was ousted from power, 56 US firms operated in Haiti, whereas by the end of 1993 there were only 8, with an estimated loss of 29,000 jobs (Horblitt 1993: 73).

We can see from the example of Haiti that democratization is not just about internal change, political participation and reform or national reconciliation. It is also about satisfying powerful international observers and allies that acceptable political systems are taking shape in the region. Democratization, therefore, could be said to have two different faces: one internal and one for the international community. This is an important distinction since regimes become acceptable to the international community if some efforts are made to introduce civilian politics and electoral practices even – without any real reduction in the power of the military *vis-à-vis* civilian society or the human rights record. Guatemala and El Salvador are examples of this happening. The Bush administration insisted in the late 1980s that El Salvador was moving fast in the direction of an acceptable democracy and claimed that the human rights record of the Cristiani government was improving and the power of the army diminishing in spite of the fact that the US Congress was expressing open concern about US policy in the wake of massacres of peasants and priests in 1988 and 1989. The *America's Watch* Report into El Salvador in 1991 concluded soberly that:

> The Salvadorean Armed Forces continue to commit abuses against civilians in the course of their counterinsurgency campaigns but the number and nature of the abuses stir little active concern from the international community. Ironically one reason for the relative silence is that when comparisons to the early 1980s are invoked, the current level of abuses seems low. This is known as improvement . . . In that respect, among others, the mass killings of the early 1980s still cause severe harm. Aside from the recurrent victimization of those who suffered themselves or lost families and friends at that time and the denial of justice to the victims, comparisons permit much of the world to see the current level of abuses as tolerable human rights. (*America's Watch* 1991: 63)

Three Central American countries, El Salvador, Guatemala and Nicaragua, are currently described as undergoing processes of democratization, if by that we mean the start of transitions (not necessarily irreversible) away from entrenched authoritarian regimes towards some form of elected, civilian government dependent on competition between political parties. So far, however, none of these countries could be said to have advanced very far in the direction of stable and consolidated democracies. Nicaragua, for example, remains divided between the supporters of the Sandinistas and recalcitrant right-wing forces who are unwilling to admit the right of the FSLN to participate fully in national debates. The result is instability and the threat of insurrection, which during 1993 broke out into fighting in parts of the country. Meanwhile policies designed for economic reconstruction came to a standstill, and the agrarian reform policies of the 1980s are slowly being dismantled.

In El Salvador, the process of democratization, which the US misleadingly insisted was under way from the time of the elections of 1982, only began in 1992 with the signing of peace agreements between the Cristiani government and the FMLN. The implementation of the agreements, which in themselves do not guarantee democratization since they merely bring an end to the war, has been slow, in particular due to the opposition from high-ranking members of the army (Munck 1993: 85). Leader of the FMLN, Shafik Jorge Handal described the Chapultec agreements as a 'programme for the democratization . . . of the country' but not a substitute for democratization (Handal 1993: 1). The clauses relating to military reform, reform of justice and administration, human rights legislation and some land reform must be implemented before we can talk about an actual process of democractization being under way. If democratization in El Salvador is to be anything more than empty rhetoric, it must include, perhaps more than anything else, the army giving up its right to oversee and veto the political arena. Two events, to be monitored through the mid to late 1990s, will indicate to what extent this is occurring: the outcome of elections starting in 1994 and in particular the treatment meted out to the FMLN and their supporters; and the implementation of policies for national reconstruction which must address the land issue and the question of the resettlement of displaced peasants and exiles who number around one million people or 20 per cent of the population (Frisk 1990).

Part of the problem is that electing a civilian government into office is simply not enough to justify the description of democratization. As Booth and Walker point out, the key question to ask in Central America is not who has nominally been elected into office but who exercises power (Booth and Walker 1993: 134). True democratization has to overcome the tendency in regional politics for powerful elites – the oligarchy or the military – to hide behind centrist politicians in government whose capacity for action is completely circumscribed. The governments of Napoleon Duarte in El Salvador and Vinicio Cerezo in Guatemala are examples of this kind of psuedo-democratization. Democratization in the region, more than simply putting elected civilian politicians into office requires a transformation of political culture, alongside some basic socio-economic reform. Democratization of the Central American political systems must incorporate changes in the way politics is conducted, including a move towards elite flexibility to facilitate negotiation and reform, and the introduction of minimal kind of social justice which the state must be seen to support. The state therefore needs to have some degree of independence from powerful local elites. The attitude of economic elites towards reform is central in the construction of lasting democracies. In El Salvador, for example, where the struggle for land continues, there can be no stable or consensual political system if this issue remains unaddressed. If we bear in mind that the key to the democracies in Costa Rica and the Commonwealth Caribbean, which though problematic are relatively stable and legitimate, is the link between the operation of the political system and some material gain for most of the population, we can see why it is difficult to imagine democracies in societies such as El Salvador where the issue of peasant rights, including the right to form a union and to formal contracts of employment, remains taboo.

If the picture is bleak for the Central American societies emerging from authoritarian rule, what of the future of those democracies already in existence in the region? The political systems of the Commonwealth Caribbean, with its unique political culture in the region, survived the crisis of the 1980s relatively intact. Governments changed hands through elections in Jamaica and several of the smaller states. Costa Rican democracy also survived the economic recession of the 1980s, though its traditional independence was brought into question as the country moved towards a position of dependence on US financial and economic aid. The Dominican Republic moved towards a slow and partial democracy, characterized by real limitations on reform and a political class separated from the electorate. Haiti's tentative transition was halted by the coup which overthrew Aristide in 1991. A resolution of Haiti's transition depends upon the economic elite recognizing – and accepting – that democratic change will not leave their power unchanged and unreformed. And Cuba, which entered a political and economic crisis with the collapse of the Soviet Union and the loss of Soviet aid, has yet to draw up plans for political reform though serious moves toward economic liberalization began in 1993. Political transformation in Cuba, however, is particularly difficult because of the terms in which the debate is shaped through US pressure. Nothing less than the dismantling of the entire political and economic edifice created by the revolution will suffice to persuade the US that democratization is under way; this is despite the fact that moves towards democratization elsewhere in the region have been introduced by representatives of the dying authoritarian state. In fact, democratization can rarely be said to constitute a complete break with the past anywhere, but is rather a slow dismantling of the structures of the previous system – with the tacit acceptance of the old political guard. This is one reason why it is so uncertain a process. Yet Washington so far refuses to view any partial change in Cuba as signs of an opening up of the system.

International support for democratization, especially from the US, is part of a wider policy-orientation linking changes in the political system to economic reform and the creation of market-based economies. The international changes of the 1980s plus the dynamic of regional politics combined to make the US an important source of pressure on governments to understand democratization as a natural compliment to liberal economic reform. Payne and Sutton see US pressure on regional govern-ments to move towards both economic and political reform as partly expressed through 'the traditional . . . carrot and stick. The carrot was announced by President Reagan when he unveiled the Caribbean Basin Initiative (CBI) in ..1982; the stick was wielded in the various structural adjustment packages imposed upon many Caribbean governments during the decade by the actions of the International Monetary Fund, the World Bank and the US Agency for International Development' (Payne and Sutton 1993: 20–1).

The enthusiastic belief of the US that democratization will come through economic liberalization has to be questioned in the light óf regional development in the 1980s. The problem with liberalizing the economies of the region is that, in the short to medium term at least, these measures do not necessarily favour democracy and in some cases may operate against it. Economic liberalization has high social costs, as we demonstrated in Chapter 5. The measures not only have alienated people from governments and made social reform impossible but in some cases have required the maintenance of an authoritarian political culture, in spite of formal political reforms, in order to implement the economic measures. The tentative political reforms of the Dominican Republic, for example, have been threatened by the costs of structural adjustment, and Jamaican democracy has been seriously undermined by the failure to use economic reform to halt the erosion of living standards on the island. The result in Jamaica is a growing propensity to violence, political apathy, emigration and an increased reliance on trafficking in illegal narcotics. In themselves, these developments cannot be seen as making Jamaican democracy unstable, especially since there is no articulated political alternative to the system. But they do not bode well for the future of the country. Huber points out that economic deterioration has historically been proved to endanger democracies in the region, while drug trafficking and laundering of drug profits weaken the state. 'The capacity of states to provide basic social services is not only important for the maintenance of formal democracy but crucial for any movement toward substantive democracy, that is toward a society where the many hold a real share of power and can use that power to improve the material conditions of life for those in the lower ranks of the social order' (Huber 1993: 94–5).

*   *   *

How do we conclude this review of the region's development prospects? It must necessarily be a sober conclusion that we offer. We have traced the efforts of the region to break out of the cycles of agrarian dependence and international vulnerability by attempting economic diversification; and we have also outlined the different struggles by the peoples of the region to control their own destiny, both internally against colonialism and authoritarian governments, and externally in a world controlled by advanced capitalist states which are motivated by their own security and development concerns. Although there have been some notable successes along the way, the events of the 1980s – recession, political conflict and violence, and international domination – indicate that the region still has a long way to go before equitable and harmonious development can be achieved. The region remains peripheral and the economies remain vulnerable. Development remains limited by the international system and it is by no means clear that the global changes inaugurated at the end of the 1980s will bring any material improvement to Central America and the Caribbean. Policy alternatives are more circumscribed than ever with the collapse of the revolutionary regimes of the region. And democracy, where it exists, is weak or limited in almost all cases. Economic elites remain excessively privileged, the democratic states are weak and some-times permeable to corruption, and political apathy is an ever-present danger. The democratic transitions are as yet uncertain. Much remains to be done if the twenty-first century is to offer to the inhabitants of the region the chances of a reasonable life and livelihood.

Guide to Further Reading

General Works and Introductory Studies

Almost all research on Central America and the Caribbean has traditionally been divided between studies of Central America; studies of the
Commonwealth, and Cuban studies with the Dutch, French and Spanish-
speaking Caribbean, receive far less attention. This bias is particularly
noticeable in the literature available in English. Some of the few recent
books which at least see the insular Caribbean as a whole, linguistic
differences notwithstanding, are J. Dominguez, R. Pastor and R. Delisle
Worrell (eds), *Democracy in the Caribbean* (Johns Hopkins University
Press, Baltimore, 1993); A. Payne and P. Sutton (eds) *Modern Caribbean
Politics* (Johns Hopkins University Press, Baltimore, 1993); and C. Clarke
(ed.), *Society and Politics in the Caribbean* (St Anthony's/Macmillan Series,
London, 1991). Dominguez, Pastor and Worrell (eds) mix a useful thematic
approach to the region with case studies of individual countries, while
Payne and Sutton (eds) and Clarke (ed.) tend towards emphasizing case
studies. One of the best edited works on the insular Caribbean in Spanish is
A. Serbin and A. Bryan (eds), *El Caribe Hacia el 2000* (Nueva Sociedad,
Caracas, Venezuela 1991). It contains chapters by important scholars from
Latin America on the international relations and the political economy of
the region, gender relations and ethnicity. For a general introductory
history to the Caribbean, see the very basic J. H. Parry, P. Sherlock and A.
Maingot, *A Short History of the West Indies* (Macmillan, London, 1987 4th
edition) or the old, but well-written, study by Eric Williams, long-time
Prime Minister of Trinidad and Tobago, *From Columbus to Castro: The
History of the Caribbean* (André Deutch, London, 1970).

Central America is best approached in the first instance by an
introductory text rather than an edited volume. One of the best is J.
Booth and T. Walker, *Understanding Central America* (Westview Press,
Boulder, Colorado, 1993, 2nd edition). Its main aim is to explain the crisis
of the 1980s. It emphasizes the causes of insurrection and the role the US
played. Much more historical in its approach is H. Perez-Brignoli's
introductory history, *A Brief History of Central America*, dating from
1985 in Spanish, but published in English for the first time in 1989
(University of California Press, Oxford).

Two much longer studies on the isthmus are J. Dunkerley, *Power in the
Isthmus* (Verso, London 1988) and V. Bulmer-Thomas, *The Political
Economy of Central America since 1920* (Cambridge University Press,

1987). Both draw extensively on material from Central America and are invaluable for detail on the politics and economics of the region. The best edited volume on the region in English is L. Bethell (ed.), *Central America since Independence* (Cambridge University Press, 1991). J. Flora and E. Torres-Rivas, *Central America*, in the series 'Sociology of Developing Counties' (Macmillan, London 1989), is also good.

The History of the Region

On Central America, see especially R. L. Woodward, *Central America: A Nation Divided* (Oxford University Press, New York, 1985, 2nd edition). A good general economic history, in Spanish, is C. Cardoso and H. Perez-Brignoli, *Centroamerica y la economia occidental* (EDUCA, San José, 1977). On the importance of coffee and the coffee oligarchy, see C. Hall, *El cafe y el desarrollo histórico-geográfico de Costa Rica* (Editorial Costa Rica, San José, 1982); E. Bradford Burns., 'The Modernization of Underdevelopment in El Salvador', in C. Wilber (ed.), *The Political Economy of Development* (Random House, New York, 1988, 4th edition); and J. Paige, 'Coffee and politics in Central America', in R. Tardanico (ed.), *Crisis in the Caribbean Basin* (Sage, Newbury Place, 1987).

On the importance of sugar in the Caribbean, see the seminal studies by Sidney Mintz, and especially *Sweetness and Power: The Place of Sugar in Modern History* (Viking Press, New York, 1985). Books dealing with the nineteeth-century history of the insular Caribbean, treating it as a unit, are especially difficult to find because of its fragmentation due to imperial rivalries. Important partial studies include the classic work by C. L. R. James, *The Black Jacobins* (André Deutch, New York, 1963); E. Braithwaite, *The Development of Creole Society in Jamaica, 1780–1820* (Oxford University Press, London 1971); and a study of a later period by P. Bryan, *The Jamaican People, 1880–1902* (Macmillan, London, 1991). F. Baez's comparative study of Cuba and the Dominican Republic, *La Formación de Sistema Agroexportador en el Caribe: Republica Dominicana y Cuba, 1525–18998* (Editorial Universitaria, Santo Domingo, 1986) is excellent but unfortunately only available in Spanish.

Politics

On the Caribbean, see especially the edited collections by Payne and Sutton, *Modern Caribbean Politics*, and Dominguez, Pastor and Delisle Worrell, *Democracy in the Caribbean*, both of which adopt an overwhelmingly 'political' approach, though in the best essays this is mixed with an appreciation of economic factors. On individual countries, see G. Lewis, *Puerto Rico: Freedom and Power in the Caribbean* (Monthly Review Press, New York, 1963); A. Payne, *Politics in Jamaica* (Christopher Hurst, London, 1988; T. Thorndike, *Grenada: Politics, Economics and Society* (Frances Pinter, London, 1985); J. Heine (ed.) *Revolución e Intervención en el Caribe: las lecciones de Grenada* (GEL, Buenos Aires, 1990); R. Espinal, *Autoritarismo y Democracia en la Politica Dominicana* (CAPEL, San José, 1987); J. Ferguson, *Papa Doc, Baby Doc: Haiti and the Duvaliers* (Blackwell, Oxford, 1987); and D. Close, *Cuba: Politics, Economics and Society* (Frances Pinter, London, 1988).

The 1980s saw an explosion of studies, monographs and collected volumes on Central America, some of which, inevitably, have dated quickly. A useful short introductory article is J. Booth, 'Socioeconomic and Political Roots of National Revolts in Central America', *Latin American Research Review*, 26 (1) 1991. J. Dunkerley, *Power in the Isthmus* (Verso, London, 1988) is of course excellent. The second part of Flora and Torres-Rivas (1989) 'The Transformation of Politics', is a good introduction to the Central American political systems. One of the best collected volumes in Spanish, though by now somewhat dated, is D. Castillo Rivas (ed.), *Centroamerica: Más Allá de la Crisis* (SIAP, Mexico, 1983).

L. Bethell, *Central America since Independence* (Cambridge University Press, 1991), contains excellent chapters on individual counties. See also T. Walker, *Nicaragua: The Land of Sandino* (Boulder, Colorado, Westview Press, 1991); T. S. Montgomery, *Revolution in El Salvador: Origins and Evolution* (Boulder, Colarado, Westview Press, 1982); J. Handy, *Gift of the Devil* (Toronto, Between the Lines, 1984); M. Edelman and J. Kenan, *The Costa Rica Reader* (New York Weidenfeld, 1989); and J. *Weeks and P. Gunson, Panama: Made in the USA* (Latin America Bureau, London, 1991).

The timid process of 'democratization' in the isthmus is a theme which is starting to excite interest. For a good early piece on El Salvador, where a lot of attention is concentrated, see T. Lynn Karl, 'Imposing Consent? Electoralism vs Democratization in El Salvador', in P. Drake and E. Silva (eds), in *Elections and Democracy in Latin America* (San Diego, University of California, Center for Iberian and Latin American Studies, 1986). For the Dominican Republic, C. Conaghan and R. Espinal, 'Unlikely Transitions to Uncertain Regimes? Democracy without Compromise in the Dominican Republic and Ecuador', *Journal of Latin American Studies*, 22, 1990). On democratic stability in Costa Rica, see John Peeler, 'Elite Settlements and Democratic Consolidation in Columbia, Costa Rica and Venezuela, in R. Gunther and J. Higley (eds) *Elites and Democratic Consolidation in Latin America and Southern Europe* (Cambridge University Press, 1992).

Economics

A good general introduction, dealing especially with the economic crisis of the 1980s, is C. Deere *et al.*, *In the Shadow of the Sun; Caribbean Development Alternatives and US Policy* (Boulder, Colorado, Westview Press, 1990). Some good essays on the economic crisis are to be found in R. Tardanico (ed.), *Crisis in the Caribbean Basin* (Sage, Newbury Place, 1987).

In order to understand the complexities of the Central American economies, Bulmer-Thomas (1987) is absolutely essential reading. J.

Weeks, *The Economies of Central America* (New York, Holmes and Meier, 1985) is also very good. For a detailed analysis of Sandinista economics, see R. Spalding (ed.), *The Political Economy of Revolutionary Nicaragua* (Allen & Unwin, London, 1987). The Costa Rican model of development is discussed perceptively by R. Franco and A. Leon, in 'Estilos de desarrollo, papel del estado y estructura social en Costa Rica', *Pensamiento Iberoamericano*, July–December 1984, vol. 6, although it does not cover the vital period of the late 1980s.

The two best studies on Cuba economics in English, though somewhat dated now, are C. Mesa-Lago, *The Economy of Socialist Cuba*, (University of New Mexico, 1981) and C. Brundenius, *Revolutionary Cuba: The Challenge of Growth with Equity* (Boulder, Colorado, Westview Press, 1984).

For Puerto Rico, see J. Dietz, *Economic History of Puerto Rico* (Princeton University Press, 1986). For Jamaica, see A. Payne, *Politics in Jamaica* (Christopher Hurst, London, 1988) or A. Payne, 'Orthodox Liberal Development in Jamaica: Theory and Practice, *Third World Quarterly* 10(3) 1988. More general essays on the economies of the insular Caribbean are R. Delisle Worrell, 'The Economies of the English-speaking Caribbean since the 1960s', and S. Quick, 'The International Economy and the Caribbean: The 1990s and Beyond', in J. Domingez, R. Pastor and R. Delisle Worrell (1993).

International Relations

Obviously, most studies of the region in this category analyse the relationship with the US. To understand where the Caribbean Basin fits in US foreign policy, R. Feinberg, *The Intemperate Zone: The Third World Challenge to US Foreign Policy* (New York, Norton 1983), is a good place to start. R. Pastor is excellent at explaining US policy; see, for example, *Condemned to Repetition: The United States and Nicaragua* (Princeton University Press, 1988). L. Schoultz, *National Security in Latin America* (Princeton University Press, 1987) is also very good and makes detailed reference to government and congressional sources. On the consequences of US policy in Central America, the best introduction is J. Pearce, *Under the Eagle* (Latin America Bureau, London, 1986, 2nd edition). See also W. Leogrande, 'From Reagan to Bush: the Transition of US Policy towards Central America', *Journal of Latin American Studies* 22 (2) 1990.

Also very useful are J. Braveboy-Wagner, *the Caribbean in World Affairs: the Foreign Policies of the English-speaking States* (Boulder, Colorado, Westview Press, 1988); J. Heine and L. Manigat (eds), *The Caribbean and World Politics: Cross Currents and Cleavages* (New York, Holmes & Meier, 1988); M. Erisman, *The Caribbean Challenge: US Policy in a Volatile Region* (Boulder, Colorado, Westview Press, 1984); and N. Hamilton (ed.), *Regional Dynamics and US Policy in the 1980s* (Boulder, Colorado, Westview Press, 1988).

On Cuban international relations, see J. Domingez, *To Make a World Safe for Revolution: Cuba's Foreign Policy* (Harvard University Press, 1989).

On relations with Europe, see J. Roy (ed.), *The Reconstruction of Central America: The Role of the European Community* (North-South Centre, University of Miami, 1992); P. Sutton (ed.) *Europe and the Caribbean* (Macmillan, London, 1991); and C. Stevens, 'The Caribbean and Europe: Endgames?', *Development Policy Review* 9(3) 1991.

Journals

The journals where articles appear most frequently are:

Journal of Latin American Studies
Latin American Research Review
Journal of Inter-American Studies and World Affairs
Hemisphere
Latin American Perspectives
European Review of Latin American and Caribbean Studies

In Spanish, see particularly:

Estudios Sociales Centroamericanos
El Caribe Contemporaneo
Nueva Sociedad
Anuario de Estudios Centroamericanos

Bibliography

America's Watch, (1991) *El Salvador's Decade of Terror. Human Rights since the Assassination of Archbishop Romero*, Human Rights Watch, New York.

Amin, S. (1974) *Accumulation on a World Scale*, Monthly Review Press, New York.

Azicri, M. (1988) *Cuba Politics, Economics and Society*, Frances Pinter, London.

Baez, F. (1986) *La Formacion del Sistema Agroexportador en el Caribe. Republica Dominicana y Cuba 1515–1898*, Editorial Universitaria, Santo Domingo.

Baud, M. (1987) 'The Origins of Capitalist Agriculture in the Dominican Republic', *Latin American Research Review*, 22 (2).

Beckford, L. G. (1972) *Persistent Poverty: Underdevelopment in the Plantation Economies of the Third World*, Oxford University Press.

Bermudez, L. and A. Cavalla (1982) *Estrategias de Reagan hacia la revolucion centroamericana*, Editorial Nuevo Tiempo, UNAM Mexico.

Best, L. (1968) 'A Model of a Pure Plantation Economy', *Social and Economic Studies*, 17 (3).

Bethell, L. (1991) *Central America since Independence*, Cambridge University Press.

Binns, P. and M. Gonzalez (1980) Cuba, Castro and Socialism', *International Socialism*, no. 8.

Black, G. (1984) *Garrison Guatemala*, Zed Press, London.

Blaiser, C. (1976) *The Hovering Giant: US Responses to Revolutionary Change*, University of Pittsburg Press.

Bonilla, F. and R. Campos (1981) 'A Wealth of Poor. Puerto Ricans in the New International Order', *Daedalus*, no. 110 (Spring).

Booth, John A. and T. W. Walker (1993) *Understanding Central America*, Westview Press, Colorado.

Bouricaud, F. (1967) *Pouvoir et societé dans le Pérou contemporain*, Colin, Paris.

Bradford Burns, E. (1980) *The Poverty of Progress: Latin America in the Nineteenth Century*, University of California Press.

Bradford Burns, E. (1988) 'The Modernization of Underdevelopment in El Salvador', in C. Wilber (ed.), *The Political Economy of Development* 4th edn, Random House, New York.

Braveboy-Wagner, J. A. (1984) 'The Politics of Developmentalism: U.S. Policy Toward Jamaica', in H. Michael Erisman (ed.), *The Caribbean*

Challenge: U.S. Policy in a Volatile Region, Westview Press, Boulder, Colorado.

Bray, D. (1987) 'Industrialization, Labor Migration, and Employment Crises: A Comparison of Jamaica and the Dominican Republic', in R. Tardanico (ed.), *Crises in the Caribbean Basin* Sage, New York.

Brundenius, C. (1984) *Revolutionary Cuba: The Challenge of Growth with Equity*, Westview Press, Boulder, Colorado.

Brundenius, C. and A. Zimbalist (1988) *Cubanology and Cuban Economic Performance*, Westview Press, Boulder, Colorado.

Bryan, P. (1991) *The Jamaican People, 1880–1902*, Macmillan, London.

Bulmer-Thomas, V. (1987) *A Political Economy of Central America*, Cambridge University Press.

Burbach, R. (1986) 'El imperialismo norteamericano y las nuevas socie-dades revolucionarias', in J.L. Corraggio and C.D. Deere (eds), *La transicion dificil: La autodeterminacion de los pequeños paises perifericos*, Siglo XXI, Mexico.

Burton, M., R. Gunther and J. Higley (1992) 'Introduction: Elite Transformations and Democratic Regimes', R. Gunther and J. Higley (eds), *Elites and Democratic Consolidation in Latin America and Southern Europe*, Cambridge University Press.

Cabán, P. (1990) 'Industrial Transformation and Labour Relations in Puerto Rico: From Operation Bootstrap to the 1970s', *Journal of Latin American Studies*, 21.

Cambranes, J.C. (1985) *Coffee and Peasants in Guatemala (1853–1897)*, Institute of Latin American Studies, Stockholm.

Cardoso, C. (1991) 'The Liberal Era c. 1870–1930', in L. Bethell (ed.), *Central America since Independence*, Cambridge University Press.

Cardoso, C. and H. Perez-Brignoli (1977) *Centroamerica y la economia occidental (1520–1930)* Editorial Costa Rica, San Jose.

Cardoso, F. and E. Faletto (1979) *Dependency and Development in Latin America*, Oxford University Press.

Casaus, M. and R. Castillo (1990) *Centroamerica 1989*, CDEAL, Madrid.

Casaus, M. and R. Castillo (1991) *Centroamerica 1990*, CEDEAL, Madrid.

Cassá, R. (1979) *Historia Social y Economica de la Republica Dominicana*, Santo Domingo.

Castillo Rivas, D. (1980) *Acumulación de Capital y Empresas Transnacio-nales en Centroamerica*, Siglo XXI, Mexico.

Castillo Rivas, D. (1983) *Centroamerica: Mas Alla de la Crisis*, SIAP, Mexico.

Castro, J.R. and D. Barry (1990) 'La guerra de baja intensidad y la militarización de Centroamerica', *Itzapalapa* no. 20 (Julio–Dec), Uni-versidad Autonoma Metropolitana, Mexico.

Ceara Hatton, M. (1988) *Las economias caribeñas en la decada de los ochenta*, CIECA, Santo Domingo.

Chomsky, N. (1986) *Turning the Tide: US Intervention in Central America and the Struggle for Peace*, ZED Press, London.

Clarke, C. (1990) 'Europe in the Caribbean: from Colonial Hegemony to Geopolitical Marginality', in A. Bryan, J.E. Greene and T.M. Shaw (eds), *Peace, Development and Security in the Caribbean: Perspectives to the Year 2000*, Macmillan, London.

Clarke, C. (1991) 'Introduction: Caribbean Decolonization – New States and Old Societies', in C. Clarke, *State and Politics in the Caribbean*, Macmillan, London.

Close, D. (1988) *Nicaragua Politics, Economics and Society*, Frances Pinter, London.

Conaghan, C. and R. Espinal (1990) 'Unlikely Transition to Uncertain Regimes? Democracy Without Compromise in the Dominican Republic and Ecuador', *Journal of Latin American Studies*, 22.

Coote, B. (1987) *The Hunger Crop*, Oxfam, Oxford.

Craig, S. (1977) 'The Germs of an Idea', afterword to W A. Lewis, *Labour in the West Indies*, New Beacon, London.

Craig, S. (ed.) (1982) *Contemporary Caribbean: A Sociological Reader*, Maracas, Trinidad and Tobago.

Debray, R. (1977) *The Revolution on Trial: A Critique of Arms*, Penguin, Harmondsworth.

Deere, C. D. (1990) 'A CBI Report Card', *Hemisphere*, (Fall).

Deere, C. D. *et al.* (1990) *In the Shadow of the Sun: Caribbean Development Alternatives and U.S. Policy*, PACCA, Westview Press, Boulder, Colorado.

Dietz, J. (1986) *Economic History of Puerto Rico: Institutional Change and Capitalist Development*, Princeton University Press.

Diskin, M. (ed.) (1983) *Trouble in Our Backyard: Central America and the US in the 1980s*, Panteon, New York.

Dominguez, J. (1982) *Cuba: Internal and International Affairs*, Sage, California.

Dominguez, J. (1984) 'Cuba's Relations with Caribbean and Central American Countries', in A. Adelman and R. Reading (eds), *Confrontation in the Caribbean Basin: International Perspectives on Security, Sovereignty and Survival*, University of Pittsburg Press.

Dominguez, J., R. Pastor and R. Delisle Worrell (eds), (1993) *Democracy in the Caribbean: Political, Economic and Social Perspectives*, Johns Hopkins University Press.

Dunkerely, J. (1982) *The Long War – Dictatorship and Revolution in El Salvador*, Junction Books, London.

Dunkerley, J. (1988) *Power in the Isthmus*, Verso, London.

Dunkerley, J. (1991a) 'Guatemala since 1930', in L. Bethell (ed.), *Central America since Independence*, Cambridge University Press.

Dunkerley, J. (1991b) 'El Salvador since 1930', in L. Bethell (ed.), *Central America Since Independence*, Cambridge University Press.

Edelman, M. and J. Kenan (eds) (1989) *The Costa Rican Reader*, Weidenfield, New York.

Edquist, C. (1985) *Capitalism, Socialism and Technology*, Zed Press, London.

Erisman, M. (ed.) (1984) *The Caribbean Challenge: US Policy in a Volatile Region* Boulder, Westview Press, Boulder, Colorado.

Espinal, R. (1987) *Autoritarismo y democracia en la politica dominicana*. CAPEL, San Jose.

Espinal, R. (1991) 'Between Authoritarianism and Crisis-Prone Democracy: The Dominican Republic after Trujillo', in C. Clarke (ed.), *Society and Politics in the Caribbean*, Macmillan, London.

Fagen, R. (1986) 'La politica de transicion', in J. L. Coraggio and C. D. Deere, (eds), *La Transicion dificil: la autodeterminacion y los pequenos paises perifericos*, Siglo XXI, Mexico.

Fagen, R. (1987) *Forging Peace: The Challenges of Central America*, PACCA, Basil Blackwell, Oxford.

Feinberg, R. (1983) *The Intemperate Zone: The Third World Challenge to US Foreign Policy*, Norton, New York.

Feld, W. and G. Boyd (1980) 'The Comparative Study of International Regions', in W. Feld and G. Boyd (eds), *Comparative Regional Systems*, Pergamon Press, New York.

Ferguson, J. (1987) *Papa Doc Baby Doc: Haiti and the Duvaliers*, Blackwell, Oxford.

Fernandez, J. (1988) *Inestabilidad Economica con Estabilidad Politica El caso singular de Costa Rica*, Editorial de la Universidad de Costa Rica, San Jose.

Fitzgerald, E. V. K. (1987) 'An Evaluation of the Economic Costs to Nicaragua of US Aggression, 1980–1984', in R. Spalding (ed.), *The Political Economy of Revolutionary Nicaragua*, Allen & Unwin, London.

Fitzgerald, F. (1978) 'A Critique of the Sovietization Thesis', *Science and Society*, vol. 42, no. 1.

Flora, J. and E. Torres-Rivas (1989a) 'The Transformation of Politics after 1945', in Flora and Torres-Rivas (eds), *Central America*, Macmillan, London.

Flora, J. and E. Torres-Rivas (1989b) 'Sociology of Developing Societies: Historical Bases of Insurgency in Central America', in Flora and Torres-Rivas (eds) *Central America*, Macmillan, London.

Flora, J., D. Benson and C. B. Flora (1989) 'Central America: Cultures in Conflict', in Flora and Torres-Rivas (eds) *Central America*, Macmillan, London.

Frambes-Buxeda, A. (1990) 'Las falsa expectativas del Plan del Caribe para la sub-región a la luz de las experiencias de Puerto Rico', in C. Gaitier Mayoral *et al.*, *Puerto Rico en la Economía Política del Caribe*, Edición del Huracán, Rio Piedras.

Franco, R. and A. Leon (1984) 'Estilos de desarrollo, papel del estado y estructura social en Costa Rica', *Pensamiento Iberoamericano*, vol. 6, (Julio—December).

Frisk, P. (1990) 'Displaced Persons and Human Rights: The Crisis in El Salvador', *Third World Quarterly*, 12(3).

Gaddis, J. L. (1982) *Strategies of Containment: A Critical Appraisal of Post-War American National Security Policy*, Oxford University Press.

Garnier, L. (1984) 'Industria, Estado y Desarrollo', *Estudios Sociales Centroamericanos* (San Jose) vol. 37 (January–April).

Garnier, L. (1991) 'Beyond Trade', *Hemisphere* 3(3) (Summer).

Girault, C. (1991) 'Society and Politics in Haiti: The Divorce between the State and the Nation', in C. Clarke (ed.), *Society and Politics in the Caribbean*, Macmillan, London.

Gleijeses, P. (1989) 'The Agrarian Reform of Jacobo Arbenz', *Journal of Latin American Studies*, 21.

Gorostiaga, X. and P. Marchetti (1988) 'The Central American Economy: Conflict and Crisis', in N. Hamilton *et al.* (eds), *Crisis in Central America: Regional Dynamics and U.S: Policy in the 1980s*, PACCA, Westview Press, Boulder, Colorado.

Griffith, Ivelaw (1992) 'The Nature and Security Implications of Drug Operations in the Commonwealth Caribbean', paper delivered at the Fourth Meeting of the Caribbean International Relations Working Groups of the Latin American Social Science Council (CLACSO), St Thomas, June.

Hall, C. (1982) *El Cafe y el desarrollo historico-geografico de Costa Rica*, Editorial Costa Rica, San Jose.

Hall, M. and H. Spalding (1989) 'Urban Labour Movements', in L. Bethell (ed.), *Latin America Economy and Society, 1870–1930*, Cambridge University Press.

Hall, S. (1977) 'Pluralism, Race and Class in Caribbean Society', in *A Study of Ethnic Group Relations in the English-speaking Caribbean, Bolivia, Chile and Mexico*, UNESCO.

Hamilton, N., J. Freiden, L. Fuller and M. Pastor (eds) (1988) *Regional Dyn-amics and US Policy in the 1980s*, Westview/PACCA, Boulder, Colorado.

Hamnet, B. (1988) 'La Regeneracion', *Historia de Iberoamerica* Tomo III, Historia Contemporanea, Catedra, Madrid.

Handal, S. J. (1993) 'Ponencia en el IV Encuentro del Foro del Sao Paulo', Havana, Cuba.

Handy, J. (1984) *Gift of the Devil: A History of Guatemala*, South End Press, Boston.

Handy, J. (1988) 'Democracy, Military Rule and Agrarian Reform in Guatemala', in J. Kirk and G. Schuyler (eds), *Central America: Democracy, Development and Change*, Praeger, New York.

Handy, J. (1989) 'Insurgency and Counter-Insurgency in Guatemala', in Flora and Torres-Rivas (eds), *Central America*, Macmillan, London.

Harnecker, M. (1984) *Pueblos en Armas*, Ediciones Era, Mexico.

Harrigan, J. (1991) 'Jamaica', in P. Mosley, J. Harrigan and J. Toye (eds), *Aid and Power: The World Bank and Policy-Based Lending*, vol. 2: *Case Studies*, Routledge, London.

Horblitt, S. (1993) 'Multilateral Policy: The Road Toward Reconciliation', in G. Fauriol (ed.), *The Haitian Challenge: US Policy Considerations*, The Centre for Strategic and International Studies, Washington.

Huber, E. (1993) 'The Future of Democracy in the Caribbean', J. Dominguez, R. Pastor and R. Delisle Worrell (eds), *Democracy in the Caribbean Political, Economic and Social Perspectives*, Johns Hopkins University Press.

Jácome, F. (1990) 'Diferencias etnorraciales y su utilización ideológica', in A. Serbin and A. Bryan (eds), *¿Vecinos Indiferentes?*, Editorial Nueva Sociedad, Venezuela.

Jacome, F. (1991) 'Sistemas politicos de la Cuenca del Caribe: divergencias y transformaciones previsibles', in A. Serbin and A. Bryan (eds) *El Caribe Hacia el 2000*, Nueva Sociedad, Caracas.

Jaguaribe, H. (1979) 'Autonomía periferica y hegemonía céntrica', *Estudios Internacionales*, (Chile), no. 12.

Kaufman, M. (1985) *Jamaica under Manley: Dilemmas of Socialism and Democracy*, ZED Press, London.

Kirk, J. and G. Schuyler (eds) (1988) *Central America, Development and Change*, Praeger, New York.

Klare, M. (1984) *American Arms Supermarket*, University of Texas, Austin.

Labarge, R. A. (1960) *Impact of the United Fruit Company on the Economic Development of Guatemala 1946–1954*, Tulane University, New Orleans.

Lapper, R. and J. Painter (1985) *Honduras. State for Sale*, LAB, London.

Lefeber, W. (1978) *The Panama Canal, The Caribbean in Historical Perspective*, Oxford University Press.

Leogrande, W. (1990) 'From Reagan to Bush: The Transition in US Policy towards Central America', *Journal of Latin American Studies*, 22.

Lewis, A. (1990) *Politics in West Africa*, Allen & Unwin, London.

Lewis, D. (1990) 'Non-Governmental Organizations and Alternative Strategies', in J. Wedderburn (ed.), *Integration and Participatory Development*, Fredrich Ebert Stiftung, Kingston, Jamaica.

Lewis, D. (1991) 'El sector informal y los nuevos actores sociales en el desarrollo del Caribe', in A. Serbin and A. Bryan (eds), *El Caribe Hacia el 2000* Editorial Nueva Sociedad, Venezuela.

Lewis, G. (1987) *Grenada: The Jewel Despoiled*, Johns Hopkins University Press, Baltimore.

Lewis, W. A. (1950) 'The Industrialisation of the British West Indies', *Caribbean Economic Review*, 2(1).

Lijphart, A. (1990) 'Tamaño, pluralismo y el modelo Westminister de democracia: implicaciones para el Caribe Oriental', in J. Heine (ed.), *Revolucion e Intervencion en el Caribe: las lecciones de Granada*, GEL, Buenos Aires.

Lizano, E. (1988) *Programa de Ajuste Estructural*, Banco Central de Costa Rica.

Lopez, J. R. (1990) *Las Relaciones Economicas Entre La Comunidad Europea y America Central Durante los Ochenta: Balance y Perspectivas*, IRELA Doc De Trabajo, no. 24.

Lovell, W. G. (1988) 'Resisting Conquest: Development and the Guatemalan Indian', in J. Kirk and G. Schuyler (eds), *Central America, Development and Change*, Preager, New York.

Lowy, M. and E. Sader (1985) 'The Militarization of the State in Latin America', *Latin American Perspecitves*, Issue 47, 12(4) (Fall).

Luciak, I. (1990) 'Democracy in the Nicaraguan Countryside', *Latin American Perspectives*, Issue 66, 17 (3) (Summer).

Lynch, J. (1988) 'La formacion de los estados nuevos', *Historia de Iberoamerica* Tomo III, Historia Contemporanea Catedra, Madrid.

MacEwan, A. (1981) *Revolution and Economic Development in Cuba*, Macmillan, London.

Manley, M. (1991) *The Poverty of Nations. Reflections on Underdevelopment and the World Economy*, Pluto Press, London.

McCreery, D. J. (1976) 'Coffee and Class: The Structure of Development in Liberal Guatemala', *Hispanic American Historical Review*, no. 56.

Mesa-Lago, C. (1981) *The Economy of Socialist Cuba*, University of New Mexico, Albuqueque.

Mesa-Lago, C. and F. Diaz-Briquets (1988) 'Estrategias diferentes, paises similares. Las consecuencias para el crecimiento a la equidad en Costa Rica y Cuba', *Anuario de Estudios Centroamericanos* (San Jose) 14 (1–2).

Millet, R. (1990) 'The Aftermath of Intervention: Panama 1990', *Journal of Interamerican Studies and World Affairs*, 32 (1).

Mintz, S. (1985) *Sweetness and Power. The Place of Sugar in Modern History*, Viking, New York.

Mintz, S. (1987) 'Indentured Labour in the Caribbean', in R. Tardanico (ed.), *Crisis in the Caribbean Basin*, Sage Publications, Newbury Place.

Mintz, S. (1991) 'De la clase hacia la identidad: una perspectiva caribeña', *El Caribe Contemporaneo*, no. 23 (July–Dec).

Montgomery, T. S.(1982) *Revolution in El Salvador*, Westview Press, Boulder, Colorado.

Moreno Fraginals, M. (1983) *La historia como arma y otros estudios sobre esclavos, ingenios y plantaciones*, Critica, Barcelona.

Mosley, P. (1991) 'Introduction and Synthesis', in P. Mosley, J. Harrigan and J. Toye (eds), *Aid and Power, The World Bank and Policy-Based Lending*, no. 2, *Case Studies*, Routledge, New York.

MrCreery, D. J. (1983) *Development and the State in Reforma Guatemala 1871–1888*, Athens, Ohio University.

Munck, G. (1993) 'Beyond Electoralism in El Salvador: Conflict Resolution Through Negotiated Compromise', *Third World Quarterly*, 14 (1).

Munroe, T. (1972) *The Politics of Constitutional Decolonisation, Jamaica 1944–1962*, University of West Indies, Jamaica.

Muñoz, H. (1980) 'Interdependencia desigual: las relaciones economicas entre los Estados Unidos y America Latina', *Cuadernos Semestrales Los Estados Unidos – Perspectiva Latinoamerica*, 2(8).

Murguialday, C. (1990) *Nicaragua, revolucion y feminismo (1977–1989)*, Editorial Revolucion, Madrid.

Murphey, M. (1987) 'The International Monetary Fund and the Contemporary Crisis in the Dominican Republic', in R Tardanico (ed.), *Crisis in the Caribbean*, Sage, Newbury Place.

Newfarmer, R. (1984) *From Gunboats to Diplomacy – New US Policies for Latin America*, Johns Hopkins University Press, Baltimore.

North, L. (1982) *Bitter Ground: Roots of Revolt in El Salvador*, Between the Lines, Toronto.

North, L. (1988) 'Democratization in El Salvador: Illusion or Reality?', in J. Kirk and G. Schuyler (eds), *Central America, Development and Change*, Praeger, New York.

Nuñez, O. (1987) *Transicion y lucha de clases en Nicaragua, 1979–1986*, Siglo XXI/CRIES, Mexico.

Nye, R. (1971) *Peace in Parts: Integration and Conflict in Regional Organizations*, Little, Brown, Boston.

Paige, J. (1987) 'Coffee and Politics in Central America', in R. Tardanico (ed.), *Crisis in the Caribbean Basin*, Sage, Newbury Place.

Painter, J. (1987) *Guatemala. False Hope, False Freedom*, LAB, London.

Pantojas, E. (1990) 'Puerto Rican Populism Revisted: The PPD During the 1940s', *Journal of Latin American Studies*, 21.

Pastor, M. (1987) 'The Effects of IMF Programmes in the Third World: Evidence from Latin America', *World Development*, no. 15.

Pastor, R. (1987) 'The Reagan Adminstration and Latin America: The Eagle Resurgent', in K. Dye, R. Leiber and D. Rothchild (eds), *Eagle Resurgent? The Reagan Era in American Foreign Policy*, Little, Brown, Boston.

Paus, E. (ed.) (1988) *The Struggle Against Dependence: Non-Traditional Export Growth in Central America and the Caribbean*, Westview, Boulder, Colorado.

Payne, A. (1988) *Politics in Jamaica*, Chistopher Hurst, London.

Payne, A. (1988b) 'Orthodox Liberal Development in Jamaica: Theory and Practice', *Third World Quarterly*, 10 (3).

Payne, A. (1990) 'La politica exterior del Gobierno Revolucionario del Pueblo', in J. Heine *Revolucion e Intervencion en el Caribe: las lecciones de Granada*, GEL, Buenos Aires.

Payne, A. (1991a) 'Britain and the Caribbean', in P. Sutton (ed.), *Europe and the Caribbean*, Macmillan, London.

Payne, A. (1991b) 'Jamaican Society and the Testing of Demcoracy', in C. Clarke, *Society and Politics in the Caribbean*, St Antony's/Macmillan, London.

Payne, A. and P. Sutton (eds) (1993) *Modern Caribbean Politics*, Johns Hopkins University Press.

Payne, A., P. Sutton and T. Thorndike (1984) *Grenada: Revolution and Invasion*, St Martin's Press, New York.

Pearce, J. (1986a) *Under the Eagle*, LAB, London.

Pearce, J. (1986b) *Promised Land: Peasant Rebellion in Chalatenango, El Salvador*, LAB, London.

Peeler, J. (1992) 'Elite Settlements and Democratic Consolidation: Colombia, Costa Rica and Venezuela', in R. Gunther and R. Higley (eds) (1992) *Elites and Democratic Consolidation in Latin America and Southern Europe*, Cambridge University Press.

Perez, L. (1989) *Cuba: Between Reform and Revolution*, OUP, New York.

Perez-Brignoli, H. (1989a) *A Brief History of Central America*, University of California Press.

Perez-Brignoli, H. (1989b) 'Reckoning with the Central American Past: Economic Growth and Political Regimes', in M. Edelman and J. Kenan (eds), *The Costa Rica Reader*, Weidenfeld, New York.

Perez-Lopez, J. (1991) 'Swimming Against the Tide: Implications for Cuba of Soviet and Eastern European Reforms in Foreign Economic Relations', *Journal of International Studies and World Affairs*, 33 (2) (Summer).

Petrovich, J. and S. Laureano (1986) 'Towards an Analysis of Puerto Rican Women and the Informal Economy', *Homines* (San Juan) 10 (1).

Pierre-Charles, G. (1983) *El Caribe Contemporaneo*, Siglo XXI, Mexico.

Pierre-Charles, G. (1988) 'El proceso democratico en Haiti y su contexto regional', *El Caribe Contemporaneo*, (July–Dec).

Poitras, G. (1988) 'Un post-mortem prematuro. La doctrina Reagan y America Latina', *Nueva Sociedad*, no. 98 (Nov–Dec).

Pollack, M. and A. Uloff (1985) *Costa Rica: Evolución Macroeconomica 1976–1983* PREALC OIT, Santiago.

Portes, A. (1985) 'Latin American Class Structures: Their Composition and Change During the Last Decades', *Latin American Research Review*, 20 (3).

Prince, R. (1985) *Haiti Family Business*, LAB, London.

Pryor, F. L. (1990) 'Socialismo via ayuda externa: la politica economica internacional del GRP', in J. Heine *Revolucion y Intervencion en el Caribe: las lecciones de Granada*, GEL, Buenos Aires.

Quintero Rivera, A. (1982) 'The Socio-Political Background to the Emergence of the "Puerto Rican model" as a Strategy of Development', in S. Craig (ed.), *The Contemporary Caribbean: A Sociological Reader*, Maracas, Trinidad and Tobago.

Rivera Urrutia, E. A. Sojo and J. R. Lopez (1986) *Centroamerica: política economica y crisis*, Editorial Costa Rica, San José.

Roddick, J. (1988) *The Dance of the Millions*, LAB, London.

Rodriguez Beruff, J. (1988) 'Puerto Rico en el plano internacional: intereses metropolitanas y reconsolidacion del colonialismo', *El Caribe Contemporaneo*, no. 17 (July–Dec).

Rodriguez, E. (1986) 'Costa Rica: inflacion y creciemiento ante la crisis de deuda externa', *Pensamiento Iberoamericano*, vol. 9 (Jan–June).

Rojas, M. (1988) 'Movimientos sociales, participacion y negociacion del conflicto en Costa Rica', in F. Barnhona (ed.) *Costa Rica Hacia el 2000 Desafios y opciones*, Nueva Sociedad, Caracas.

Rosenberg, M. (1989) 'Obstaculos en los Estados Unidos a la politica de Reagan en Centroamerica', *Sintesis* (Madrid), no. 7 (April).

Rotberg, R. (1988) 'Haiti's Past Mortgages its Future', *Foreign Affairs*, 67 (1) (Fall).

Rovira Mas, J. (1982) *Estado y Politica Economica en Costa Rica 1948–1970*, Editorial Porvenir, San Jose.

Rovira Mas, J. (1988) *Costa Rica en los años 80*, Flacso, Costa Rica.

Roxborough, I. (1979) *Theories of Underdevelopment*, Macmillan, London.

Ruccio, D. (1987) 'The State and Planning in Nicaragua', in R. Spalding (ed.) *The Political Economy of Revolutionary Nicaragua*, Allen & Unwin, London.

Safa, H. (1986) 'Female Employment in the Puerto Rican Working Class', in J. Nash and H. Safa (eds), *Women and Change in Latin America*, Bergin & Garvey Publishers, Massachusetts.

Safa, H. (1989) *Women, Industrialization and State Policy in Cuba*, Helen Kellogg Institute for International Relations, Working Paper 133.

Samuel, W. (1990) 'Regional Cooperation as an Element of Caribbean Development Strategy', in J. Wedderburn (ed.), *Integration and Participatory Development*, Friedrich Ebert Stiftung, Kingston, Jamaica.

Sankatsing, G. (1990) *Las Ciencias Sociales en el Caribe. Un balance critico*, UNESCO, Nueva Sociedad.

Schlesinger, S. and S. Kinzer (1983) *Bitter Fruit: The Untold Story of the American Coup in Guatemala*, Anchor Books, New York.

Schoultz, L. (1981) *Human Rights and US Policy Towards Latin America*, Princeton University Press.

Schoultz, L. (1987) *National Security and US Policy Towards Latin America*, Princeton University Press.

SELA (1991a) *Proposals for Latin America and the Caribbean*, Caracas, Venezuela.

SELA (1991b) *Guidelines for Industrialization The Latin America and Caribbean Industrialization Programme in the 1990s* (August), Caracas, Venezuela.

SELA (1991c) *The External Debt Situation in Latin America and the Caribbean* (September), Caracas, Venezuela.

SELA (1991d) *La Dinamica y los dilemas de la integracion en America Latina y el Caribe* (September), Caracas, Venezuela.

SELA (1992a) *The Caribbean Basin Initiative: Assessment of the Experience Since 1984* (September), Caracas, Venezuela.

SELA (1992b) *The Lome Caribbean and the European Community* (March).

SELA (Sistema Economico Latinamericano) (1989) *Trade Newsletter*, no. 26, Caracas, Venezuela.

Seligson, M. (1980) *Peasants of Costa Rica and the Development of Agrarian Capitalism*, Madison, Wisconsin.

Serbin, A. (1984) 'Nacionalismo popular y nacionalismo populista en Trinidad y Tobago', *Mundo Nuevo* (Caracas) Año VII, no. 23–24 (enero-junio).

Serbin, A. (1987) *Etnicidad, clase y nacion en el Caribe de habla inglesa*, Editorial Unvesitaria, Caracas.

Serbin, A. (1990) 'Drugs in the Caribbean Basin', *Journal of Interamerican Studies and World Affairs*, 32 (2).

Smith, C. (1990) 'The Militarization of Civil Society in Guatemala', *Latin American Perspectives*, Issue 67, 17 (4) (Fall).

Sojo, A. (1989) 'Costa Rica: el desarrollo economico y social ante el año 2000', *America Central Hacia el 2000*, Nueva Sociedad, Caracas.

Solis, L. G. (1990) 'Costa Rica y Estados Unidos', in F. Rojas Aravena (ed.), *Costa Rica y el Sistema Internacional*, Nueva Sociedad, Caracas.

Sollis, P. (1990) 'The Atlantic Coast of Nicaragua: Development and Autonomy', *Journal of Latin American Studies*, 21.

Spalding, R. (1987) *The Political Economy of Revolutionary Nicaragua*, Allen & Unwin, London.

Stahler-Sholk, R. (1987) 'Foreign Debt and Economic Stabilization Policies in Revolutionary Nicaragua', in R. Spalding (ed.), *The Political Economy of Revolutionary Nicaragua*, Allen & Unwin, London.

Stavenhagen, R. (1970) 'Classes, Colonialism and Acculturation', in I Horowitz (ed.), *Masses in Latin America*, OUP, New York.

Stevens, C. (1991) 'The Caribbean and Europe 1992: Endgame?', *Development Policy Review*, 9 (3) (September).

Stone, C. (1973) *Class, Race and Political Behaviour in Urban Jamaica*, University of West Indies, Kingston.

Stubbs, J. (1989) *Cuba: The Test of Time*, LAB, London.

Sunkel, O. and P. Paz (1979) *El subdessarrollo latinoamericano y la teoría del desarrollo*, Siglo XXI, Mexico.

Sutton, P. (1991a) 'Politics in the Commonwealth Caribbean. The Post-Colonial Experience', *European Review of Latin American and Caribbean Studies*, 51 (Dec).

Sutton, P. (1991b) 'The EC and the Caribbean: Main Dimensions and Key Issues', in P. Sutton (ed.), *Europe and the Caribbean*, Macmillan, London.

Swingewood, A. (1979) *Marx and Modern Social Theory*, Macmillan, London.

Thomas, C. (1988) *The Poor and the Powerless: Policy and Change in the Caribbean*, Monthly Review/LAB, London.

Thorndike, T. (1985) *Grenada Politics, Economy and Society*, Frances Pinter, London.

Thorndike, T. (1990) 'Teoria y práctica del poder popular', in J. Heine (ed.) *Revolución e Intervención en el Caribe: las leciones de Granada*, GEL, Buenos Aires.

Thorndike, T. (1991) 'Politics and Society in the South-East Caribbean', in C. Clarke *Society and Politics in the Caribbean*, Macmillan, London.

Torres-Rivas, E. (1987) *Centroamerica: la democracia posible*, FLACSO & EDUCA, San Jose.

Torres-Rivas, E. (1989) *Centroamerica: Politica y Sociedad 1929–1989*, Documento de Trabajo, FLACSO, San Jose.

Torres-Rivas, E. (1990) 'Centroamerica: Guerra, transición y democracia', *Iztapalapa*, no. 20, (Dec) Universidad Autonoma Metropolitana, Mexico.

Torres-Rivas, E. (1991) 'Crisis and Conflict, 1930 to the Present', in L. Bethell (ed.), *Central America Since Independence*, Cambridge University Press.

Torres-Rivas, E. and D. Jimenez, (1985) 'Informe sobre el estado de las migraciones en Centroamerica', *Anuario de Estudios Centroamericanos*, 11(2).

Touraine, A. (1989) *America Latina Politica y Sociedad*, Espasa Calpe, Madrid.

Tulchin, J. (1971) *The Aftermath of War. World War One and US Policy toward Latin America*, Weidenfield, New York.

United Nations, (1992) *Human Development Report*, Oxford University Press.

United Nations, (1993) *Human Development Report*, Oxford University Press.

Vilas, C. (1989) *Transicion desde el subdesarrollo*, Editorial Nueva Sociedad, Venezuela.

Vuskovic Pedro and R. Escoto (1990) *Peqeños Paises Perifericos*, CRIES, Nueva Sociedad, Caracas.

Walker, T. (1991) *Nicaragua: The Land of Sandino*, 3rd edn, Westview, Colorado.

Wedderburn, J. (1993) 'Analisis y perspectivas de la situacion politica, social y economica de los paises del Caribe: Jamaica', in Fundacion Federich Ebert *Los Paises del Caribe y Las Relaciones con la Comunidad Europea*, Madrid.

Weeks, J. (1985) *The Economies of Central America*, Holmes & Meier, New York.

Weeks, J. (1986) 'An Interpretation of the Central American Crisis', *Latin American Research Review*, 31 (3).

Weeks, J. (1987a) 'Panama: The Roots of Current Political Instability', *Third World Quarterly*, 9 (3).

Weeks, J. (1987b) 'The Mixed Economy in Nicaragua: The Economic Battlefield', in R. Spalding (ed.), *The Political Economy of Revolutionary Nicaragua*, Allen & Unwin, London.

Weeks, J. and P. Gunson (1991) *Panama Made in the USA*, LAB, London.

Whiteford, L. (1991) 'Debt Crisis, Birth Crisis', *Hemisphere* 3 (4) (Winter).

Whitehead, L. (1987) 'The Costa Rican Initiative in Central America', *Government and Opposition*, 22 (4).

Whitehead, L. (1988) 'Explaining Washington's Central American Policies', in B. Larkin (ed.), *Vital Interests: The Soviet Issue in US Central American Policy*, Lynne Reinner, Boulder, Colorado.

Whitehead, L. (1990) 'Soberania, democracia y socialismo: refleciones sobre la experiencia de Granada', in J. Heine *Revolucion e Intervencion en El Caribe: las lecciones de Granada*, Gel, Buenos Aires.

Williams, E. (1944) *Capitalism and Slavery*, Chapel Hill, London.

Williams, E. (1970) *From Colombus to Castro: the History of the Caribbean*, Andre Deutsch, London.

Wilmore, L. and J. Mattar, (1991) 'Reconversion industrial, apertura comercial y papel del estado en Centroamerica', *Revista de la CEPAL*, no. 44 (August).

Woodward, R.L. (1984) 'The Rise and Decline of Liberalism in Central America: Historical Perspectives on the Contemporary Crisis', *Journal of Inter-American Studies and World Affairs*,, no. 26.

Woodward, R.L. (1985) *Central America: A Nation Divided*, 2nd edn, Oxford University Press.

World Bank (1991) *Development Report*.

World Bank (1992) *Global Economic Prospects and the Developing Countries*.

Zunder, A. (1976) 'The Changing Caribbean Bauxite Industry', in H. Chin (ed.), *The Caribbean Basin and the Changing World Economic Structure*, Wolters-Noordoff, The Netherlands.

Index

Note: 'n.' after a page reference indicates the number of a note on that page.

261